I found this book relatable and entertaining. It offers the reader a wonderful, and sometimes hilarious or quirky, insight into the 'real' life of a real estate agent. A 'must read' for anyone in the industry.

Linda Upton
Sales Consultant

I thoroughly enjoyed reading 'Sold on The Dream', it highlights both the glamorous and not-so-glamorous side of real estate—it is a captivating read! In this reveal-all expose of our industry, 'Secret Agent Michael Blackmoor' has managed to capture accurately and wittingly what makes the real estate world so unique, as well as describe the behavioural traits of some fiends—I mean, 'friends' — in our industry! I would highly recommend this book to anyone who has had to deal with a real estate agent ... or unfortunately knows one. This is a light-hearted take on a profession that changes day to day, and always has a riveting story to tell.

Cate Arnold
Principal I Real Estate Agent

This is a very insightful, honest, raw and, at times, humorous look at Real Estate in Queensland. I enjoyed reading the stories and anecdotes from the author, which added immensely to the book.

Trish Springsteen
Author I Public Speaking Coach

Having worked with Michael, and experienced the emotional roller coaster ride of real estate with its highs and lows, this book is perfectly relatable. A witty and honest take on the day-to-day grind of our industry for many, that debunks much of the pretence and glamour. Plenty of times we have both recounted our experiences, over a coffee, on the quirks and oddities of our chosen profession. Michael has been able to capture this amusing content in a way that is not only funny, but also a true indication of the many facets of the complex role of an agent. Enjoy a glimpse of life on the inside!

Carlton Stokes
Sales Consultant

SOLD On The Dream

Michael Blackmoor

SOLD On The Dream
Copyright © 2023 Michael Blackmoor
First published 2023

Disruptive Publishing
17 Spencer Avenue
Deception Bay QLD 4508
Australia
WEB: www.disruptivepublishing.com.au

Editing and layout by Jo Scott

Cover design by Disruptive Publishing

Cover image by Michael Blackmoor

ISBN# 978-0-6457459-2-4 Print

SOLD On The Dream

Michael Blackmoor

The Poor Man's Guide to a Life in Real Estate

Dedicated to my wonderful wife and family who have faithfully supported me throughout the up and downs of my real estate career.

Also, to the many friends and colleagues I have shared this unique journey with.

And to Jo, a past client who has become a dear friend and inspiration with her own writing exploits and enthusiasm.

TABLE OF CONTENTS

FOREWORD

When Michael Blackmoor first shared with me that he was writing a book about his experiences as a real estate professional, I immediately looked forward to reading it. Having known him for many years, professionally and then personally, I knew that this book would be nothing less than truthful, revealing, informative, entertaining and worthwhile.

How did I know this? Many years ago, I attended an open home for a property on the outskirts of Brisbane, and in doing so had the rare and delightful experience of dealing with a *perfect* real estate agent. Nothing was too much trouble, he was polite, professional and personable. Hmm ... that's enough alliteration for the time being. My initial impression, as a potential buyer, was that this agent was knowledgeable, efficient, proficient, and ... honest.

Michael had no way of knowing that the mumsy middle-aged woman who was enquiring about a thoroughly modest home, albeit on a sizeable block of land, was in fact a property tragic, a repeat offender and serial renovator who had been quietly building a portfolio with a predominantly buy-and-hold strategy, across Australia over many years. And yet, Michael treated me with utmost respect and gave me nothing less than exemplary professional attention. Needless to say, the whole purchasing experience was faultless, in fact it was the most positive experience I'd had dealing with an agent over many years as an investor.

So, I made a mental note then that the next time I needed the services of a selling agent, there was no question I would use anyone other than Michael Blackmoor. True to his style as a real estate professional, he kept in contact with me over the following years, and when the time came to liquidate my property portfolio the task could not have been in better hands. This self-proclaimed less-than-elite agent wrangled multiple offers over a number of properties, securing many quick sales at well over the asking prices. Now that's an elite result, by any measure.

But back to the book ... to the inexperienced, stepping into the world of real estate can feel like navigating your way through a mirrored maze, but it needn't be. Believe me, it's a whole lot easier and far more agreeable with an experienced guide to lead the way. To have someone alerting you to hidden perils, and helping you to avoid mistakes, save time, and conserve your precious energy is a gift, indeed. In *SOLD On The Dream*, Michael Blackmoor demonstrates how real estate is an entrepreneurial adventure deserving of your energy, your time, and your conscientious application to the task. It offers rewards that are rich in life experience, in friendships made, and the best of true success ... however you measure it.

There has never been a greater need for this book than now. In this modern era, property has become a national obsession, it feels as though home ownership is considered our patriotic duty, and yet it has never been less attainable. And so, an alternative title to this book could have been *Everything you ever wanted to know about (a career in) real estate but were too frightened to ask*. In his inimitable and irreverent style, Michael lifts the lid on the machinations of the (sometimes) murky world of property sales to dispel a few myths ... and confirm a few others. It's a light-hearted, but wickedly truthful, insider's guide to the property arena beginning with starting out in the industry, to how to survive and thrive as a property professional, and right through to a prescient look at what the future holds for the profession and real estate in general.

And don't be fooled by Michael Blackmoor's self-deprecating humour, he is one of life's natural observers, an affable raconteur and a great teacher. Learn from his wisdom. Read the book. It won't be taxing because Michael's writing style hits the sweet spot between being incredibly informative and wildly entertaining. I howled with laughter as I read his anecdotes about buyer and seller behaviour and recognised myself in many (okay, most) of the scenarios, guilty of all the transgressions described.

SOLD On The Dream is a must-read for anyone who has ever, or will ever, sell or buy a property; it's for anyone thinking about a career in real estate, or is new to a career in real estate ... or is just real estate-curious! I commend this exceptional book to you.

Lesley Oliver
Property Investor, and Author of *The Gilded Cage*

INTRODUCTION

Spoiler alert! Before we start, I will put my cards on the table. You see, I do not for one minute pretend to be a definitive authority or elite achiever in the wonderful world of real estate. That path is already well-trodden by many others who are only too keen to impart their expert knowledge based on their *proven* success (apparently). I am happy to concede I have always been more of a 'consistent plodder'. In making such an admission, I feel this represents the more realistic side of this profession for a great many of its participants. My best achievement might simply be sticking it out for 16 plus years and working for just three different companies in that period. Plenty of time in which I have slowly come to comprehend the fascinating internal workings of this intriguing industry.

I worked in international finance in London for many years before moving to Australia with my Queensland-born wife and young children in 2006. Without a job on arrival, I initially considered pursuing a similar career path in Brisbane, but with opportunities a little more limited at the time—and perhaps swayed by my new tropical surroundings—I started to yearn for a fresh direction that this big life change might offer me. Real estate was never a prior idea and, to a degree, only presented itself as a viable option due to being a quick and obtainable career transfer. This realisation dawned on me after attending a careers expo in Brisbane. Furthermore, here was something I could challenge myself with as a newly arrived Englishman attempting to sell Australian homes to Australians—okay, well *some* Australians at least, intermingled with many other inbound nationalities as it turns out, much like me—and utilise to integrate into, and understand, the diverse local culture. I admit my own pre-conception of the industry both in the UK and — presumably by default—Australia was one where the accountability and professionalism of most agents was questionable. (As compared to the structured world of finance I had come from.) And I felt that this could also be an opportunity to apply my 'cultured' past business life into a more professional offering, as my winning point of difference.

It is important to acknowledge, at this point, that things are moving rapidly and even since starting to gather these observations and memories together, the real estate landscape has evolved. The rise of technology and its digital disruption to established practices, coupled with the emergence of the millennial customers with different demands and expectations, has forced change. Tighter external scrutiny and regulation of employment structure and performance, combined with harsher economics, has also contributed to shifting standards.

As I write, we have just started to move out of a long period of unprecedented low interest rates and historically low amounts of stock (properties) for sale. On top of this, the recent impact of COVID-19—as with so many businesses—has further impacted cashflow and activity levels. I commenced my career in slightly simpler times, for example, the relative ease of gaining an initial position in the industry has probably decreased. Some of the descriptions here should be viewed in relation to perhaps a more carefree era but, nonetheless, are still important to note as a backdrop to what follows on. Things will continue to develop at an ever more increasing pace, yet certain basics remain constant in terms of human interaction and behaviour which, after all, is where the fun starts!

The intention of these collected personal observations is not to provide some detailed disclosure of how things operate at the pinnacle of the profession, as there are far better qualified elite operators to do that, and I would not profess to match their achievements. Sorry, but this is not another 'Guaranteed Success' or 'Fast Track to Big Earnings' blueprint or bible! Thus, anyone hoping for a get-rich-quick handbook of handy hacks and tips for a swift rise to the top will be sorely disappointed! Nor is it meant to ridicule the industry tirelessly either, just simply cut through many of the extensively deployed smoke and mirrors to highlight, at times, the hypocrisy and many idiosyncrasies. This will also demonstrate how many of the practices and methods people often question have originated with sound reasoning to combat the unregulated chaos that is (frankly) dealing with the public!

There remains a lot of pompousness and ego-driven behaviour, underpinned by a desire to never ever admit you are struggling. This sometimes masks a good deal of honest work going on below the surface. Ultimately, as I try to break a few things down into areas of common anguish, we attempt to understand both the client's and agent's perspective of what goes into this big melting pot of emotion, stress, and ambition! To that end, my hope is these assembled tales will be of some interest and amusement to a wider audience, beyond just my weary fellow exponents! Firstly, we will need to understand the steps and environment needed to establish yourself before opening out into all the wonderment and excitement that follows (if you can last that long!).

No doubt those talented top-performers working in the best offices will wish to paint a somewhat different picture, and may even suspect some sour grapes on my part, but statistics repeatedly show they represent a relatively small percentage of the industry in total. I will always acknowledge these individuals and be in awe of their achievements and work ethic. Nonetheless, believe me, there are plenty of others to go around! This then symbolises the plight of these foot soldiers, and the overriding mood is certainly intended to be light-hearted as opposed to overly critical of a profession that has ultimately kept me afloat thus far in this great country and provided many new friendships and memorable experiences along the way.

1 | LET US BEGIN

Wow, where on earth do we start? Good question, and the big one that confronts most fresh-faced— and some not-so-fresh-faced—individuals as they embark on their glittering new career in the exciting and endlessly rewarding 'theatre' of real estate. In truth, if they are just starting out, it is usually answered very quickly: sit down, shut up and cold call these 300 numbers a day (that no one else in the office wants to do) until you get a lead you can hand over.

First things first, what really *is* the job? This book primarily covers the experiences and observations of a sales agent role. As the name suggests, this relates to the *selling* of houses rather than the *letting* of them, which is typically conducted separately in most organisations by property managers. Okay, a career in sales then? However, this is one in which, critically, you have absolutely no product to sell until you go out and get it yourself. This splits the job into two very defined parts: *Listing* and *Selling*.

Listing involves prospecting for potential stock (properties) to then market and sell. Prospecting consists of various activities to establish contacts with people, such as traditional 'cold calling', door knocking and flyer dropping. In this digital age they are now combined with more dynamic electronic endeavours, such as social media blogs and other Internet-based exposure. Mind you, the age-old pursuit of sucking up to the principal in the hope of being given some free leads can be another avenue as well. You are still effectively selling in this first stage, the product simply being yourself and your company. Listing is key and your absolute lifeblood (no stock, no cash!), so most employers will place a higher value on an agent listing property than selling it. Also remember this 'stock' once acquired has no unit or 'recommended retail price' and you must research/guess/make up *(*delete as appropriate)* its correct market value yourself—in conjunction with the owners, perhaps—for potential buyers as an individual commodity. As with any product, price it too high and no one will buy it.

Selling relates to the marketing of a property once listed and the subsequent negotiations and agreement of a contract of sale. Both functions must be completed to achieve a commission, but it is the listing aspect of the job which ultimately determines your success going forward (and sinks many a hopeful). A good house, priced correctly, will sell almost regardless of the agent's performance at that stage, but have no house to sell in the first place and you are dead in the water!

A sales career in real estate is many things: challenging, complex, frustrating, and yet equally rewarding and highly satisfying when things go well. If you are a 'people person' then there is great opportunity to meet and assist a broad cross-section of the community in different stages of their life journey, all with unique stories to tell. Perhaps reflecting this, the job itself is culturally diverse and genuinely open to 'all comers' young and old. This, coupled to a relatively easy entry pathway, makes it a favourite for mid-life career changers as much as for aspirational young starters.

'University of Life' experience has as much currency here as anything slightly more cerebral. It can make for a fascinating collection of people when you work in a team with a rich mixture of ages, backgrounds, and personal aspirations. Certain characteristics are more common across the spectrum in those who have managed to stick around. Being naturally self-assured, strong-minded and outgoing are desired attributes. Of course, there is sometimes a thin line between such values and just being egotistical, high maintenance and self-centred, as we shall see!

It is important to note my personal experiences—and the related stories contained in this book—are all based on Queensland legislation. As with many things in the good old United States of Australia there are some significant differences in local practice between individual jurisdictions which would impact aspects of initial training and subsequent processes. In Queensland, for example, we prepare—albeit using approved templates—and execute contracts ourselves as opposed to the legal fraternity, who typically just get handed the resulting paperwork to convey (much to their indignation sometimes!). The overarching structure relating to registration and conduct is regulated via the Office of Fair Trading (OFT) in Queensland. Nonetheless, most of the general observations and human traits highlighted remain true and comparable across any state lines. Regardless, the objective here is not to get bogged down in detailed technical or legal finer points (much like some agents I have known!).

Just what was involved to get a start in Queensland? At the time I enlisted, to become an entry level sales agent this encompassed a straightforward five-day training course at the Real Estate Institute of Queensland (REIQ), or other registered training facility, to learn the broad basics of the industry through a number of defined modules, followed by an open-book exam (some attempt to make sure you were listening). Assuming you passed this first go—and if you didn't, *seriously*, abandon any aspirations immediately!—you then just needed to get a provisional position with a registered agency. Historically not too difficult, but certainly becoming harder as discussed in the introduction. From there, you applied and paid for a sales agent licence—which normally comes back from the OFT after police checks within three to four weeks—and assuming you haven't robbed a bank or murdered someone recently, hey presto! You now have the keys to the Ferrari, having only just passed your driving test, so what could go wrong?

For those talented and hardworking individuals who can really excel and ride the wave, real estate sales extends exceptionally good rewards, but contrary to popular belief, for many other honest grafters it offers, at best, only moderate to low income with plenty of self-funding—and self-doubt—along the way. It provides flexibility in a way most office or factory jobs can't, and yet can have you working unscheduled and unsociable hours at any point in time at the beck and call of clients, just to chase the next paycheque.

You must be of a certain mindset for sales. If you want structured nine-to-five-only with a guaranteed salary, you really need to look elsewhere (or at least to the Property Management Department!). Whilst many people bemoan their perception of agents and their 'easy' lifestyle, the truth is 95% of them would not put up with what your average agent must endure in terms of income fluctuations, combined with random hours, and constant accessibility 'on demand'. Forget a quiet day off, well unless you have absolutely no stock!

To the outsider there is a certain romantic allure, of course. This cut and thrust, slightly shadowy industry where there is good money to be made through potentially nothing more than your own guile, confidence, and gift of the gab. There are plenty who will try their hand for this alone. It is all in the show and if you talk the talk, the world is yours! Of course, the small print is ultimately whether you can also walk the walk. Bluff and bluster may get you so far initially, but only consistent efforts and results will ensure a future. If you are perhaps already known in the community all the better, hence a steady flow of ex-sportspeople and local councillors/politicians getting in on the act. Nothing better than already being a local 'identity' to get the ball rolling. Indeed, a perfect starting point if you already have some contacts, but that alone will not create a career.

There is also an undeniable buzz when you win your first listing or close a sale, which can become quite addictive, and not something that every routine job can replicate. However, a word of warning as this can seductively pump you up very easily and get you way ahead of yourself. I find a golf analogy quite relevant here (something else I must graft at!). You start learning the game and frankly you are a hacker, but then out of the blue, on the fifth tee of an otherwise poor game you finally connect perfectly and hit an absolute cracker down the middle of the fairway into the distance. Oh boy, how you immediately walk tall and tell yourself, 'Bang! I've arrived. Cracked this game', only to revert and play the rest of the round like the donkey you are! Beware, as beginner's luck and naive enthusiasm must stand the long test of time and multiple rejections!

By the very nature of the core activity—people interacting with other people—there are inevitable social side effects, and agents can be depicted by those they have dealt with as absolute champions through to the scum of the earth (quite often through circumstances beyond their control). Heroes and zeros all here, although as mud always sticks, it tends to be the zeros we hear about to form our somewhat one-sided opinion upon. In today's instantly judgemental world of social media, Google reviews, etc., plenty of extra petrol is available to pour on a time-honoured fire by faceless keyboard warriors and the 'wronged'. Of course, good old stalwarts like certain current affairs programs have their hackneyed diary note once a week to run the latest despicable, uncaring real estate agent story!

The relative ease and speed of entry into the profession, whilst attractive, potentially adds to the image problem given there are several fledgling agents who may be learning 'on the job' at any one time, and who may be opening themselves up to possible problems and misunderstandings that—with the hindsight of—gained experience might avoid or eliminate. As mentioned, things are perhaps changing in this area due to new regulation and strained economics, but historically there have always been easy openings for the fair-weather 'give it a crack' brigade. For every well-run company that has a defined and tough selection criteria—for new agents to ensure a good culture fit and demonstrated experience/results for potential earnings—there have been many loose offices operating a 'more the merrier' approach to sales staff, who will pretty much throw anyone a bone. Bums on seats time!

Another problem here is the very nature of how things are financially structured. Rest assured, in most small to mid-size offices there won't be much in the way of a Human Resources Department! It's congratulations from the boss, you're onboard, swiftly followed by, "the team will show you the ropes". Unfortunately, 'the team' in question are other agents either on commission-only or debit/credit remuneration, which means they are focussed only on themselves and on where the next dollar is being extracted to live on. Helping you out doesn't pay the bills, buddy. Add to this the inherently insecure nature of most agents, and why would they assist someone else who is effectively now their direct competition within the office?

If you are lucky there might be a sales manager with a specific brief to assist you. However, don't get too excited, as in my experience many 'Sales Managers' are just another (favoured) agent pumped up by the principal with a mock senior title and extra retainer to keep them sweet. They will typically still be selling themselves and whilst they may give you some lip service—even a weekly 'one-on-one' meeting—for appearances sake, don't hold your breath on learning anything too enlightening.

It's probably worth clarifying at this point the differing pay structures. Experienced and successful agents are typically employed as 'commission only'. As this suggests, no salary is taken, just proceeds from settled sales. The percentage retained will be higher, but there is no income backup. No sales, no pay! 'Debit/credit' is where a basic retainer is paid—thus ensuring a regular paycheque—but this is offset against future settlements, that is, you do not receive any additional commission-based income until outstanding debts are covered first. This is the more likely option for inexperienced new recruits—or the occasional favoured starlet—although the debit figure can rack up quite quickly if things are slow. Finally, you may just be salaried if performing a specific role (manager, etc.) with or without the possibility of additional commission. Most agents fall into the first two categories, hence the insatiable need for properties to sell!

Although there is some external reputational risk with novices, the flip side is these unsuspecting and oh-so-keen new recruits— who will generally do anything to get a start—are perfect cannon fodder to do the unpopular 'urban myth' tasks many established agents try to shy away from. Yes, we all know what we are supposed to do every day—and all maintain we do it—but really, give me a break! Why subject yourself to the drudgery and outright desolation of cold calling random numbers all day long when these lemming new recruits can do your dirty work instead. They can take all the abuse and negativity because, after all, "we all had to do it when we started". If by some miracle they get someone with a pulse who wants to talk, they can then be made to either hand the lead over, or a more experienced agent will 'mentor' them as they are clearly too inexperienced to do it on their own yet. (Mentor, as in your established colleague completely takes over and grabs the headlines, all the glory, and most of the money.) Think of it as a pawn sacrifice in chess, the kings and queens will stay back and come more into play when things start to get interesting.

One of my past offices, for a while—wanting to boost listing numbers—had a procession of new 'trainees' starting, all put through the rigorous phone farm. Almost all followed the same path. For the first two or three weeks they would genuinely hammer the lines. I was even cold called at my own house by a couple of them at different times, not realising I was their work colleague. Not really the best look or fine tuning of data! They would usually jag a few (weak) leads/appraisal opportunities and we would be told how good they were in the following week's sales meeting (and how we should follow their example).

However, nearly all would burn out by week four through the sheer grind of it all, and would either leave or start playing up. Their call numbers would suddenly drop off, along with the so-called opportunities. In this case they would be quietly shown the door and the next one rolled in. If any questions were asked, there would always be a specific reason for their departure, not related to the fact it was inevitable due to the soul-destroying nature of what they were doing.

My own experience of starting was, to a degree, along typical lines. On day one the principal welcomed me and after a brief chat handed me over straight over to his sales manager. He was a fair bit younger than me, actively selling himself, and seemed almost bemused as to what he had to do with me. In his relatively short time in this lofty role, it would appear he had only dealt with people with some prior real estate experience, so this 'blank page' entrant was something new. We had a quick meeting in which he enquired whether I was comfortable with a younger line manager—no problem, I indicated—and then I was handed some pre-existing notes on what was needed for an ideal week as a newbie. A sort of ABC of sales prospecting. I was told to read through this and then go and drive around my new 'farm area' to note any *For Sale* signs already there, to build an understanding of the existing activity in what would be my patch, and that was pretty much that!

The notes covered making so many calls per day, combined with door knocking individual streets, etc. Off I stumbled, following these generic instructions of how to proceed. On day two, however, the agent whom I had been seated next to in the office quickly introduced me to the *Dark Side*. He smiled at what I was collating from my sign spotting the previous day and asked to read through the notes I had been given. "What's the information you gathered going to be used for?" he enquired. "So I will have an idea of the market profile and other agents share," I repeated parrot fashion from what had been explained 24 hours prior. "Is that it?" he remarked ruefully, "You'll never earn any money just doing that. You can follow this guide and achieve a little, very slowly, or cut to the chase and make some real money. Come with me for a drive!".

He grabbed my newly-typed list and headed for his car. "You have to do the uncomfortable, direct things that actually make money and ignore everything else—waste of time," he advised. "We are only going to door knock the properties with existing 'For Sale' signs on your list, and then try to get them to change agencies".

This seemed at odds with my REIQ training where it was indicated that we couldn't 'jump' other agents signs and approach them directly about the same business. Thus, in these very early days there was already a demonstration of the two potential paths that lay ahead: the more respectful, but slower, accumulation of sustainable contacts with which to develop a database and opportunities from, or the quicker and dirtier route of slightly less ethical 'smash and grab' of anything that moves, regardless of reputational risk.

I went along for the ride, so to speak, and unbelievably the first house we knocked at had just come out of an exclusive agreement, and the owners invited us in for a chat! *Wow, I thought, perhaps this guy has the answers!* Well, yes and no. He most certainly had a fearless, no-nonsense, direct approach that is an asset in many respects when your livelihood depends on creating new opportunities. However, if the result thereafter was not immediate, his attention span was limited. In this case the owners weren't prepared to commit to another exclusive listing and only offered an open list with no new advertising money, which he had no interest in, and nothing ultimately eventuated. Also—as I subsequently observed often with other agents of similar approach—he didn't ultimately achieve anything more by his methods because he was plain lazy! His motto was simply, 'Why do in five days what you can do in two?'. Fair enough, except turn that around and ask, 'Why then, go missing in action and waste the other three days?'!

I am not ashamed to say, therefore, despite possibly earning less in the short term, I rejected the *Dark Side* and stuck to what I felt sat well with my own character (oh, you weak dog!).

Perhaps it was due to my slightly more senior years on entering the industry, coupled with existing life experience but, with the benefit of hindsight, my first office seemed a good environment to start off in. The basic structures were outlined, and the principal was knowledgeable and generally approachable if needed. Yes, of course you were expected to make calls, get out and about door knocking, go flyer dropping, etc., yet there was not the absolute micromanagement or flogging you to death on 300+ calls a day with somebody standing over you. Which is good, because I wouldn't have lasted! This allowed me to develop a style and method of work that felt right for me. The most *productive* model? Some would say no, but I could at least sleep at night knowing I hadn't overstepped the mark anywhere. I was also communicating with people genuinely as me, not as some overly scripted robot with a (very) thinly veiled dialogue that suggested only self-interest with little real empathy or interest in the client.

From what I subsequently saw with new starters, particularly the young ones—and after gaining a broader understanding of how some companies operate—suggested I may have just got lucky, as most were put through the intensive call, call, call, battery farm first. There is a certain well-known brand infamous for this approach. Even their more established agents have to demonstrate tangible 'outcomes' every day from hammering the phones, otherwise they are not leaving. This requirement forces some of them to become quite creative about what constitutes a win, and when to hold things back for 'use' the next day! For their style of operation this intensive method works for new recruits, to a degree. Just like any elite army selection, you either break them quickly, or those who do survive are of the 'right stuff'. I know of some people who didn't last a week (even a day!) in this environment and others who came through relatively unscathed and were now suitably conditioned for what they had to do going forward. Me, I would rather eat my own arm than work in that type of oppressive atmosphere, but then again, here I am writing this!

Ultimately, on entering this industry you are laid bare relatively quickly and the mantra is quite straight forward, *'You have no database of contacts and are of no use until you do'*. And so, the learning curve begins.

2 | BLUNT INSTRUMENTS AND THE BLOB

Still keen? Okay, so assuming you have managed to secure a starting position somewhere and have a toe in the water, how is the new office going to support you? In any profession staff procurement and management is vitally important. In the corporate world many firms spend considerable money on assessing and profiling potential staff and ensuring their ongoing wellbeing. Motivation is critical, obtaining the correct balance between encouragement, support, control, and optimum performance.

Nonetheless, for some reason in many real estate offices there appears to be a certain 'dumbed down' dynamic in this area. Often petty issues or grievances with sales agents are raised in the public open-air forum of the office floor in a sort of builder's yard or military boot camp mentality of heated exchanges. (Mind you, a few principals are ex-builders!) As this is somehow considered easier—and *less* confronting—than a grown-up discussion behind closed doors. It's never good witnessing an agent being sacked on the spot and asked to clear their desk, directly in front of you, whilst you keep your head down and pretend you are suddenly busy on the phone and strangely oblivious. It is ironic that in an industry centred around complex interactions with customers, it is somehow difficult for many principals and sale managers to do the same thing effectively with their own staff.

Quite often there are few *carrots* either, only ever *the stick*! The basic holding position being that you are always underachieving unless proven otherwise. The rudimentary form of 'encouragement' nearly always falls back to, "Joe Blow at Such & Such is doing more business than you lot, and we are looking to bring him in because he's a champion,". Moreover, there's not much attempt at any meaningful, in-depth analysis either. I did five appraisals last week: "You're a legend; listening and doing everything right". But I only managed one this week: "You're underperforming and you need to raise your game quickly," etc. This two dimensional or 'blunt instrument' management, as I see it, is perhaps all that is needed given the constant revolving door of staff in some offices, i.e., you don't need to get too close and personal, as they won't be around long enough!

This conceivably comes back to the aforementioned 'bums on seats' policy operated by many small to medium size offices over the years, that is, *the more agents employed, theoretically the more sales for the office*. Would-be applicants were probably put through no more taxing questioning than "Why do you want to join us?" "Err, because I would like to have a shot at real estate," comes the informed and well researched reply. "Okay, well we'll give you a desk and see how we go". Bingo, you're in! Again, things are changing in this area but, in all honesty, some of the motley crew of (at best) ill-advised new recruits I have seen over the years has highlighted this lackadaisical approach.

Once you are in and have had your exhaustive 10-minute introductory training, keeping you in check on a regular basis from thereon is quite often done via the dreaded *Weekly Sales Meeting*. Time honoured 'name and shame' techniques are deployed here, as we go around the room painfully, slowly, one by one with each agent having to tell the class what prospecting they did this week, how many appraisals conducted, listings signed, etc. Into this mix is the occasional curveball question, like naming your 'win for the week' (hopefully a bloody short meeting!). Of course, the simple premise is the public embarrassment and humiliation of admitting your gross under achievement to all your colleagues is the only possible motivation you ever need to get out there and be a success. That, and the fact it is much easier for the principal/sales manager to do this for everyone in one go (in 30 to 60 minutes), and they are then admonished from any further hands-on management for another week!

This leads to a couple of unwanted outcomes. Firstly, resentment and fear of the meeting itself which should be a positive environment in which to share advice, recent experiences, and property information. The second is an overwhelming pressure to produce *something.* This ensures the quality and genuine potential of some of the appraisals brought to the table are questionable at best (e.g., I did Auntie Dot's house yesterday, just so I had one to mention). After all, if you have some BS to show-and-tell you can probably get away with it for another week. Not worth the risk of having *nothing* and becoming the next target of the blunt instrument.

A common embellishment around many a meeting venue are the whiteboards. Not only can your lack of results be verbally dissected, but they can also be put on display for all to see (just in case anyone was still wondering). Top performers table, monthly sales totals, active appraisals, and individual agents stock/time on market/list price, are all prominent in black and white as a subtle backdrop to proceedings. Furthermore, required actions can be debated as a forum and indelibly written up against your name so there is no escape. 'Agreed then, you *will* get that price drop by next week.' Some were higher tech and attempted to provide printouts of recent activity, but this was only as good as who had bothered to enter their appraisals on the in-house CRM (customer relationship management) system that week. Typically, not many, either through being lazy or secretive (okay, both). Whatever method is employed, the objective is essentially the same: open-air theatre with quick and simplistic management to *get results*.

At present, while working more independently with my current employer, I am spared this weekly ritual. Nonetheless, I have endured my fair share of it over the years in many office-based environments. I equally loved *and* loathed these meetings. They were tedious and confronting when you were going through a slow patch. Yet, they were great for seeing the different approaches and character traits of individuals. There were the relentless peacocks who miraculously always had something wonderful happening and wanted centre stage to bore everyone else to death with overly detailed and elaborate stories about, often, not that much. The trick here is to ramble on for 10 minutes so it sounds like you have been *very* busy, and people might forget by the end you have only spoken about one thing.

Then there were those who would come out fighting and want to deflect things back on the management as soon as any criticism was levelled. Finally, there were the 'keep quiet and hope nobody notices you this week' contingent (the numbers here could vary depending on whether you had nothing positive to talk about!). Conversely, if you did have a great week with a couple of sales and couple of new listings, you couldn't wait for the next meeting so you could sit there, oh-so-smugly—for once—detail your successes and be a hero, just for one day (apologies Mr Bowie). The blunt instrument swings the other way in this instance, and you are immediately hailed as excellent by the principal for what you have achieved, and what a shining example you are to everyone … well until next week anyway.

Whether it be via the sales meeting, or if you are really lucky and have the luxury of a more private one-on-one session, there is a predictable and well-established hierarchy of layered criticism that can be implemented at each turn, irrespective of who you are or how well you are doing. Effectively, if you are starting to make progress at something, that just highlights your next problem. It's a bit like an old-school computer game where, as a new recruit, you ascend each level only to be met by a further second-rate challenge as you slowly climb up towards the summit. The added bonus is, this is 'one size fits all' and can also be retrospectively applied, regardless of how long you have been working in the industry and where you are in the learning curve. It goes something like this.

Begin Game: Start Career

- Level 1: **"You're not making enough prospecting calls"** *(You make more calls - Proceed to level 2)*
- Level 2: **"You're not creating enough database contacts from all those calls"** *(You create more contacts in the database - Proceed to level 3)*
- Level 3: **"You're not converting enough contacts into appraisals"** *(You create more appraisals - Proceed to level 4)*
- Level 4: **"You're not turning enough appraisals into listings"** *(You create more listings - Proceed to level 5)*
- Level 5: **"Your listings are all overpriced"** *(You get price reductions - Proceed to level 6)*

- Level 6: **"You're not converting enough listings to sales"** (*You give up) No, just kidding! - Of course, you learn how to 'close' deals properly!*

If you pass Level 6, you may just keep your real estate life intact and continue playing to finally rack up some points (well, earnings). However, also be aware of the hidden trap at this more advanced level of play.

- Level 7: **"You're finally making sales but, because of this, you're now not making enough prospecting calls again"** - *Lose all your lives and go back to Level 1*

Busted!

You never ultimately escape the game anyway because there will always be some aspect you can be pulled back on. As much as everyone will talk about consistency and the 'ideal week' timetable of balanced activities, for many it never quite works out like that. As a newbie it can be daunting, but even for established agents you are always braced for either, "Great sales month ... but you need to urgently get prospecting again for new listings," versus "Excellent prospecting and listings this month ... but you need to get this existing stock moved on and sold,". It is a constant see-saw with a life all its own. To understand this simplistic approach we need to delve a little deeper into the bigger picture of how most regular sales agents are viewed in general.

You see, before you get too settled in and start to think you may just become a valued lifelong member of the sales team, let us address the reality. Firstly, the industry-wide average 'life' (to be 'long' with!) at any one place is probably about 12 months. Secondly and crucially, there is no 'I' in team, right? Big clue right there! You see, in many offices there really is not much of an individual status for your journeyman agent. The term 'team' is an over-elaboration, as you are simply part of an autonomous blob of 'salespeople' that needs to churn out a certain amount of dollar production every month. The actual contents of the blob are, to a degree, irrelevant to senior management as long as it produces results. Sometimes the blob gets bigger, sometimes the blob gets smaller, but as long as there is a blob that's all that matters. Someone leaves (or you sack them), easy, just assimilate some other willing new recruit into the blob.

It's borne of a vicious circle. Agents tend to move agencies quite often, because if things are not going to plan it is easier to cling on to the hope it will be different somewhere else, i.e., it's not *your* fault. They may leave quite suddenly and in some cases with an outstanding debt owed for agent paid advertising or debit/credit arrangements. This means many principals are wary of being burnt and often do not see many agents as long-term employees to nurture, simply *current* employees doing an easily replaceable job. This creates an inevitably constrained relationship, the essence of which filters through to the agents, who retain limited loyalty with the view that they do not really owe the firm anything as they have never been close. To a degree this insulates both sides and, in many cases, ensures there aren't too many tears shed by either party when someone leaves. Hence, the only constant is the blob itself, certainly not the members. It's always good fun when the annual full team photo is taken, to have bets on how many faces will be left by the next one!

Now in saying all this, if you become an *exceptional* performer then you can transcend the blob and move to a higher level of consciousness—well, senior agent or sales manager—because the only time you develop individuality and real profile is when you can offer the boss the BIG dollars, baby! Then you are suddenly on a pedestal in front of the blob as a shining example of what can be achieved if you work hard. Wondrous things start presenting themselves to you free of charge or question, and life seems better. However, another good saying to remember at this point is you are only as good as your last deal, so do not rest on your laurels too much, or get cocky, as you can still be re-absorbed into the blob. Your newfound status and apparent chumminess with the principal can disappear again as quickly as your last paycheque.

The blob can very occasionally be treated and let out *en masse*, only when it suits of course. Most of the bigger franchise groups have regular self-indulgent awards evenings and—if you are lucky—the principal will promise free alcohol in return for your attendance. They can then hold court on the night at a large table populated by all their fawning staff. It is an unspoken competition to see who has the biggest entourage of apparently loyal and dedicated staff (to subliminally demonstrate how wonderful they are as leaders and what a clearly happy ship they run). Any suggested allegiance displayed by the blob is typically more to the booze on offer and any after-party antics, however. Also, it's a golden opportunity for the show ponies to glam up for the night (and my God, do they!) with every member of the blob equally basking in the shared glory—if there is any—of the office, even though some of them have not contributed to it and are only there to make up the numbers, literally!

In moving from a world of structured career paths and long service recognition, this was probably the biggest single thing I had to get my head around. The realisation of the blob culture and having a very generic and interchangeable role was certainly a departure. Perhaps I am a delicate flower, but I found being referred to collectively as just 'the salespeople' all the time quite derogatory and almost a public affirmation of the removal of individuality from the equation.

Yet the paradox with this is ultimately whatever team structure is seen to prevail. In truth, you are always a business within a business, and essentially must promote yourself and create outcomes as an individual in real estate. That is not to say some form of genuine team ethic and interaction isn't still highly beneficial. In terms of having appropriate reliable cover in the event of sickness or leave, and increased opportunities for cross selling of other agents' stock within the office, having a good group of likeminded colleagues is critical. Nonetheless, when many are confronted by the harsh reality they are primarily judged individually, and earn only based on the results of their own actions, this often ensures 'the collective' is relatively loose at best.

3 | Look At Me, Look At Me!

Yep, that's right. It's all about me! All the time! THE END. I mean now you're in the game, you must get noticed—and quick! Seriously, do you *really* need my face on your open home directional sign? Of course not, unless—shock, horror—it is not there purely to guide buyers safely to your front door?

Relentless self-promotion is about as fundamental as an oxygen supply in real estate. This is borne out of essentially two things. From a practical perspective, it is a basic requirement to keep your name out there and to garner attraction business. People have very short memories, so if you don't remain in their face, you don't exist. By supplying a constant drip feed of marketing featuring yourself, there is an outside chance to keep in people's conscious thoughts when it comes time to sell. However, the second factor is more intriguing: personality and ego! By definition, to enter and prosper in the industry you ideally need to be self-confident and outgoing. Quite often this comes with a built-in need to be constantly fed with your own self-importance.

I believe the best agents have the absolute right to mindfully let you know how good they are because they have damn well earned it (and chances are they will deliver you an exceptional outcome, over and above the average guy). Ironically, these high-end performers can generally let their sales and listings do the talking for them, as genuine success is very apparent. That's the point, real and sustained achievement is easy to see in the level of consistent listing engagement and subsequent results within a local community. Whilst you may still manage your brand effectively, for a top performer a considerable amount of attraction business will flow simply through the public profile of sold properties and successful auction campaigns, plus word-of-mouth recommendations from satisfied vendors. Such individuals are already busy and confident of their own ability/track record, so are less likely to need or resort to constant 'white noise' updates about, err, not much.

Therein lies the big problem with self-promotion. There are way too many average guys who want you to believe they are also the elites. For them the game plan is always *perception is reality*. Create the illusion you are a leader in your field and some mug punter will believe you at face value. Unfortunately, it doesn't stop with the potential client! There is nothing more dangerous than the mediocre agent who genuinely believes their *own* vastly inflated hype! After all, you can be almost anything you want to be in your head, but it's what you do on the ground that ultimately pays the bill. The road is littered with those who have talked big and earned small!

Today technology should really empower the end client, more than it does, to call this out. It amazes me how highly exaggerated statements of activity and apparent success are consistently peddled at a time where actual results are freely available online to those who simply take some time out to investigate. Go for your life, say what you like, but if you have only six sales to your name—on portals like *Rate My Agent* or *realestate.com.au*—at the end of a year, that's pretty much what you did!

Talk of technology brings us to the wonderful world of Facebook (FB) and the joys of social media in general. At its best, a valuable new tool in the modern arsenal of multiple marketing channels, however, more typically a delightful portal of pointless and unregulated self-obsessed drivel. The key word there is unregulated (yes, and drivel!). In the good old days of only having print media available via the newspaper or office printed flyers there tended to be—a little—more control on the content at a management or independent editorial level. Also, the very construct of the newspaper advertising sections—alongside others in the marketplace—to a degree ensured a more professional format and exposure for any self-marketing. By contrast, the web offers a free environment that has virtually no restrictions on quality or style of initial content. Just say what you like, who can really check? Happy days!

The first common area for offenders is over exaggeration or bending the definitions slightly to increase impact. "I've done four contracts already this week - going off!" proclaims the gung-ho agent via their social media page. What they don't say is they were simply low *offers*, not completed contracts, so two didn't get agreed by the owner and one withdrew their interest, hence they have only completed one full transaction! *"Three offers already this morning, and it is only 11am!"* That's because two of them are just in the form of verbal feedback from call backs and count for little, perhaps?

As a rule, always be highly suspicious of the oh-so-busy agent that is never *too* busy to update their Facebook status as the very first priority, before the ink is even dry on the paperwork. You can also double and triple dip on the same thing to create a veritable fog of activity! For any listing you can have the 'Coming Soon' post, followed up by a 'Just Listed', then a 'First Open

Home', followed by 'Contract Secured', 'Unconditional' (SOLD sign up) and 'Settlement'! At least six posts for the same piece of stock!

To be honest though, it generally works because most people see things pop up in their feeds but don't necessarily register much of the detail, so they become vaguely aware that this agent is really busy, posting updates all the time with listings and sales. If you then add in—very generously—sharing your fellow agents' listings as well (because most people won't actually realise they aren't yours) then the possibilities are endless! That is assuming we have got something tangible—i.e., completed contract, new listing, etc.,—to talk about, as most of the time bold assertions are created out of much less!

The second theme, therefore, is to talk up other activities to mask the lack of a true result. The supposed point of difference post style is a classic example of this. "Working on Sunday, unlike other agents, but that's what I do for my vendors," smugly announces the agent ... once! Well *clearly* it's not what you usually do otherwise you wouldn't feel the need to tell us all specifically (or would have a similar update *every* Sunday?). The true translation is, "Shit, some idiot wants me to do a bloody inspection on Sunday. No real interest, but outside chance of a payday—and desperately need it—so I will reluctantly do it for 20 minutes if they fit in with me. Anyway at least I can look good on Facebook". Chances are nothing comes from the inspection as they are tyre kickers, but that shouldn't get in the way of a good post opportunity (and God forbid, if they do commit and you get a Sunday contract, there's another two or three solid gold posts at least!).

If you don't even have any inspections to play with then you have to get a little more creative: "Out and about today delivering flyers to my local community and having some great conversations," accompanied by a photo or—even worse—shaky handheld video of said flyers in your hand with a suitable street scape before you. Wow!

Now you may have indeed walked all morning and had some exchanges with unsuspecting people—who walked out into their garden at the wrong moment—or you may have just walked for five minutes for the photo opportunity ... who knows? Exactly! Pictures of your open home about to start are another good one with either the exterior decked out in all its finery—flags, directional signs, branded car—or the inside with (if you are diligent and can be bothered) your prepared brochures, flyers, and general welcome presentation on display.

The final well-trodden route is when you give up completely with linking your output to specific business-related activities and go *'off-piste'* so to speak. The world then becomes your oyster with random arty pictures of flowers or the sunset in your local area. Shout outs for other local businesses—gee, thanks—so you look community spirited and not in any way self-obsessed (if only they knew!). Recipes, general observations on life, all are fair game. You can also turn economist and start giving 'well' researched market updates, either cut and pasted from someone else who might know what they are talking about or—as a back handed promotional tool—based purely on what you and your wonderful office is doing at any given point of time (which is a fully rounded picture of the whole market, of course).

Now I admit this is somewhat of a contentious area. Myself, I don't want a recipe from a real estate agent (I would use a cookbook written by a chef, funnily enough). Likewise, your average salesman from the high street is probably not the greatest philosopher, economist, or professional photographer for that matter, so I personally tend to steer clear from too much of this output. This is directly at odds with most social media training gurus (much more on these guys later!) who will tell you it is vitally important your content isn't totally business oriented and you should talk about other things to show your human side and personality. I do get it, but still honestly wonder whether most people really care. If you can establish a potential contact through someone feeling they know you a little better or have an area of common ground, all well and good, but professional integrity, results and—very much so now—fees still are the key areas people want to know about, not so much whether you are as good at making a lasagne as Jamie Oliver.

I guess the basic take out with social media is simply always try to read between the lines and take everything with a substantial pinch of salt (oops, cooking tips again). After all, it's easy enough to post, "Two contracts already this week," as if this is just the causal norm, but if you then fail to post anything similar for the next few weeks, it's obvious you were desperately cashing in on the only bit of business you have done in the last months! Still, that's the game and, yes, we *all* have to play it!

Before leaving the vast arena of peddling things you are not expert in, I have to mention another blossoming modern genre, the injection of comedy and 'light entertainment'. Whilst some of this material is still delivered through social media channels, it also infects professional online video content, related to selling the property itself. Apparently, you must be a bit different or quirky to stand out and just not so damn boring and professional (you know, just like those seasoned news readers appearing with red noses and revolving bow ties to liven up informing us of the latest riots or economic downturn).

Enter the comic video, belly laugh as the jovial agent wise cracks all the way to the front door of his latest listing. Funny guy, he should be on the stage (but then, strangely enough, he isn't). Again, I am going against some of the 'dynamic' training, but we are selling a house, the buyers are buying a house and want to see it—and, I believe, professionally delivered information about it—not some clown self-indulging his secret aspirations to be a second-rate cruise ship entertainer. Moreover, if the agent has done their job with marketing costs, the owner is paying!

Now, *of course,* it is not about selling the house at all (but don't tell the aforementioned cash strapped owner that). This, ladies and gentlemen, is all about those other potential sellers out there seeing the video as well and somehow being wowed by all this fluff *(Too funny! Wish he could do that for me!).* This creative genius isn't contained if you don't have an immediate listing to sell, why not create a social media post of comical 'bloopers', outtakes from your previous shoots—no stop it, you're killing me, seriously!—or some quirky market update.

Now, there are a couple of agents for special mention in dispatches—they know who they are—who have become well known at both ends of the spectrum in this field. One, selling elite homes has gone down the route of full Hollywood production values and 'main feature' approach typically using hired supercars and a number of glamorous models—ladies that is, not the types of cars—to approach and then populate said luxury pad. I kid you not. Full marks for taking things to the extreme! However, my genuine and *only* favourite is another agent who posts regular monologues to camera, whilst driving between appointments, essentially parodying various situations and the irony of how both clients and agents act. Now this *is* comic gold, for one reason: he is not taking it seriously and is calling out the BS!

As touched on briefly in the last chapter, the endless procession of completely meaningless franchise-based internal sales awards falls squarely into the self-marketing, ego soothing category as well. We all know the agent who loves to give you a flyer proclaiming they are the (wait for it) *'Third best auction listing agent in November for Queensland (South)*—What the? Oh, and they got *Company X's 'Special Bronze Badge'* award because of it. Well, that is just peachy! *'Best Northside Office - Quarter 1'*— out of how many, just your franchise?—by what criteria? Who bloody cares! The general rule of thumb is everyone can be good at something if they try hard enough to come up with a category for it *(e.g., 'Best Marketeer'?!* Always a cracker!).

Again, the problem is one of genuine quantification, quality control and consistency. Theoretically, an award for pure sales commission generated, or number of houses sold, should be a true reflection. In most cases they are for the best performers, but I have still seen a few books 'cooked' just prior to an annual awards night to edge a favoured person over the line (adjustment of reported commission numbers, transfer of extra sales from departed ex-agents, etc.,). Other hollow awards often nominated by principals are there just for show, and are nothing more than vehicles to reward the current 'chosen one'—if they haven't qualified through other practical means—and give them something to modestly plaster over their next flyer and social media push.

The big franchises love their self-indulgent 'elite' performer clubs as well and give them great names like the Admiral's Club or Platinum Plus Agents. Even the poor old property managers can normally get in on this one with special membership of their own niche groups with commanding titles like Diamond Standard (or an occasional Greek God). This does incentivise internally and motivates employees to a degree, no issue there, but to your average punter on the outside world these awards and imposing names don't count for too much, I feel. Always the same, the team goes to the annual 'glittering' awards night and then the next day comes the flurry of social media posts about what a fabulous evening it was and all the awards they won.

Wow, what a surprise, but not really because you wouldn't have gone if you weren't getting something (don't want to be on the losers table). Shame we never hear about the *real* awards for the night: 'Pissed Before Arrival' award for outstanding pre-loading, 'Stays On Tour' award for most audacious drunken coupling of the night back at the hotel—or venue toilet—and finally the coveted 'No Hope' award for being face down in the fountain by 10 p.m. with no shirt or shred of dignity left.

I may be wrong, but I can't remember the last time the local baker advertised specifically how many bread rolls they made this morning. Perhaps it is because it's *their job* and they just get on with it! Yet many agents think this profession somehow gives them a divine right to *relentlessly* tell the world what they are doing and how damn fantastic they are. Saving people's lives on a regular basis as a paramedic or fireman, being an overseas aid worker in a war-torn region—perhaps there are professions we should really care to hear about, but doing 10 minutes of paperwork sitting at a comfy desk after a 20-minute house viewing ... really? Does the entire population need a bloody running commentary of your own self-magnificence?

Some of you may also be familiar with agent review websites, where customers and clients can post agent testimonials and rate their overall service. There is some genuine benefit in this of course as—by and large—it is independent narrative, as opposed to self-indulgent twaddle. One of the main sites has an annual awards system, for those agents who have achieved a high number of 5-star reviews. From an agent's perspective you do not need to have sold the most homes necessarily, simply have a good number of high-quality assessments within a specific area. This hopefully rewards those who go the extra mile, rather than the churn and burn brigade.

All good, and indeed I fully encourage people to use such sites, both when selecting agents and, if they are happy with the agent in the transaction they have just completed. The clever bit is that these awards are done by every single suburb, so in reality there are a great multitude of recipients. Winners are grinners, none more so than in real estate, so the company knows they will get good exposure for their brand and website because, guess what? Every single winning agent will immediately bombard the airwaves with their new shiny 'Agent of the Year' title, for whichever patch they have been awarded. Nothing particularly wrong in that, but just quite amusing at the same time each year we suddenly get a flurry of posts from a seemingly endless number of Agents of the Year.

Again, do the public really understand what that means? I am 'Agent of the Year (for Cheaptown)' all my communications now declare. The default assumption would probably be that is the most successful agent in terms of number of sales or commission earned. Who knows, it could be like a Rotten Tomatoes review, and I might simply be the best dickhead in the area by number of complaints, for all most people would check. Now reviews are a good thing to be judged by, so there is no harm done in this case, but nonetheless this title is pushed for all it is worth and often with deliberate vagueness as to what it represents in the hope it will imply all things to all people in terms of untouchable achievement.

Another angle that promotes the feeling of importance and *obvious* success is that of the selling 'team'. Instead of plain old John Smith, you can list your house with 'Team John Smith'. Wow, the combined talents of multiple agents, that sounds impressive. Perhaps, until you realise Team John Smith is still just plain old John Smith after all, with an underpaid—and under experienced—trainee (or his son) doing some of his donkey work when he can't be bothered himself. Not so much double strength as watered down.

You might see John at listing time to get you signed up but, come inspections and open homes, some other muppet will turn up instead (sorry didn't he mention that at the listing presentation?). He might get involved at the end again if an offer has to be negotiated (after all that's where the glory lies, not with running dead-beat tyre kickers). The selling team has become somewhat of a *vogue*, but in many cases it doesn't offer much over a single, dedicated and hardworking agent. As just covered, often the 'team' is created around one established individual who wants those list/sell numbers without being bogged down with everything that goes with it, so gets some cheap labour in. All good, as it looks important if you surely have enough business to warrant a team.

Another common reason is two individuals wanting to share the load and joining forces. Quite often this can be a husband-and-wife team, with one covering for the other on the school run, etc. Again, you might think two agents sounds better than one, but if the team is suggesting it consists of two fully functional agents then they should be doing twice as much business as a single agent! Another case of a somewhat arrogant, and condescending, opinion that the public care or hang on every aspect of your persona, so 'Team' will automatically make you seem super important and successful. Depressingly, of course, it sometimes works and that is why it is done. Just check the numbers first and ask who will be fronting the property when it is showtime: the organ grinder or the monkey? Before they rage, the true elites will often have teams around them as well—as they *really do* have too much business!—but this is slightly different as they will be handpicked and generally will have to make a solid contribution to an already high-performing group. No problems here, you just need to be careful and separate the wood from the trees.

Now you may think, at this stage, I am against all this self-promotion malarkey. Far from it, I am only frustrated by too much poor, lazy or misleading ego driven indulgence. The harsh reality is we all need to be marketed in some shape or form to be in that shop window for consideration. Of course, I use social media and have indeed created all manner of new listing, open home and sold posts over time. However, I like to think in the main they remain primarily factual and relatable to real business taking pace.

Upping the ante a little, one senior ex-colleague of mine from a previous company is a fine exponent in the consistent saturation approach. He creates the obligatory posts and tweets around transaction-based activity but, additionally, will never go more than a few hours with something new hitting the airwaves. Updates of open numbers/buyer behaviour, analysis of changing market trends, plus other 'valuable' discussions and interactions undertaken. In addition, some wholesome lifestyle posts of gym work/running or inspiring quotes to fill in the occasional business-related gaps. To credit him, they are generally all a reasonable quality, and it takes some discipline to keep up this consistency with anything meaningful. In isolation does this work to a greater degree? Do some people react to a photo of you still at your desk at 8 p.m. 'on the phones' and immediately think you're their guy. Potentially (if the price is right!), but I believe having a proactive office around you doing much the same thing is the real game-changer.

As we shall see later on, agencies that adopt an office-wide approach to this, with solid investment in properly structured ongoing advertising, unsurprisingly are more successful and garner a great deal of attraction business (potential clients actively contacting them, i.e., unsolicited). Agencies that do not, have a greater reliance on making the initial contacts first through the more traditional methods—phone calls, door knocking, etc.,—or simply hoping their individual agents will self-promote enough for them. As demonstrated above, to a degree most will, but typically short of spending too much of their own money on it (principals' job, right?). Talk is cheap, however, so the ultra-positive persona never stops, whether speaking to clients/customers, other agents or the pet dog for that matter.

Given all of this, here is a free tip: never waste your breath asking a sales agent 'how's business?'. No point, because the answer will always be the same come rain, shine, impending bankruptcy, nuclear attack or the general end of mankind. "Fantastic mate, really good —on fire at the moment!" (well maybe that's just the aforementioned nukes?). Ironic, but unaltered, the same response still comes when asked by one of your own colleagues or competitors in idle small talk at a social event (yet they already know the real answer, they just wanted to hear what you would say!). Remember, you can't kid a kidder! Still, remain ever present and ever positive. Never talk it down, never expose any weakness and never suggest any economic concerns, just brazen it out! After all, as every good trainer will ram down your throat—*there is no such thing as a bad market, just new opportunities* (to lose money and be an underperformer).

4 | First Contact

O kay, with some self-marketing done you have your face out there and you really can't put it off any longer, time to start creating some action! Unfortunately, this now means talking and dealing with the great unwashed of the general public. A scary proposition at the best of times as, let's face it, nobody out there likes agents, right? Where would any self-respecting survey of 'least trusted professions' be without the usual suspects heading the table. Real estate agents alongside our fellow brothers-in-arms in used car sales and the odd politician or two. Apparently, we are *all* annoying, devious and generally dishonest.

Is this fair? In truth, not, as agents are no more, or less, a reflection of society in general. There are good operators and there are bad operators. Warm, genuine and trustworthy professionals with an amazing work ethic, countered by mischievous, slack wasters! However, therein is the inherent problem. You see, our potential customers are *also* very much a reflection of the same society. Some are open and genuine, wanting—and listening to—good advice and guidance, yet others are far from fair or appreciative and in some cases darn right deceitful.

There is also a hierarchy problem as some people believe they have a right to treat you with disdain because they look down their nose at your job. Agents, unfortunately, are fair game to be used and abused, as 'that's what they deserve'. Perhaps some do, but the vast majority do not. It stands to reason that over time certain 'damage limitation' strategies are put in place by the average agent, through bitter experience, and in anticipation of what will be thrown at them next. As will be seen, there is a curious element of self-fulfilling prophecy created by those who complain about certain traits of agent conduct yet unwittingly are the very architects of such behaviour (which is simply being deployed as a legitimate countermeasure to said client's behaviour).

First contact for a newbie is more likely than not through cold calling or door knocking, at least until you are more established and can generate higher value connections through other activities like open homes and enquiries on your own stock. Unfortunately, this is about the worst end of the spectrum to start, as defensiveness and disdain run in equal measures. The last thing most people want to do—in particular at dinner time or the other annoying times we are drilled to call 'because someone will be home'—is to speak to another clown that's just phoned them out of the blue. Just like all those other parasites with a now predictable patter about 'being in their street this week', and the importance of knowing 'the current value of your home', with the killer and highly original close, 'even if just for insurance purposes'.

Most who bother to answer—and don't just ignore via caller ID— will be very short and non-committal at best, and it can become soul destroying. Very occasionally, someone caught off-guard might seem half interested and tentatively make a booking under pressure. Success! Well, maybe, but here's our first lesson: agree now, defer later! Just before your booked appraisal time they will call and cancel, or just message you that 'something has come up' and they will have to do some other time—*i.e., never*— and they will 'get back to you'. They had no real intention or interest to go through with the appraisal, they just agreed originally to get you off the phone more easily, until they could come back later with a decent excuse (need to de-scale the kettle over the next couple of days, so too busy, etc.). It's much the same for door knocking, they'll either hide and pretend they are not home or politely tell you to bugger off (well mostly).

I had a hilarious example of this once, going to pick up my son from the house of one of his school friends, after work. I had never met these particular parents before and was still in my work uniform, complete with name badge, when I knocked at their screen door. The front door itself was open and I could see the family in the distance sitting in the lounge at the far end of the house. Looking up and being able to discern there was an agent knocking at their door, they bravely dispatched their 10-year-old up the hallway to utter, "What do you want?". I assume had I answered as expected about wanting to speak to mum and dad about their house, he would have been prompted to say, "They are busy". There's nothing like getting the kid to do your dirty work and avoiding any direct contact! However, when I answered that I was here to pick up my son, the parents jumped up straight away, came to the door, welcomed me in and struck up a friendly conversation! I had passed from the dark to the light in one reply!

I digress slightly here, but my own experience of both cold calling and door knocking has never been great. You sit there forlornly looking at a list of meaningless downloaded numbers, knowing a third of them are out of date, a third will not answer and the final third will be very short with you at best, mildly abusive at worst. Of course, we are told this is a necessary evil to find that one 'right place, right time' person who will be ready to sell. I am not going to say that never happens, but it is a bit like panning for gold in your local creek. Targeted cold calling around listings and sales has the potential to be marginally more productive, but when starting—unless doing this on behalf of an established agent—you do not have anything to work with.

As already indicated, there is great deal of hypocrisy around mass cold calling. Everyone must do it at some point—primarily when starting out—but in my experience *nobody* likes it and the moment you gain any momentum via other means, you quietly drop it whilst maintaining to your colleagues that you are still doing it (and, of course, in any KPI review). Principals are not stupid—well most of them at least—and they know this all too well, hence the attempts to corral staff through scheduled mandatory group calling sessions. Gimmicks such as free pizza after two-hour evening call sessions or little prizes for each appraisal gained try to make this a 'fun' activity, in much the same way as going to the dentist is.

Channelling Dennis Denuto, *it's all about the vibe!* The idea is if everyone is in it together battling away side by side, it isn't so bad, right? Well, yes, it is. One of my offices had a dreaded two-hour call competition every Tuesday afternoon. It would hang heavy over you all day prior. The principal would sit in their office, door open and listen, occasionally shouting out, "Can't hear many calls being made!" when it was obvious there was no flood of eager conversations, more of a laconic trickle. If you got a win, typically through saving up a secret call-back you already knew would yield a positive response from an earlier discussion—so wasn't even a true cold call, but hey, whatever gets you through, right?—you got to ring a little bell and be given a chocolate for your trouble (and bask in 15 seconds of adulation before back to the phones).

To add further excitement, we had a quarterly competition to see who could get the most cold call appraisals—via the call competition sessions—with an even bigger prize (probably two chocolates, I don't know, having never won it!). We had a league table on the wall with weekly numbers and a running tally. Great if you jagged a few somehow, but somewhat demoralising (the idea) if you did not. Zero *again?* Go see teacher to explain! It is no coincidence the boss is called a principal in real estate because it is sure as hell like being back at school!

Door knocking is not much better. At least you are out in the fresh air, but there is always a suspicious number of houses with no one home—despite the TV being on in the background!—punctuated with the occasional curt answer or angry dog. On the one hand, it is slightly more personable than a call, but on the other you are directly invading people's space, crossing their property boundary to confront them head on (if you are lucky).

Again, apathy and lack of consistency, combined with a more enlightened awareness to security in recent times—e.g., not asking a female agent to door knock at odd hours by themselves in some random neighbourhood—leads to abortive attempts at making this a group activity as well. The blob drives to a predetermined location and then fans out and covers multiple streets at a time. Every office-based agency I have been at has tried this at one time or another with usually very limited success. Some would at least trust the sales staff to go out on their own and self-regulate as a group, whilst one agency would employ the sales manager to circle around constantly in his car to ensure you were doing your job, street by painful street (and not sitting in the park for a quick smoke). Trust, hey? I would say terrible, but of course some would bunk off if they thought they could get away with it!

You see it is apparently all about creating a pipeline of ongoing people you can speak with, leading them ultimately into your listing 'funnel' (the favourite white board diagram for every training occasion). 'Everything happens for a reason', at least we would like to think so. In real estate terms that should be listing a home (and subsequently selling it) because from a first point of contact with somebody you have tracked them, worked on them, and ultimately 'processed' them to the point of tangible business. Indeed, this concept is constantly used to justify any and all activities. It doesn't matter if after 1,000 cold calls you only have three harassed, and not overly interested, people to show for your efforts, they are 'valuable' contacts who will eventually progress to becoming sellers one day, or so the story goes.

Returning to our beloved public, as things develop and we start to have better conversations through other channels, surely matters should improve? Ideally, but the more complex situations in which these discussions can happen ensure more trickiness and disappointment with people's behaviour. Thus, we protect ourselves, and any number of common grievances over supposed agent conduct can be attributed to established tactics adopted simply to minimise distress! *'Buyers are liars ... and sellers are worse'*, so we are told by our more experienced colleagues as we embark on our journey. Turns out, they are not just embittered, in a lot of cases they are dead right! Now that may sound harsh and, in fairness, most do not set out to be deceptive, but as circumstances change around an individual, so their requirements, motivation, engagement and communication can all alter dramatically. To demonstrate, let's take a couple of classic scenarios and look at them from both sides of the coin.

As a buyer, you go through an open house and potentially give the agent details of exactly what you are looking for. Then you became very frustrated as you are emailed details of houses that don't match your specific criteria. Didn't the agent listen to me? They are now sending me things that are totally different to what I asked for! Surely the agent should only send exactly what the buyer is looking for, so as not to upset them and for the best chance of a match? Annoying? Ignorant? Well perhaps, on the surface. However, the reality of the situation is very, very often the buyer does not end up purchasing something that matches their original criteria.

Again, this is not through being deliberately deceptive, but simply whilst looking, something turns their head in a different direction and before you know it all bets are off on the original idea. Unfortunately, the agent who respected their wishes and only sent limited properties—perhaps also spending a good deal of time tracking down extra possibilities that matched their exact criteria—has probably now missed out, whilst the agent who hedged their bets and sent them a much broader selection regardless, has inadvertently still provided them with something that fits their amended plans.

Now here's the rub, a person who gives you their original criteria and only wants precise matches will *never* call you to advise if their criteria changes, so unless you have a sixth sense you will also always miss out. Conversely, a person who might moan initially that you aren't respecting their wishes will instantly forgive and forget if you still happen to match them with something else they end up buying.

Even knowing this well, it is still easy to fall into the trap from time to time. I had a buyer I knew from a previous transaction who was very definite on a *four bedroom, two bath, brick low-set requirement in two or three specific 'good areas' locally.* I tried to line up entirely matching homes and got him through a couple that were apparently 'close', only to discover a day later that he had put a contract on one of my colleague's properties in a relatively rough area of a completely different suburb. As if that wasn't enough, it was a *three bed, one bath, Hardie™ Plank high-set!* About as far removed from his criteria of two days previously as you could get! His reasoning—when I called him after the event—was he had only gone to that property to support his son who was viewing it (also looking to purchase a property). He decided on the spot he liked the look of it himself and it was a lot cheaper than the other things he was viewing! Okay, then (not like I wasted my time or anything).

Another favourite bugbear, this time from a potential seller's perspective, is once they have had an appraisal conducted, then being constantly hounded by the agent every day as to whether they are ready to list yet. At the time of the appraisal, it was made quite clear that they weren't listing yet, they were 'just getting an idea', so why doesn't the agent listen and leave them alone?! Seems reasonable? That depends on whether you must earn your living from ensuring you get the listing! You see, a lot of people will try to insulate themselves from having to decide on the spot. By stating they are not ready yet, they hope to dampen the agent's inbuilt eagerness for an immediate outcome.

Truth is, in many cases they are actually ready to decide—otherwise they wouldn't be inviting this random person into their house—but they just don't want the agent to know that until they have called a few in and had time to determine the best option. In this case, the agent who respects the seller's wishes on face value, so doesn't hound them and 'will call in a month's time' runs a very high risk of missing out.

The agent who repeatedly calls regardless, *may* piss the seller off in the short term, but may just as equally wear them down and be 'Johnny on the Spot' when they decide in the next few days. Add to this, a principal or sales manager breathing down your neck constantly asking you if you have followed up again on that promising lead and there is a genuine need to harass! Despite this, I freely admit I have long been guilty of the *do not overly intrude* approach, only to miss out on a few listings to those who are more aggressively recontacting.

Unfortunately, with many conversations and social interactions the potential for misunderstanding or misdirection is large. Another buyer favourite, "Oh, I put an offer on that property first and the agent didn't even get back to me. He sold it to someone else". Terrible! Really? Until we drill down a bit deeper to find out their 'offer' was a low-ball verbal-only offer that the agent simply advised the owner would not consider—or counteroffer—unless the buyer put it in writing and was prepared to up the initial indicated figure. The buyer thinks they can play the game with the agent so refuses to do either, but insists they leave their interest 'on the table'. Given, at this point, there is effectively no formal interest to go forward with, the agent legitimately moves on and ends up selling it to a serious buyer (who commits an offer in writing with a reasonable starting figure). There is no requirement to go back to the initial buyer first either, who then gets the shits when they miss out— i.e., their little ploy didn't work—so somehow blames it on the agent.

Trouble is, that people hear the superficial story and always assume the agent must have acted unreasonably when, in fact, on behalf of their seller—who they work for!—they have done exactly the *right* thing. The first buyer has created the situation by wilfully refusing to commit to a formal approach or sensible starting price, in the hope of getting the property on the cheap (regardless of whether they might have had some vague intention to increase the offer later).

Having had my own experiences with several buyers like this over the years, the irony is the pattern typically repeats and they *seemingly* miss out on several properties they have supposed interest in. Either all the agents they are dealing with have the same dubious traits and lack of apparent communication or perhaps—more likely—this minimalist, non-commitment approach is somewhat flawed?

Another constant frustration is when an agent just won't tell you what the owners actually want in terms of a price, "Mate, come on, what's going to buy this? You must know!". Surely, if the buyer is keen, give them the genuine bottom line and there is a very good chance of a swift agreement? Wrong! Well, firstly—as just mentioned—we work for the seller and are attempting to get the best price and won't hamper this by giving away the bottom line immediately *(well, perhaps!).*

In some instances, however, the owner needs a quick sale and is happy to divulge a minimum sell figure. Great, except buyers think agents are liars as well—as a default position—so the irony is even if we do give the genuine figure of where the owner is at, the buyer will then take that and *still* offer a figure below, essentially not believing the agent or simply now trying it on (as the owner must be able to move a bit more). What is the point?

"You can't handle the truth!". Correct, Jack. Hence, never give them the real bottom line and always add a bit on top. The very thing the buyers think we are doing anyway! Ah, so goes the endless cycle of mistrust!

Even something as simple as when someone calls on your mobile can be distorted. You are on a landline—or with a client—and it goes to message bank, and they leave a voice message. Fine, but being impatient on possibly missing out on their dream home or having their offer heard, they then call the office reception number *instantly* afterwards and complain they have been *'trying to contact the agent'* about a property, *'but he is not returning their calls'*. Give me a bloody chance!

One aspect of the way people interact is often wanting to take the easy route out of an otherwise difficult or uneasy conversation. A seller might withdraw the property from sale with you and say they are *'just taking a break from the market for a while'* hoping to exit quietly, only to list it two days later with someone else. They did not have the courage to admit it directly to you. This can be quite amusing at times, people scrabbling for soft responses or throwing their partner under the bus to save themselves! "Oh, I liked the property, but my wife has said no, sorry" (so please don't shoot the messenger). Of course, if you could speak to the wife independently her story would probably be, "I didn't mind it, but hubby isn't keen to go that high on our budget".

This is all bad enough at a superficial level, but things can sometimes get a bit darker when problems and disagreements occur within a contract, with potential financial and emotional fallout. The sad fact about being the middleman is whenever there is a dispute the buyer or seller will, if possible, want to ensure no attachable blame comes their way (with any legal/monetary repercussions). When your back is to the wall, just too tempting, try to blame the agent!

Yep, here comes that bus again, except this time *you* are under it! When two sides are talking, primarily via a third party, then the most likely scapegoat is usually said third party (who *clearly* misunderstood something or got a vital issue 'lost in translation'). How convenient! Amazing how recollections can dim very quickly when expedient. Whilst I am not suggesting everyone takes that route, I have experienced numerous such instances. Even with people who have been perfectly reasonable to that point, but then panic under pressure or when optimum financial outcomes might be slightly endangered.

To avoid confusion, perhaps we should add to the list of services provided under a listing agreement: 'Official stooge for disputes and general punchbag, as required'. In truth, not a bad option as most agents and agencies will not risk a public dispute or legal action as is it not a good look, regardless of their convictions. Easier to absorb a small fee adjustment or other action to 'fix' a situation rather than make a big and costly production out of it.

In closing, I'll sight an example of client behaviour that happened to me only relatively recently. I had sold a four bedroom home achieving both a street and local estate record. Yes, sorry, that sounds like typical ego talk but, nonetheless, it was a record, albeit during the pandemic madness where—as will be covered later—just about any joker could get an amazing result due to mass buyer hysteria (not that you tell Joe Public that).

Indeed, I duly executed my local area 'Just Sold' flyers promoting this achievement, in the hope of follow-on business. For once (!) this did result in contact from a neighbour across the street who got my correspondence and noted the SOLD sticker going up on the opposite side of the road. This owner had realised the sale had happened quite quickly and was very impressed to find out the figure we had achieved. They didn't yet have their house suitably prepared for marketing photos/public sale but were definitely intending to sell and wanted to explore the opportunity of seeing whether I had buyers left over from the previous sale that I could recontact and run through 'off-market', i.e., without needing to openly advertise or prepare the house to show conditions.

This is a legitimate technique potentially saving the owner marketing costs and giving already qualified buyers the opportunity to view something before it goes 'public'. During the heightened COVID-19 market this method became quite common as agents had a good source of keen buyers, and sellers realised they could potentially utilise existing competition for a higher sale price without going through more expensive and complex activities.

Having met the owners and inspected their house, I was both pleased they had recognised my success with the other property —and shown faith to contact me—and that the property itself was entirely compatible for the many buyers I did, indeed, still have on the books. Wonderful! What could go wrong? Well, my first—frankly rookie—mistake was to be slightly too confident of my position (and too accommodating). The owner wanted to explore the off-market opportunities first and then, if this didn't produce anything suitable, consider a separate normal market listing.

I suggested we just put in place a very basic open list agreement for the off-market stage with no advertising, etc., simply to give me the essential legal authority to contact buyers about the house and run them through. In the event this did not produce the desired effect, we would then negotiate/sign a separate exclusive agreement with associated advertising as normal. In my past experience, many owners are wary of getting locked down in an exclusive arrangement for months, before they are ready or have assessed the agent performance (in particular when an unknown agent contacts them, claiming they have a 'buyer for the property'). I fully understand this, so in offering an open arrangement for the off-market stage, I demonstrated I was focused on that process first, and was not just using it as a convenient *trojan horse* to tie the owner down to something else. Of course, in demonstrating your virtues, you assume the owner will appreciate this and effectively reciprocate in how they act. I judged these owners to be genuine, friendly and keen to do business, so where's that harm?

With the listing authority duly signed, I went about contacting around 30 qualified buyers directly from my database (who had been interested in the previous property), including some underbidders in the multiple offer situation we recently had. After a week or so of careful work, I had identified and shortlisted around eight groups with serious interest, four of whom were highly motivated to inspect as soon as possible. We arranged a closed inspection session one Saturday afternoon and brought each group through in turn. During this time the owners seemed impressed with the response we were getting and my communications as to how things were progressing.

From the four inspections, we received three subsequent offers on the day, including one exceptionally good offer from a lovely young couple who had already been looking in the area for several weeks. I worked through getting the best figures from each group and at the end of the process the young couple offered a figure slightly higher than the property over the road (thereby another potential street/estate record). This was also very close to the 'dream' price the owner had indicated they might dare to hope for in this crazy market. Whilst their house was bigger than the previous one, the presentation and condition was certainly not as good, so I felt the offer was again an exceptionally good outcome (given we were off-market and not advertising in any way).

We should never count chickens, but I was confident this was in the bag already. As it turned out, however, this was the high point of the exercise and things started to slowly unravel from there. The owners, presented with this all-round excellent offer—they also wanted a long settlement period, which these buyers could grant—on the Saturday evening, initially indicated they needed the weekend to consider and just check in with their bank regarding finances on Monday morning. They were building a new house and wanted to double-check that the swap-over numbers worked with this offer. Also, the bigger decision was a bird in the hand—i.e., this offer—versus could they get more money by the extra competition of going to the open market and advertising?

There's no correct answer to that, but it would cost them to find out, both financially and in preparation time for the house. It was somewhat frustrating they hadn't already worked this through, but I duly accepted the situation, advised the buyers, and held the offer through until the start of the following week. Monday came, no updates. After some chasing, the owner advised he had been too busy with work to speak with the bank yet, so it would be another couple of days now for a final decision (so could I just hold the buyers a little longer).

That uneasy feeling started, but given there was not much alternative, I advised the buyers in good faith, being open with them and explaining the seller's situation with their bank (and building their next home, etc.). In doing so, I did stress to the owner that the longer they kept these buyers hanging, the more chance they might come across something else or simply lose patience, so time was of the essence. It appeared the only decision was either taking this excellent off-market offer or risk going fully to market instead.

Things dragged on—I'm now starting to become really concerned—then finally on Thursday afternoon (after more chasing) the owner responded indicating that, after initial discussion with the bank, the current offer figure was 'workable' for them, so I could advise the buyers. However, they were waiting on some 'written confirmation from the bank', so the only proviso was they could not sign the formal contract until the following Monday morning (that being nine days since the original offer was made). As frustrating as this was, we appeared to have an agreement. So, I advised my very tolerant buyers their offer figure, and their generous settlement conditions, were verbally acceptable to the owners. We should be formally signing off on the Monday, once the final bank documentation was available to the owners.

Slow process, but all was at least good now. Yet as any seasoned agent will tell you, never get too excited until the ink is dry on *all* signatures! Oh yes, and my bubble was burst really quick! Having advised my buyers of the 'good news' on the Thursday evening, I took a concerned call from them on the Friday morning. Had anything changed overnight, they enquired? No, all good from my side.

Then came the sucker punch. The buyers informed me they had just had a call from *another* local agent inviting them to an 'off-market' viewing opportunity the next day at, you guessed it, the SAME house! Somewhat dumbstruck I suggested perhaps there was some confusion, and it was in the same street—as mentioned, this had become a more common method—but no, it was very clearly the same property. I was confused and somewhat embarrassed to be hearing this from my buyers who, I had effectively advised the night before, had bought the house!

Furthermore, the other agent was one I knew, who had a less-than-glowing reputation and used all the tricks of trade. I apologised to my buyers and said I would contact the owners to find out what on earth was going on. Clearly sensing things were now not as they appeared, I thought I would give these owners one chance to 'come clean' by their own hand. Having called, I initially relayed I had spoken to the buyers, advised them their offer figure was now acceptable and they were excited and ready to run with the contract on Monday. I waited … nothing. The owner simply acknowledged that was 'great'.

Okay, they had their chance! "Before I go," I said, "just one other thing. These buyers are a little concerned, as they have just been invited to a private viewing at your house tomorrow, by another agent." Dead silence. After a seemingly lengthy and very pregnant pause, the fumbling started. The owner admitted he had spoken 'some time ago' to another agent—who had sold a house further down the street—and they said they had a database as well, so they *may* have contacted some of their buyers (but he didn't realise they would contact mine as well, *sorry*).

Firstly, I put him straight on the concept that no one owns buyers and despite all the fanfare and BS about special databases, by and large, we are all talking to the same people in the same area. However, more importantly there was still no mention of anything else. I pushed again, "Straight question, do you have another agent doing counter inspections at your house tomorrow?" Dead silence again. Followed by some mumbled half acknowledgement, but only as an 'insurance policy' because they didn't know how well my inspections might go in the first instance (even though this was a week later and they had an excellent outcome!).

Trying to defend the position, it just got worse. They would 'probably' still go with my buyers but they just wanted to 'double-check' things first, but they weren't wasting time as only buyers that were of the 'same level as the offer' were coming through. I saw a red light immediately, as it was now apparent they had divulged the details of my offer to the other agent, despite the fact that figures should not be public knowledge in private treaty negotiations.

I was incredibly angry, not that the owner might seek to get the best outcome they could from more than one source, but the duplicitous and devious way they had gone about it. If the second agent had not, by sheer coincidence, contacted the same buyers as I already had, we would have been absolutely none the wiser and in blissful ignorance (which is exactly what the owner wanted until he had all his options on the table).

The whole Monday 'bank confirmation' was a smokescreen to buy time for additional inspections without my knowledge. The owner had used the loophole of the open agreement to sign a second open agreement and hedge his bets. Fine, but with no explanation to me, and certainly denying me any effective right of reply, the other agent had a massive advantage in knowing what the target was and being 'last in'. I also knew this particular agent would have the knack of ensuring, *somehow,* they got a slightly better offer on the table to blow me out of the water, come what may (even if it was from their Uncle Bob, with generous get out clauses for later).

Indeed, this agent even contacted my buyers again and tried to coerce them to withdraw their offer with me and resubmit with them 'for a better chance'! (which they refused to do). Long story short—thank goodness, you say—after a further couple of days of delaying tactics the owners miraculously got a marginally better offer and immediately took it instead, leaving my poor loyal buyers (and me) high and dry.

The point? Being highly deceptive, untruthful, not responding to calls and chasing the last dollar, are surely all things those terrible agents do? Yes, for sure sometimes, but understand there are plenty of clients they serve who will give them a very good run for their money! For what it's worth, there was an interesting postscript to this tale. A few months later—allowing for the long settlement—I rechecked the ownership of the house and it had not changed hands and had not sold after all (and hasn't to this day). Perhaps the alternative contract price was too high—and the buyer flaky on finance and/or building and pest results—or perhaps it was indeed just Uncle Bob. Perhaps, there just is karma ... occasionally.

5 | To Price, or Not to Price

Assuming you have made some tentative headway on creating new contacts, hopefully before too long you will start getting some requests for appraisals. Great, but if you think that means things will start to get any easier from here, or your first sale is already in the bag, there are plenty of hurdles to come. First and foremost is what are you going to do in terms of a price evaluation?

With any property, there are two types of assessment an owner—or buyer—can usually receive. There are formal valuations, typically used for obtaining bank approvals for purchase loans or re-financing. These are conducted by independent qualified valuers working to a reasonably regimented structure of property size and directly comparable recent sales. Valuations cost a fee and are generally only done when needed, as part of the aforementioned financing process or for an independent assessment in situations like mortgagee sales or asset disposal (marriage separations, deceased estates, etc.). By their nature, on balance, they tend to be slightly more conservative (unless the latest unofficial 'directive' from the banks is we want to give money away more easily for the next six months).

Enter the real estate agent, at this point, with the alternative free and fun-filled option of a market appraisal. Unlike the valuation, there is little structure or conservatism needed here! You are fully 'qualified' as well, of course—with your whole five-day REIQ course and 10 minutes with the boss when you started—and you are *free*. So, most owners will get an appraisal rather than a valuation, unless they are forced to for legal reasons.

Appraisals can use more 'artistic license' with—hopefully—some reference to directly comparable recent sales, but a greater degree of interpretation by the agent through their 'expert' local knowledge of the real-world market (apparently) and their gut feel for what the property can really achieve. Problem is—unlike the valuer—you are not *very* independent as, ultimately, the appraisal, for you, is just a means to an end, i.e., getting the underlying listing, if the client is thinking of selling.

Hence, accuracy and detail are the first casualties of war, up against ensuring you get the follow-on business. In most cases appraisals tend to be higher than equivalent valuations and, interestingly, if a legal process is using agent-based appraisals—rather than a formal valuation—typically the client is asked to obtain at least three to ensure representative price evidence (the legal fraternity isn't so trusting!).

Funny, isn't it? In virtually any other walk of life when you engage someone for their professional opinion, that's:

i. what you want, and
ii. expect to get

After all, ask a doctor about the results of a critical scan and you would probably want the truth, warts-and-all so to speak, rather than a fluffed up, 'all good' non-committal answer (and fingers crossed you won't die soon). Why then, in real estate, is the primary objective of many agents, and their corporate training, centred around doing everything possible to *not* provide a specific price opinion?

On the surface, some may sight slack agents who don't want to put the detailed research in, or those who are simply not confident or experienced in the market. In most instances, however, this is not borne of tardiness or lack of knowledge, but the bitter experience of most sellers not actually wanting to hear the very thing they have asked for! "All we want is an honest opinion," says Mr and Mrs Seller as you sit down with them. Guess what? Oh no you don't!

'Don't lose it on price' is the much-worn mantra of many a sales manager and principal when an agent is about to set off for a listing presentation ... and with good reason. You see, people will *eventually* accept the inevitable truth about the real value of their beloved home, but not usually up front. Don't listen to the nagging voice of reason, much better to go with the smiley, ultra-positive guy that says the market is *just pumping* and the property is worth every cent you want and more! ("Just sign here – NOW.")

Time and time again the diligent (sorry, naive) agent gives a genuine assessment based on detailed and comparable research, only to be beaten to the punch by the guy that fluffs up the numbers or *somehow* avoids the whole price opinion thing altogether, and just talks themselves up, regardless. This again is another example of how the industry has evolved to counter a problem created by the end client. The common complaint is agents always 'talk things up' and cannot be trusted on price, and yet, this is exactly what they must do in a lot of cases to ensure they have some chance on winning any business they may be in competition on. Frustrating it may be, but when you are commission-only and your livelihood depends on it, constantly taking the moral high-ground can send you broke very quickly!

The good operators can work somewhere in the middle, providing credible relevant research, then using specific examples—with crafted wording—to effectively draw out of the owner what their price mindset is, without them even realising. To some degree, they can then position themselves accordingly in their responses. The key here though, if allowing the seller the potential to pursue their ideal price in the first instance, is ensuring—at the point of listing—you engineer an agreed mechanism to review price feedback (and adjust accordingly) if this is not obtainable. This may be via an auction process with a scheduled reserve determination, or simply building a formal price review in after an agreed period of one to two weeks.

We will cover auctions in more detail later, but it is probably worth looking at the associated price strategies at this point, as discussion around this is generally linked to the appraisal figure reveal (or lack of it!). Without stating the obvious, there are essentially two routes to consider. Listing with a price, or without.

Listing with a price has several variations. All fall under the term 'private treaty' which means any presentation of offers and subsequent negotiations are not conducted in the public domain—as with an auction—but instead on a one-on-one basis via the agent. At its simplest, a straight list price can be placed on a property (e.g., '$450,000'). Unequivocal, the buyer knows the exact—worst case, for them—figure the owner wants, so has more confidence in terms of that property being within their budget. The owner, however—unless the market is highly active and receives multiple offers—is probably capped at the indicated figure, as most buyers will not feel they need to exceed it unless under the pressure of direct competition. They will most likely try negotiating against the stated figure, but everyone is clear on the starting point at least.

In this case, unless specifically instructed, the agent should not— in the first instance—be indicating immediate negotiation below the list price is possible.

"Mate, how much will they take then?"

"Well, I know my clients will take $450,000, as stated."

Unwavering execution of this principle is patchier in practice, but it sounds good in theory! The softened version of this strategy is when the owner is open to approaches around the stated figure and is happy to indicate such (e.g., '$450,000 Negotiable'). This again indicates the upper end to a buyer, but also shows openly they can make reasonable offers against it, which the owner will at least consider. Without immediate competition, the owner— to a degree—is probably giving away the $450,000 in this instance, as everyone will now feel they can negotiate unless backed into a corner.

Now we come to the more contentious price indications. A method that has gained a lot of use in recent years is **'Offers Over'**. Not necessarily popular with buyers, however, many of whom have been burnt by this strategy and see it as divisive. The premise is it still provides a general price guide as to where the sellers sit, but—from their perspective—doesn't cap the upside potential in the same way as a fixed figure, effectively asking people to go up from the number stated, rather than negotiate down from it.

That's fine, but the problems start with how this is utilised in practice. All good if the owners will seriously look at any offers over the stated figure, but too many times it is used to artificially cheapen the house and attract inspections when the stated figure is much lower than that which the owners will accept. To put this in context, the example $450,000 house I would probably have as 'Offer Over $445,000' or 'Offer Over $449,000'. This softens the price slightly—placing it 'below' the $450,000 benchmark from a buyer's initial perception—whilst opening up potential above $450,000, but crucially, from a buyer's perspective, is still indicating a price level from which the sellers will be talking seriously.

Nonetheless, this can easily be abused and there are agents—and agencies—that would list this at 'Offers Over $419,000' for example, knowing fully well their seller still wants $450,000, but tempting buyers with a false sense of price point. The perceived benefits are better viewing numbers for the agent and feedback that probably enables them to start wearing down the owner on their starting price. However, the 'sell' to the owner is this will create extra competition and they will easily be able to bring the final price paid up to $450,000 through buyer demand and rivalry. To a point perhaps, if you are lucky, but most buyers are not too impressed when they put in a genuine offer around $420,000 say, to be told the counter position is at least $450,000!

There are a few other variations along this theme such as 'Suit Buyers Over $450,000', 'Suit Buyers Mid $400k+', etc., all doing much the same in terms of softening, but with some form of guide price retained. The irony of all this is nowadays most buyers have access to past sales and online valuations—not to mention having inspected many houses in the local market—and will simply offer what the perceived value is, regardless of the price label.

Therefore, does 'Offers Over' work? Well, that depends where you position it and what the owner wants. If the figure is below the likely general market valuation, then people will indeed pay over the stated figure without too much drama. Likewise, if the offers over figure is above the general market feel for the property, people will come in below it and simply ignore the figure (sometimes the criticism of this method from a would-be seller). Pitched correctly in relation to the true property value a good connection/outcome is likely. But pitch it $40,000 below the (unrealistic) price the owner wants—to disguise this—and it's highly unlikely you will get anyone coming up to the figure that the owner thinks you are still going to get for them.

The governing authorities—in principle at least—also take a dim view of deliberate price misrepresentation through low offers over pricing, although in practice how often this gets pulled up is questionable. I have heard many horror stories from buyers, over the years, of attempted offers on other properties with significant variance between the indicated price and the owner's true requirement.

Listing with no price, as the name suggests, removes any indication as to what the owner is wanting. Auction is the main vehicle for this, but equally a growing trend in unpredictable markets is for private treaty listings to also display 'no price' (at least initially). Offers and negotiations will still be dealt with confidentially—and there are generally no fixed deadlines imposed—but a degree of wider competition and assessment of market feedback is attempted, as with an auction process. Properties can just be advertised as 'For Sale', or 'Price By Negotiation', 'Inviting Offers', and so on.

Although most agents will not admit it, before the recent pandemic market—see below—this was primarily used when the owner's starting figure was too high, and you didn't want to put that figure on the house (but not lose their listing either!). Hence, we go down the line, 'Well, let's see if that's out there without *burdening* the property with a set price'—nice! Simple translation: *Crap, I am not putting $520,000 on a $450,000 house!* It's a cop-out because if you are really chasing a better outcome, confidently through no price competition, you would go down the auction route and be done with it. But that is more costly and involved, so just suggest no price for the first few weeks until you can come up with plan B. In my experience most buyers hate a non-auction property listed with no price and either skip it completely or assume the seller's expectation is too high (usually correctly!).

Ultimately, however you choose to dance around either the appraisal price or subsequent proposed list price, as mentioned, you must ensure to build in some form of agreed review mechanism if the seller's price is too high. As we will cover in a later chapter, the danger is without this you blindly sign the listing off at too high a price and there it stays until the next cherry-picking agent comes along and takes it from you!

In saying all that, the recent COVID-19 situation, and the unexpectedly strong sales in the housing market resulting from it, made things quite interesting for a while. We will cover this in more detail later, but in summary, during the period of the pandemic we had reduced stock—lack of people going to market—yet strong buyer activity (cheap bank loans and a healthier economy than first feared). The simple economics of low supply, coupled with high demand, led to extreme competition for many residential homes and some exceptional prices being obtained.

This somewhat skewed the usual model, as you could probably run with an inflated appraisal figure and have much more chance of getting away with it! Mind you, a self-perpetuating chasing of the tail situation was inevitably created. With stock in noticeably short supply, the competition for listings amongst agents became even more intense than normal. Knowing the market is hot for the sale— if you can just nail down the property—what do you do in this situation? Add twice as much on top as usual, of course!

Better still, promise almost anything is possible, the sky is the limit in this crazy market! In short, succumb to whatever fantasy world the owner is living in, with little or no resistance because:

i.   you absolutely cannot lose the listing, and
ii. there is an outside chance some desperate buyer will pay a *drug-money* figure anyway

Even if not, competition should be intense, and you can use all this ample feedback to position the seller quickly and get the thing gone before anyone else has a sniff. By and large this worked very well for a while and those who—even in normal circumstances—had no qualms about accurate price determination were often rewarded, regardless.

'Offers Over' and, most certainly, 'No Price' suddenly got a new lease of life as it was quite possible to get in excess of $50,000, or more, on top of pre-COVID expectations. I had success during this period with multiple offers on a number of 'Offers Over' listings with outcomes ranging from $7,000 to $35,000 over indicated base price. The key here (at least initially) was still grounding the 'offers over' price at a realistic level to create strong interest and inspection numbers, then letting the competition drive the final price up through natural buyer anxiety and fear of loss.

In my experience during 2020, buyers were prepared to contest and pay more, but only for something they considered to initially be reasonably correctly positioned, price wise. Buyers were certainly anxious, but not completely stupid (or so we thought).

No, complete insanity then ensued from early 2021 when all common sense departed, and some figures being achieved bore absolutely no relationship to the property they were attached to! This further escalated the approach from some agents to the point that any half-hearted attempt to give an appraisal figure (no matter how farfetched) was thrown out completely in favour of simply, "Name your price, Mr and Mrs Vendor, and I will get it".

This approach transcended those looking to sell already, and was applied to anyone, as a form of prospecting. Knock on the door and ask the owner (whilst they are not intending to move) would they consider selling at *any* price. Some would give a fantasy figure and the agent would take this and offer to achieve it if they could advertise the house, even just for a couple of weeks. Carrot dangled and, bang, a listing out of nowhere. The scary thing is, this was quite often working. Turns out their fantasy figure *wasn't,* and some (or many) were willing to pay it in a market on speed! He who dares, wins!

Even I succumbed to the dreaded 'no price' marketing for a good deal of 2021. In part, because the buyer competition and resulting upside was so intense, trying to pin an accurate 'price' tail on the donkey before you listed was almost impossible. Also, because you knew every other clown was going that route and you couldn't afford to be the odd one out. For a while during this period, trying to find any property advertised with a price on it was virtually impossible.

There you have it, it's not just the agents getting carried away. Owners fuelled by attention-grabbing media talk of a seller's market and frenzied buyer activity, have their eyes light up and their own expectations exponentially grow. Mainstream news channels *(I use the term reasonably lightly)* love a good real estate 'which suburbs are hot' soundbite story to anchor the end of the bulletin (and keep those punters watching in fervent anticipation). Under normal circumstances there might be a bit of a control applied by the industry to counteract this, but with little or no push-back from all the listing-hungry agents vying for limited business and instantaneous gratification, the brakes were well and truly off for a while.

Even the usually cautious bank valuers seemed to get swept along on this tidal wave of price growth, with most bloated sales achieving finance approvals. Once a few settlements have gone through and set a new high-water mark, they in turn become the 'comparable' data used for future reference and pricing. Hence, just go the 'no price' route and hope for the best, it will probably happen!

The slightly disappointing news—for anyone joining the industry now—is these unprecedented times have already come to an end thanks to the emergency stop applied by the Reserve Bank through interest rate increases. Bugger, yes once again we need to have some form of (semi) accurate price determination and advice back in play to ensure a sale. Oh well, it was good while it lasted.

6 | Cheap & Cheerful

Assuming you have now managed to negotiate through the tricky subject of how much the precious house is worth, the next drama will be your charges. Commission, the fee we are paid to perform our services, is always a lively topic. Before going any further, it is worth breaking down how this fee is typically utilised, as there seems to be this general misconception that it all goes to the 'flashy' agent to finance his AMG Mercedes fetish.

In a typical 'bricks and mortar' franchise agency environment, i.e., your common high street brands with local offices, there is a minimum four-way division of the headline figure paid. Such operations are not cheap to run, either at a corporate or local level, and the sales income forms part of that funding (along with property management fees for rental homes).

Firstly, by law the quoted fee a seller pays includes the GST component, which has to be deducted. An amount is then taken off the top which goes directly to the franchise corporate head office. This is generally around 10% and covers the provision/use of corporate email and CRM systems plus brand support and back up. Of the remaining fee in many agencies—in particular for newer members—there might be a 50/50 split between the office and the agent themselves. Hence a simple example Queensland commission payment of, say, $11,000 will look something like this to the agent:

Commission Paid $11,000 ($10,000 + GST $1,000)

Deduct **GST:** $11,000 - $1,000 = $10,000

Deduct **Franchise fee** (10%): $10,000 - $1000 = $9,000

Deduct **Office fee** (50%): $9,000 - $4,500 = $4,500

AGENT'S PROPORTION (before tax and expenses) = **$4,500**

As can be seen, the agent's cut is not a great deal more than a third of the original total. Still pretty good I hear you say, but this is gross. Once tax is deducted and—very typically—with some agent-paid advertising (owed to the office) that was incurred to win the listing under competition, the figure is probably well below $4,000.

Again, if you are selling quickly, and in higher volume, that is still a fair chunk of money. But when you consider that the truth of the industry is the *average of sales* are around 11 properties per year per agent, that's an income of around $50,000 at best, before tax and expenses. The point here is not to ridicule this figure or demean anyone who earns that sort of money, but simply to demonstrate the notion that every agent is earning $200,000 or $300,000 in some kind of champagne lifestyle at *your* expense is simply not true. A good many are struggling just like everyone else. Less Mercedes and more second-hand Mazda. Add to this the average time on—non-pandemic— market of between 45 to 60 days in many areas, which means on balance the agent *isn't* selling every property quickly and is investing considerable professional time and travel over the course of several weeks to produce a successful outcome.

Nonetheless, most people still want something for nothing *(sorry, 'value for money')* and this remains an area of intense competition and constant downward pressure fuelled by the rise of the cut-price agencies and de-regulation of the market, coupled to the relentless need for new stock to sell, and limited supply. Historically, there are varying rate structures in different states due to different sales processes and regulations, so rather than dwell too much on specific rates we'll look at general trends and observations.

One of the biggest problems, I feel, is most people fundamentally don't really understand what they are paying for. As we will cover later on, there seems to be a misconception that somehow it must be related to the physical amount of work and/or time undertaken, to some sort of common standard. That's all well and good if the sale price outcome of every home was fixed, but it is completely variable. Therefore, commission represents the fee paid to a professional marketeer to achieve the best price outcome.

In simple terms this means the vendor should consider the commission fee *in conjunction* with the likely sale price they feel the agent can confidently achieve through their experience and service offering. Too many people ignore the latter and only concentrate on the black-and-white commission rate on the listing form. The irony is, at listing time *all* agents are essentially the same, and you are paying NO commission until you get a sale anyway! That is, except for one previous brightly coloured company that didn't charge 'commission' apparently, until they went belly up.

My first principal always used to say, "Why do people get so hung up on commission at the beginning of the process, as that isn't when they need to worry about it?" Wise words. Indeed, they will only ever pay it out when they have arrived at a result they are happy with, which means there is a built-in mechanism to act as a balance. In signing a contract, by definition, the seller will have likely calculated their walk away or 'cash in hand' figure—sale price less commission—so will only move forward if this net figure is acceptable. The higher the commission, the higher the sale price needs to be to meet a certain net figure for the owner. That all said, informed scrutiny and easier comparison is inevitable in this digital age and the landscape is evolving rapidly.

Does the old adage, *You get what you pay for*, hold true here? In my opinion, yes (and no!). I feel there are now three tiers of operation within real estate sales. As touched on with the earlier commission calculation example, there are the large established brands that have existed for many years and have multiple franchised high street offices nationwide, supported by a central corporate operation. They typically remain at the slightly higher end of the commission scale but (should) offer the security of a highly recognised and trusted name with a long and proven track record, combined with a team of experienced, successful agents utilising the latest technology. Many do, with the most successful offices in these companies fully justifying their billing with energetic principals running large, motivated teams with great support and cutting-edge systems provided through their corporate connections. With established procedures, good market share and local attraction business, they represent a good investment with the potential of a strong price outcome.

That's the good news, problem is the brand name alone does not guarantee all of this. For all the celebrity offices in the fold—typically, but not always, the larger ones in key city or coastal locations—there are a few small to medium ones that are not that dynamic at all and are essentially just trading off the name. They begrudgingly pay their corporate fees, but don't really exploit all the available systems and support, and have a more slapdash approach to hiring of agents, etc. Yet crucially they still charge the going corporate rate because you are, after all, paying for the superiority of their 'name'.

Truth is, you should be paying for all the higher-level service and experience that is *implied* by that name, not for the name itself. Too many average offices with mediocre sales staff hide behind their brand name as if that gives them immunity from delivering a poor service. This has seen a few underperforming smaller franchise offices close down in recent years as independent competition grows—offering keener pricing and service—whilst the corporate teams of some of the big boys, at times, seem more pre-occupied with desperately trying to hold on to past historic market share, rather than ensuring there is dynamic creation of new business *throughout* their branch network.

On that note, remember these are franchised offices and, as such, are completely independent of each other. The quaint notion of a 'nationwide network' of offices might be physically true, but don't get too excited about your details being shared around and buyers coming freely from other offices in the group. Offices, like agents, are their own profit centres and have no real interest in helping out the 'opposition' even when it is dressed in the same uniform!

All of which leads us to our next collective. There are now a growing number of independent boutique agencies forming, quite often with principals and agents who have become disillusioned with the larger franchise brands, and who want more independent flexibility and dynamism in their approach. This new breed offers a middle tier, typically a little cheaper than the big boys, courtesy of no franchise fees to pay, fewer overheads and no corporate directives set in stone *("Thou shalt not sell for less than 2.5% or be damned," etc.,)* yet still offering fully comprehensive services—often more contemporary and creative—with experienced agents. If you can take a leap of faith away from the supposed comfort of a recognised big brand name, then this new breed can be an excellent option. This sector will continue to grow, as more sellers look beyond the traditional offerings, seeking best price versus good service, whilst the continued migration away from office-based interactions to fully-online renders multiple shopfronts less relevant and less cost effective.

For the first 12 years of my own real estate journey, I worked entirely for franchise offices—under two of the biggest brands—and for most of that time I genuinely believed they offered the best opportunities, both for clients and for the agents employed by them. However, as the market started to evolve in recent years, it became apparent to me that certain brands where not evolving with it (at least not consistently with all their offices). In my last office of this nature, I felt we were hanging on to the name, and associated charging structure, in some sort of aloof ivory tower without actually seeing how poor some of our service offering had become (and how flexible the growing 'no name' opposition was becoming).

This, combined with a clear drop in walk-in or attraction business generated through either the office location and/or name, raised real questions. As the previous example shows, a considerable amount of commission is paid away by the average agent to the office/brand, and if the benefits from this cease to exist, then it becomes an expensive overhead. Again, it depends totally on the individual office, location and drive/philosophy of the principal and management. In my case I moved to an independent in

2019, maintaining virtually all my past clients in the process, which reinforced my belief the brand name above my head contributed less to the decision-making process, on average, than other aspects. It has been a breath of fresh air and, importantly, I know that I have still been giving 100% of the service I ever did, just in a more cost effective and flexible way.

This new and sustained pressure on the big brands—although they won't openly admit to it—has inevitably led to a quiet reduction of some of their fee boundaries, so ultimately if you do your research and choose wisely, the best rates and service offerings shouldn't be widely different between these first two tiers of operators. Too dear, still? Fear not! Enter the final group, the cheap/fixed-price low budget boys!

These guys target those aforementioned people who are obsessed with the headline rate on the listing form. Their rate will be considerably lower or there will be a cheap fixed fee, so it seems like a big win for the seller, right? Probably not. Again, it costs a lot of money to run a good operation with reliable, modern systems and good staff. None of which can be easily funded by an income stream that starts 50% to 60 % less than the more comprehensive competitors. The agents themselves receive much less for each transaction, which means it is all about quantity, not quality, to make ends meet. As an agent, you are relying on churning through as many leads/listings as you can and then needing to sell them on as quickly as possible. There is little time for developing relationships and, indeed, most clients are only coming to you for no other reason than because you are cheap.

A true cut-price agency doesn't put a lot of effort into the marketing or have highly motivated agents. It might appear at least $3,000 or $4,000 cheaper on paper at the beginning of the process. However, if they sell a property for $10,000 less than an experienced agent—through lack of good competition or the serious hunt for prime buyers—then the seller has lost $6,000 - $7,000 from their best walk-away figure. Simple concept and maths, but very hard for most people to grasp, particularly if they don't know, or can't differentiate, between agents.

There were, not so long ago, some new cut-price disruptors on the scene, of course. They boldly claimed they didn't even charge commission! Great, until you appreciate what that means. Commission is a variable fee (based on the final sale price) applied to a completed transaction. Therefore, if the agent doesn't deliver a result and can't sell the house, you pay no commission. A non-commission, cut-price, 'fixed' fee arrangement may be lower, but is typically payable *regardless* of whether the subsequent sale occurs or not. No problem if a house sells quickly, but if it doesn't and you don't like the lack of effort or service from the agency—or you simply have to withdraw from sale due to a change of circumstances—too bad, you've paid them a few thousand regardless! Not so cheap now? Purple pain!

This particular agency, despite their best efforts and nationwide TV advertising, didn't last too long in Australia because the service offering, ultimately, was just too poor (regardless of the 'cheap' price). So yes, you do get what you pay for. My only caveat on that is, *do your research*, as a good agent is worth paying a fair and decent commission to, because they will give you a better service and a better result. However, don't just blindly assume a recognised brand name above the door will guarantee that. In truth, it is as much about the individual, as many clients will follow a good operator wherever they go, because it is the *individual* they have the relationship and trust with, not the organisation. Big name or 'no name' is not as critical as the operator.

The final mention here is market cycles. The cheapies always do better, and appear in greater numbers, in a strong seller's market. When stock is short and buyers are desperate for anything, a monkey could probably sell the house if priced vaguely right. Hence, some sellers, particularly of high-end homes, take more of a risk with the agent under these circumstances. They believe their house will sell *come what may* in the first few days, so it doesn't matter if the agent is a bit of a dick *(i.e., just put up with them and we will still save thousands!).*

As my first principal once said—again he of wise words—'A buyer will buy a house *despite* an agent, not because of one'. Conversely, when it is a buyers' market with an oversupply (and properties take much longer to sell) the cut-price guys struggle because the owners need much more analysis and detailed feedback to ascertain their ongoing strategies in terms of pricing and marketing. This level of service can only be offered properly by the 'full price' agencies with better processes and systems in place, plus the cashflow model to support extended listing times.

As with the previous chapter, however, there is a postscript to all this created by COVID-19. Lack of stock and desperate times called for desperate measures. The established commission structure was, to a degree, temporarily thrown out the window by the need to secure anything at any cost. No one will openly admit to such things but, trust me, even some well-known players were 'dropping their pants' to get the next sign up. In Queensland, commission figures with a '1' at the front, for so long scorned, have become widespread during the pandemic.

The returns are smaller but if you can sell very quickly—as has been the case—you can justify this and move on to the next one (well, if there is one!).

Agencies that were once the bastions of upholding commission rates because of the perception of how superior they were—regardless of whether that was true—in some cases, have had to abandon the moral high-ground and get down and dirty like everyone else. The problem is once the genie is out of the bottle, it is not going easily back any time soon. People talk and if cheaper rates have been doing the rounds for a while, it is difficult to suddenly persuade someone to pay a higher figure. Just like listing prices, easy to reduce, but difficult to put back up! Therefore, the industry may well have created a rod for its own back.

Even before the pandemic, I had a perfect example of this. Another colleague and I had executed an off-market sale, utilising an existing buyer on our database, in a prime pocket of our local farm area. As there was no marketing or formal sales process associated, we offered the seller a reduced 'one off' commission rate reflecting this. A few weeks later I got a similar listing in the same area. I touched on the same process as above as a first option, but the owner wanted to advertise on the market regardless (but was still interested in who was on our books).

Hence, we did both exercises in parallel. We did contact an existing buyer who came through the first open home and subsequently put an offer in. This progressed and a contract agreement was provisionally reached very quickly. The price was strong and, given we had also commenced a full program, I felt our stated commission rate was justifiable. However, it turned out this owner was friends with our previous off-market seller, who had bragged to him about the commission deal he got with us, disclosing full details. He took it upon himself that the situation was now identical, and we should match this previous deal, given how quickly things had happened (and I had initially mentioned sourcing an existing buyer, with possible commission reduction).

Crucially, it wasn't really the same as we had engaged a full marketing program with an agreed rate (it just happened that the first offer came from someone we already knew). Nonetheless, he was adamant and got quite nasty about things. Needless to say, of course, for:

   i.   a quiet life, and
   ii.   timely completion of the deal, and
   iii. any reputational damage limitation, we agreed and set the same commission figure

There it is, once you put something out there with one person, treat it as in the public domain! Also, this demonstrates people do not care too much about the finer points of differing circumstances, they just see a figure and want to ensure they can match what their neighbour got (and not lose face). Whilst the pandemic may have been the unique catalyst to subtly reduce commission rates, most will quietly forget this and only focus on an ongoing figure.

Hence, as the real estate market slows, it appears the agent now wants to up their charges for (probably) a longer and less lucrative outcome than 12 months previously. Not a great look and somewhat of a challenge to justify. Thus, as stock levels significantly increase and time on market lengthens, there may be a lot more work required for potentially a lot less income.

Got all that? If commission levels and the associated justification isn't demanding enough for the newbie agent to convey and negotiate, you are not there yet! Guess what, now you need some advertising budget!

7 | Hurt Money!

Right, having defended, and hopefully agreed upon, your commission rate, you are potentially close to securing the listing—great! However, you now need to ensure the property will be highly visible and you can promote it (but more importantly yourself by association, of course).

Advertising! Probably the biggest scourge for your average seller. You already know the drill, "You get enough money in commission, I am not paying for marketing as well!" Fair? Well, again we need to dissect this from both sides of the equation.

Firstly, some terminology. Although often freely interchanged, as above, the true definition of *marketing* is the process of identifying a customer's need and determining how best to meet those needs. In the case of selling a house, that is typically recommending several activities, among which is advertising the property (as opposed to directly contacting past buyers etc.). *Advertising* is the exercise of promoting the product itself— that is, the property—through paid channels. In other words, advertising is a component of marketing. We discuss the overall marketing campaign with the owner, but the costs associated are typically for the advertising components.

Why isn't advertising covered by the commission then? The well-worn and trusted analogy often used here is a car repair. Commission is effectively the charge for the mechanics labour, that is, the agents experience, skill and time to deliver an outcome, whilst advertising is the charge for the parts, that is, a fixed third party incurred cost such as an advertisement in the local paper, etc. The analogy works quite well to highlight the difference and can then be closed with the kicker, "You wouldn't expect the garage to pay for your car parts would you?". Also, the amount of advertising needed (or sought after by an owner) can differ considerably from home to home and it is easier to treat this as a separate scalable commodity.

From the seller's perspective it does genuinely seem like this is just an additional burden on top of the large commission figure they will have to pay at the end of the process. At that point the agent will surely have plenty of money to pay off this bill, so why on earth should the owner have to do it? Unlike commission, however, these costs are not conditional on success or charged at settlement, but at the beginning (time of listing) by the relevant companies—online real estate portals, local/national newspapers, etc.,—in relation to when the appropriate advertising is first published.

That is where we run into the first problem. The agent or agency must pay these bills in the first instance. In an ideal world where *every* home listed sells very quickly, it might be argued an agency can hold these costs and then offset it against the commission. However, the reality (as we have already touched on) is many homes start off at unrealistic prices, as stipulated by the owners. There is no guarantee that each listing taken will sell within the agency period, particularly if the owner is either intransigent on price or has a change in circumstances (and withdraws from the market).

If an agent starts covering the cost of marketing on a series of listings and then only half of them sell, they are left with a big advertising bill and no means of covering it from the original property. Ultimately it is a recipe for financial disaster. The seller may not care about this, but they should because as such a debt grows the agent is under mounting and very real pressure to try and push through any offer just to get a sale to recover their expenditure. Their impartiality to uphold the best outcome for the seller is impaired as they have a vested interest in returning a quick sale.

The second problem is we need a real commitment or *hurt money* from the owner. This means they are then far more invested directly in the overall marketing process and are more likely to listen and react to what needs to be done to achieve a sale. The irony is, we might feel if we give the owner everything for free they will like us more, but the reverse happens, and this unwittingly ensures the seller is free of any commitment or financial stake-holding to be realistic about price, etc. With no 'skin in the game' they are more likely to employ another agent if the property hasn't sold, as there is no monetary penalty in doing so at that point.

The car analogy still holds as well, quite simply, why should the agent pay the owner's costs? It is not their house, they are simply providing a service and need these 'parts' to enable the job to be completed properly (as does a plumber, electrician or anyone else). As already covered, the commission is spilt several ways and far from being some outrageous fortune that can easily pay for additional costs—with enough small change left over for a six-month cruise—the returns can diminish quite quickly if stretched to cover other costs like advertising.

This is where it starts to get more complicated and murkier, however. As with commission, competition is intense and agents really don't want to lose an opportunity to list if they can help it, should advertising costs be a big stumbling block. Hence there are several strategies around this, some good, some not so.

The best option is to achieve upfront *vendor paid advertising* **(VPA)**. The strong agents can generally demonstrate the quality and success of their advertising campaigns and can secure the owner to pay for this at the beginning of the process. This ensures an appropriate level of high-quality advertising is achieved with commitment from the owner and no burden on the agent, allowing them to strive for the best outcome possible. Payment should be in full, paid either by credit card or via a formal payment structure scheme.

Where that is not possible, a 'pay on settlement' style agreement may be suggested instead. In this situation the owner still commits to a similar level of advertising, but the payment is deferred and charged to them at settlement—offset against their settlement proceeds—meaning they don't have to find upfront funds. Sounds good in principle, but this has several problems. From a seller's perspective this option is quite often deliberately underplayed by the less scrupulous agent. "Don't worry, nothing to pay (now)", is all the agent will dwell on—and all the seller will hear—rather than the major caveats in the form of still having to pay the bill if the property doesn't sell or you withdraw it from the agency.

In some cases, this actually becomes a cleverly positioned backstop, making it less likely the owner will withdraw or change agents because they suddenly realise they still have a large outright bill to pay (with no settlement to offset it). From the agency perspective, whilst this might secure more listings, there is a danger of running up a large overdraft until linked settlements occur (third parties still require their fees paid upfront!). In the event of a property being withdrawn without selling, it can sometimes get very messy when pressing the owner for the retrospective payment, effectively after the event (and with no result).

A recent variation on this theme is the wonderful new world of *buy now, pay later* providers and the like. The seller still doesn't pay upfront, but the debt is transferred to a third-party company—who then pays the agency—and the seller enters into a separate agreement with this specialist lender. They subsequently recover the money over time through a number of smaller interval payments. The main advantage to the agency is they don't carry the debt anymore and don't have to chase up late payments (and look like the bad guys). Instead, you just become a financial services salesman as well and find another thing to tie the client up with.

The other less appealing option—for the agent!—is offering free advertising. Sounds too good to be true and, typically, it is. This can also take a couple of forms. The first is where the agent/agency themselves is paying for some enhanced advertising—*agent paid advertising (APA)*—the vendor would otherwise pay for. This might be for a promotion, returning client or perhaps under extreme competition (as a carrot to get a signed listing over the line). In this scenario, the seller is at least still getting the selected benefits of a reasonable advertising campaign, however, as already mentioned, does run the risk of the agent's impartiality being somewhat diminished chasing a quicker return on their own investment.

The alternative is *actually free advertising*, or more precisely very basic advertising, that can be done at little or no cost by the agency (and then dressed up as something more exciting for the would-be seller's perspective). This involves no fees for the sellers, but in truth is only giving them virtually entry level exposure. A standard listing on one well-known real estate portal, for example, can be offered as 'Free Internet Listing', but it is buried at the bottom of page five, as opposed to a higher profile uplift. Free newspaper advertising can sometimes be offered, but often is nothing more than a thumbnail size mention on a general agency promotional advertisement, as opposed to a dedicated quarter, half, or full page through a separately paid advertisement.

Do we need enhanced advertising as part of our overall marketing? Well, the truth as always is somewhere in the middle. The old adage is *'you can't sell a secret'*. Quite true and undoubtedly, to create maximum interest—and therefore competition—good levels of exposure are strongly recommended, as this should be repaid with the best possible price outcome. In the case of auctions it is vital, and where half-hearted campaigns of this nature struggle it is often because insufficient paid advertising has taken place in the run up.

I am a strong believer in advertising, but targeted and smart, spending the owner's extra dollars wisely. High quality professional photos and upscaled internet exposure are a must on almost every property and should be the default position. However (for example), a picture signboard is ideal for a home with strong drive-by traffic, or to showcase the interior or the rear yard with stunning pool, etc. Put some of these photos on the sign and there is a real chance someone passing might just catch their eye and subsequently look the property up on the internet for further information.

Conversely, if the property is buried right at the back of an estate at the end of a cul-de-sac, chances are anyone reaching it will have done so only by finding it on the internet already—and reviewing the photos online—so the picture sign is less relevant (and that spend could be invested in social media or another stream). Marketing in general is essentially about—sorry, another industry analogy—putting multiple lines in the water or casting a big net to catch more fish, rather than just a single rod and reel. The more advertising channels you make the property easily visible by, the wider the potential audience.

Equally, make no mistake, property exposure is also highly beneficial for agent/agency brand awareness and profile (and often the main objective for getting it!). As already touched on, in this industry you must keep making constant noise to be seen and remembered. This can become quite costly over time, so what better way than getting your owners to pay for advertising that passively promotes you as well (at their expense). Perceived success is what must always be projected, so by getting your listings highlighted in the public eye, you are linking your 'brand' with activity and popularity.

In terms of selling the property, undoubtably printed media has lost ground to online-based mediums over the last few years, in particular with younger buyer. And yet there is still a persistence with some agencies to push for sizable budgets from the sellers and to 'go large' in print. Admittedly, with a coveted capital city newspaper full-page advertisement, for some high-end owners this is simply making a 'statement', but always in the seller's best interests? Who am I to say, but my wise old past principal was quite open about this and referred to the newspaper as a 'listing tool' and that was the only real reason we attempted to chase down vendor paid advertising to frequent it.

In this day and age, a well photographed property backed up by a strong online campaign—including social media—is likely to reach the majority of the target audience. There might be a few oldies around who still only look through the paper supplements over afternoon tea. At least the newspapers ensure some conformity for design and presentation with advertisements remaining professional and primarily property based. Some localised free papers and community news offerings are not so regimented, however. And—with good income to be gained— they happily hand over 50% of their pages to various local agencies trying to outdo each other with garish advertisements that may (or may not) have some vague relationship to any properties they are selling, but will principally bang on about how good *they* are.

Which brings us to the most important lesson in all this and a word of warning:

Be you the agent or the seller, advertising alone will ultimately not sell the property, only realistic pricing will.

Buyers are educated these days—by that very same medium of the internet—and generally know their price ranges and local market quite well. You can spend $20,000 on advertising if you like with your 'Hollywood' videos, hired designer furniture, etc., but if your house is $100,000 overpriced it will make little or no difference to the likely outcome (or lack of one). Buyers really do not care how much money you have blown on bringing your precious house to them, they are just interested in what represents fair and reasonable value once they have seen it. The reverse logic also applies, and some properties will sell relatively easily without elaborate marketing because they are priced more aggressively in the first place.

Ultimately you will need to demonstrate to the owner that you will put to very good use every dollar they invest in advertising to maximise the potential final price they receive. Most people would invest $1,000 to make $10,000 and (conceptually) this is the suggestion, through better exposure, buyer competition and higher price outcome. Perhaps stating the obvious, but do make sure you know your products well, if you are asking someone to pay for them!

Again, successful agents will know the full 'ins and outs' of each advertising facet they are utilising and have the belief and key statistics to back it up. This creates confidence in the seller's mind, so they are much more likely to agree, with a demonstrated potential outcome. Equally, I have witnessed quite comical situations where an agency has a certain advertising package they wish to peddle, aspects of which some of its staff members may not even bother to research or fully understand.

When algorithm-based social media boosters first came to the fore, everyone wanted to push them, but most could not explain to the owner how they worked or what they really did. Instead, "You must have this, err, it helps get you on Facebook and stuff like that, err ... better,"—thanks for that! The prominent online real estate portals produce a wealth of statistical information to support their pricey upsell options, as you might expect. Therefore, it is good practice to utilise this material when you are trying the very same product upsell! "This $1,000 internet upgrade will get you a premiere position in local searches and maximise photographic impact resulting in eight times the overall viewing traffic and 35% more direct tailored enquiries. Plus, appearances in secondary search results for all surrounding suburbs, where similar property criteria are entered, resulting in a much wider audience exposure," sounds a little more composed than, "Err, your pictures are a bit bigger and near the top, mate,".

In my experience, if the case is reasoned and well-presented most people will commit to some form of VPA to achieve the best perceived result. The amounts may vary on several factors, but even a smaller commitment is still a commitment. I will digress slightly here, as during all good corporate ear-bashing sessions, sorry sales training, we are always told you can get the same VPA wherever you are based and whoever the clients are— location is just an excuse. That's fine, in relation to some of the basic principles for sure, but realistically in a low socio-economic area with medium house prices of $300,000 you are not getting the same VPA as in the inner city or beachside where $2,000,000 and $3,000,000 properties are commonplace (yes, you guessed it, old sour grapes here never worked those sort of areas). Aspirations are different as well, some who can afford it want big, brash 'exposure' advertising for their mansions, while others just need to sell their humble home at any cost due to financial, or other, problems.

Personally (and I can hear the groans) I have always been open to putting a small contribution in myself—provided the owner is making a much bigger one and is realistic on price—as a sweetener and to demonstrate confidence in my own ability to sell the property. Ultimately, however, it is vendor funded and well-structured advertising that is a necessary part of taking any house to market correctly and ensuring your brand remains front of mind with the general public.

8 | BOOM OR BUST!

Whether you want to or not, before your would-be seller finally signs on the dotted line, there is an elephant in the room that you should theoretically address at every listing presentation. Furthermore, many driven agencies will insist you discuss it and, indeed, adopt it as your passionate default position.

Yep, you guessed it ... *AUCTION!*

The very word that ignites and inspires the chosen few, whilst striking fear into the hearts of others. Why? Well, in a nutshell, a properly structured and executed auction program conducted by a competent and hardworking agent should potentially produce an excellent outcome, whilst an ill-conceived and poorly delivered auction will produce precisely—zero. Contrary to some people's belief, there is nothing inherently flawed with auctions, as many consistent and exceptional results stand testament. It comes down to the desire of *both* the agent and the seller to fully embrace and engage in the process. In almost all real estate training or coaching, auction is promoted as the primary means for selling a property and the method you must advocate and aim for as your listing goal. There is a fair bit to unpack here, but if managed and executed correctly, it does indeed represent the best process for both agent and seller.

Let's start with the agent's perspective (because it is all about us, after all). Auction first and foremost provides structure. The agent can map out a four-week campaign culminating in a set auction date. This provides certainty and takes the pressure away from trying to achieve a result at all costs in week one. Instead, you are free to concentrate on the process rather than be pre-occupied with the outcome. There is a set of standard procedures that can be created, and skills honed around this predictable timescale, which are then transferable to any auction listing in the future, providing confidence and efficiency.

Whilst offers may or may not be considered prior to auction date, there is no obligation for the agent to push early approaches, and interest can be controlled and driven towards a single point in time to create maximum competition. It provides a strictly controlled timetable for marketing, with urgency placed upon potential buyers (who cannot dither beyond the auction date, for fear of loss). It genuinely takes away the initial price burden on a property, allowing the agent—and seller—to promote the home and review the market feedback prior to auction day and ultimately position the property accordingly for maximum outcome versus maximum engagement (well, in theory at least!).

This process typically carries the largest associated marketing spend of any listing type, so the agent gains excellent exposure for their own brand and—if the auction is successful—a good deal of positive press ('SOLD under the hammer!', etc.). Furthermore, if you do achieve a sale with auction conditions there is no subsequent messing around waiting for buyer's finance approvals or building and pest inspections, as the property is unconditional immediately—'as is, where is', baby!

From the seller's perspective they, likewise, do not have to stress about whether to take that first, early offer because the process gives them more time to understand the market (they can save up all their stress for auction day!). A fixed date and process gives those in need of certainty with perhaps a set deadline to meet—

for example, starting a new job interstate, etc., —a much greater opportunity to complete a transaction within a set timeline.

A big attraction for higher-end and luxury homes is not limiting the price potential. Where a property has many exclusive and desirable features—which can include things like location—the owner may be hesitant to put a set price in place, as the competition from emotional buyers wanting something unique may push the bidding up in the heat of the moment. It is no coincidence high value city and coastal properties have a much higher percentage of auctions taking place.

In saying that, auction is the perfect vehicle for homes at the other end of the scale, too. Those in very poor condition or in need of work can be put to market 'as is' and the buyer has no set price to inevitably push back against—because of the 'work needed'—and has to arrive at a fair valuation for exactly what they see. If the owner is realistic as to what this range is likely to be, come auction day, then chances are the property can be sold simply with no obligation to repair or renovate. This is ideal for deceased estates and (non-cooperative) marriage separations where a property may need to be disposed of quickly, but the parties involved don't have the time or motivation to address any outstanding issues beforehand.

In these circumstances—with perhaps multiple parties that need to split the proceeds—it provides the most open and clearest indication of true market price. Indeed, the legal profession commonly prefers this method due to the public and fair nature of price determination, and it is very commonly used with mortgagee sales, aforementioned separations, or bankruptcy asset liquidations.

The corporate line is 'auctions work everywhere regardless of location, socio-economic demographics, and so on'. This is technically quite true—if done properly—but is also driven by the preference of management to perpetuate auctions, because what is good for the goose *(agent)* is good for the gander *(brand)*, i.e., higher profile, unconditional contracts, etc.

Nonetheless, there are undoubtably some other factors that can assist in a positive environment for auctions. Some agencies are fundamentally auction-centric in their mindset and approach. This means the team will have a higher level of collective experience, and resources will be more freely available to support creation of a good campaign (as opposed to an agency where this happens very infrequently). The flipside, of course, is there will be greater pressure to ensure an auction listing is secured over a private treaty, and this can lead to problems if either the agent or seller is unconvinced of this choice for a particular property.

Despite what those on high would have us think, I firmly believe geographical location does impact auction listing likelihood and success. Not necessarily at an individual level, where I accept a confident and experienced auction-minded agent should be able to explain and convince a seller to go this route and obtain an outcome in most circumstances and settings. Nonetheless, there are undoubtably areas—metropolitan and beachside as previously mentioned—where the auction ratio is much higher than elsewhere and, therefore, the public (as either buyers or sellers) are much more conditioned to this.

The conversation is a lot easier to have if the concept—in particular, that good results can be obtained—is already in the consciousness of the person you are dealing with. Prestige areas will have prestige requirements (keeping up with the Jones's next door who sold their home *by auction* for $2.4 million) and hopefully a prestige marketing budget to go with it. Likewise, outer suburbs and more dispersed locations may have historically experienced much fewer auctions—as a ratio of total sales in the area—and potentially more perceived failures. It is much more difficult having the same conservation when the entrenched position across the table is 'auctions don't work'. Of course, if you raise this observation, it's treated as an excuse because you simply aren't good enough at explaining the benefits. Perhaps, but many of the super-agents or motivators telling you that still come from the city or coast!

Auctions never work? Of course, they do, but in these areas where they are not so prevalent and well supported, there will be many more failed examples from which people will determine their viewpoint. Failed is also a relative term, as the full auction process actually runs for eight weeks plus, and has a third stage—if needed, after auction day—of bringing in conditional offers, that is, those whom for whatever reason (finance approvals, etc.,) could not bid unconditionally at auction. This stage accounts for at least a third of overall sales from the total auction process, yet not selling under the hammer on the day may look like a potential failure.

In my experience, all too often auctions—in these areas—are suggested more for self-promotion or as a 'get out of jail card' by unsure agents. They don't want to address the whole price issue up front with the owner through fear of losing the listing: *list it first without price, worry later*. That's fine, but if you don't then undertake the process properly, you have simply deferred the difficult price discussion to four weeks down the track. By then it's too late to educate the seller for a realistic auction day reserve price and you will almost certainly have no result.

There are two vital aspects the agent must follow. The first is to diligently gather good feedback and price indications, and then report this information to the **vendor** via ongoing and regular meetings prior to auction. The second aspect is 'running' **buyers** over a period of three to four weeks, with regular communication to hold them in place until auction day. The latter can also include things as simple, and crucial, as ensuring they know how an auction works: finance pre-approvals, building inspections completed prior, access to a sufficient deposit, etc. They can be as keen as mustard, but if they don't turn up on the day correctly prepared, they can't bid (the greatest agent misdemeanour of all!).

Buyers have a sixth sense in this area, too. If you, as the agent, have *genuine* belief from day one that the property is going to auction to sell, and you have the energy, conviction and structure around the listing to convey this, buyers will pick up on it. Once *they* believe the property will most likely sell at auction—and potentially at an advantageous price due to clear seller motivation—they will turn up and they will bid if they really want the home. It's not rocket science! That's why mortgagee auctions always go well because the agent already has conviction they will sell at auction—only the bank to please—and so do the buyers, who sense a bargain, hence they turn up!

Equally, if your body language and comments suggest you are just 'going through the motions' with an auction property, chances are most buyers will detect this. They will sit back and wait to see what price goes on the home once the auction is (inevitably) passed in. Very few people want to stick their hands up at auction and be the centre of attention in front of everyone unless they really have to, that is, if they don't bid, someone else will buy it. If they are confident the property will still be there after auction date, chances are you won't see them until then. There is a fine line between momentum and result versus lacklustre and anticlimax. Nothing worse than an auction with more agents standing around from the office than punters, and everyone awkwardly looking at their feet until the auctioneer ends the misery and passes the property in!

I have never had the luxury—or ball-and-chain, depending on your view—of working in a strong auction-centric office, nor in the city or glitter coast for that matter. Nonetheless, the majority of my own auction experiences have been quite positive, and I believe the process works, when the circumstances are right. The reason these campaigns have generally been successful is not because I am some self-styled guru, but simply because they were only undertaken on a limited number of *suitable* properties (the majority of my listings have always been private treaty, i.e., listed with a price).

For me, there must be one of three simple tick boxes checked:

i. The owner must need to sell very urgently and, therefore, meet the market quickly, or
ii. The property is entirely unique and has nothing comparable, so accurate pricing is very difficult and could cap potential outcome, or
iii. There is a legal aspect (mortgagee sale, etc.) warranting an open and public sale price determination

If none of these three conditions *clearly* existed then, typically, I would not promote auction heavily unless the owner specifically was interested. Without the commitment of the seller, both in terms of sufficient advertising spend and understanding of essentially abiding by the process, then the risks are high for a fizzer!

The best auction (and result) to date I have executed was textbook in every aspect. By that I mean the property was a perfect example of why you should auction something (effectively, as was the vendor). I will cover more on the background to this particular property in a later chapter, but essentially it was a somewhat run-down rural home on just over a hectare of land. However, it was located in a future high-density housing development area, provisioned for in council planning, but not yet enacted in terms of detailed structure planning or establishment of services needed for subdivision.

The previous owner had *land banked* (acquired for future sale or development) this property, but had then gone bankrupt and the property had now come under the control of administrators to dispose of and recoup funds. Hence, here we had:

i.   A home *in need of much work.* However, the circumstances did not allow this, and

ii.   A property that was *difficult to price.* The present rural value was much lower than the potential future value as a development block, but this was subjective based on the timing of when development could take place, and

iii. The administrator, who had a large marketing budget, *required a quick sale* in an open and public manner

With every box ticked on this one, auction it was! We employed multiple advertising channels including newsprint at local, regional, and even national level with a highly disciplined and structured four-week campaign. During this time, we had numerous open homes, and I worked with a growing number of interested buyers—providing information and guidance as to bidding conditions etc., —towards auction day, as each week went by.

The condition of the house became a non-issue because there was no price set for which to complain about value for money. It became apparent early on there were two types of buyers: those looking for a possible cheap rural home to do up—who didn't care about the future subdivision potential—and those wanting to land bank and develop at a later stage. This presented two differing valuations depending on your point of view. Furthermore, as the advertising mentioned 'the administrator', there were also those just interested in the notion of something (anything) discounted at someone else's misfortune! Always feed the greed!

I made sure I worked all the potential buyers to be in position for auction day, in particular, two notable parties that were in it purely for the future development. Auction day arrived and a good crowd turned out. One of our corporate auctioneers was on hand and (as is often the case) things started very slowly. Reserve price was set around the top end of the rural or 'as is' valuation/feedback of around $560,000. Any higher was deemed to be speculative because the development potential was still in the future.

After a vendor bid or two to 'warm up' the audience, bidding started amongst the couple of groups looking to buy for a rural retreat. This started at early $500,000s and slowly, incrementally increased towards the reserve. Fine I thought, we should at least creep over the reserve threshold. As we approached the mid $500,000s, however, one of the potential developers suddenly stuck in a higher bid, and so it started! The other would-be developer responded in kind and the bidding accelerated dramatically, leaving the rural buyers dead in the dust!

These two heavyweights slugged it out, bid and counter bid, on and on. I tried to keep a perfect poker face but couldn't believe quite how far this was going and going until ... $965,000 finally topped out the bidding, a cool $400,000 over reserve! The auctioneer dropped the hammer, congratulated the winner and then cast his eye back at the ramshackle house, whispering to me, "Where the hell are the drugs? Hidden in the walls?!" An extreme example caused by a perfect storm, nonetheless, demonstrates why auction can be an amazing vehicle in the right circumstances. This property would have most likely had a list price of around $600,000 at best.

I had another administrator auction where I had run a couple of buying groups for a couple of weeks prior and was convinced a trio of local investors were my boys for an under-the-hammer sale. They duly arrived on the day ready to act. However, another couple—a colleague of mine had mentioned the auction to them in passing only the evening before—turned up just as the bidding was about to start. They did a two-minute look through the house (hadn't seen it prior) came back out and started bidding themselves! Blew the local guys out of the water and bought the house there and then. Again, that's the excitement and unpredictability that an auction can produce.

Just for balance, I have occasionally had less-positive experiences! One mortgagee-in-possession sale left me sick in the stomach. Again, I had my A buyers lined up, who I knew wanted the house. I was sure they had a budget to mid $400,000s at least. Our usual corporate auctioneer was not available, so head office provided a replacement. He rocked up about 30 minutes prior to kick off and I started my run through of the house and the buyers to be aware of. Reserve had been set around $420,000 and I was confident we would clear that. Unfortunately, this new auctioneer seemed somewhat distant to my information and was more interested in talking about *Black Caviar* being about to run at lunchtime.

I gave him the bank representative's details and off we went. One vendor bid in, and my A buyers put in a $400,000 opening bid to start the ball rolling. With no other immediate alternative bids, the auctioneer couldn't wait to halt proceedings and instantly got on the phone to the bank. I was suggesting these buyers would easily come up if pushed, but instead he put the frighteners on the bank representative first saying bidding was limited and there was a real risk of losing the unconditional interest he had (not even having spoken to them!).

He promptly got a reserve drop to $410,000. The banks quite often have the backup option to reduce the reserve slightly on the day if things are close. He knew this and pursued this line before applying any pressure to the buyers. He then went over to them and asked if they would increase to $410,000 and the house would be on the market and most likely theirs. Almost bemused by how easy that was, they agreed. He restarted the auction, confirmed we were selling and now had a bid of $410,000, after which with undue haste he brought the hammer down.

My colleagues all suspected this was too cheap and slightly awkward congratulations followed for a sale under the hammer, but we had undersold the house. The buyers were, not surprisingly, ecstatic and even said to me they were expecting—and willing—to pay more. As an agent there is nothing worse than this, as we work for the seller. I was annoyed with the auctioneer, for taking the easy route ... and with myself for allowing him to. The bank was happy enough, as the seller, but I couldn't help thinking about the previous owners who had been repossessed. I knew they had bought the house not that long before for around $440,000 and the lazy approach from the auctioneer might have been the difference between no debt owing to the bank afterwards or an ongoing legacy. This demonstrates another key aspect of auctions, finding (and then hanging on to) a great auctioneer. They can sometimes be the difference between an average result and an exceptional one.

Finally, the one time I broke my own rules and did suggest an auction out of desperation, the inevitable happened! This particular rural property had already been listed for a few months and was not selling. Presentation was okay, but nothing special; however, the (separating) owners were just very set on their price. I suggested removing the price and injecting some new impetus through an auction campaign; this would also give a timeline for conclusion. There was insufficient additional advertising budget and they had no real buy-into the new process, and ultimately still did not move much on price.

The result? A few of us standing around gazing down at the grass, wishing (in this case) the auctioneer *would* wrap it up very quickly! Even the usual close in these circumstances, along the lines of, "Just because there are no bidders today don't mistake this for no interest, as there are conditional buyers waiting in the wings and we invite them in now," sounded hollow and wasn't fooling anyone!

Being an occasional marathon runner, I feel that there is a valid comparison here. If you completely respect this event as unique, and you have the discipline to train and structure yourself for it accordingly, almost anyone has the potential to achieve a finish (and feel wonderful having done so). Equally, if you cut corners, are lazy in your approach, and treat it like any other 'run' you will collapse before halfway and possibly die on the road. An auction is no different, you just die on the front lawn in front of a few more people instead!

9 | ALWAYS BE CLOSING

Having hopefully executed a faultless listing presentation, during which you have diligently explained the various options and covered all bases, what is left to do? Well, unfortunately, the hardest single thing. Getting the clients signature on the paperwork!

Without a formal commitment all your good work counts for very little—both practically, and with the boss—hence much emphasis will be placed around your ability to convince this potential seller of your worth and obtain their agreement. Of course, this is true of any sales position. But with the acquisition of stock being critical in real estate, it is the capability to convert a promising presentation into a secured listing that is probably of greater significance than any subsequent offer creation or contract negotiation skills.

Given, as we have already addressed, most people's natural default position, initially at least, is to put off a final decision until they are fully comfortable—be it by comparing multiple agents first or simply creating some breathing space to decide without feeling pressured—it is vital you try to overcome this and gain an agreement at the first opportunity. As we shall see, there are some structured techniques for this, matched inevitably by many less polished or professional, but sometimes equally productive, methods.

The overriding principle is as simple as ABC: **A**lways **B**e **C**losing! Again, a common sales-related acronym, but what does this mean in practical terms? Essentially reducing the options for objection or delay as you go along, theoretically leading the potential client to a point where their agreement is inevitable because they have nothing left to contest or push back on. This is done through a combination of carefully worded questions that generally need a closed answer, coupled with predetermined and rehearsed responses to typical objections that will be raised by would-be clients.

Much of the real estate script and dialogue training centres around this concept and it starts right from the beginning of the process. An *open question* allows a free format answer from the recipient and is not ideal. Example, "Would you be interested in an appraisal?" A *closed question* requires a specific answer. Example, "I am conducting free appraisals in your area. Would Monday or Tuesday be better for you?" I use these examples on purpose because it starts at the point of first communication, long before you have got in the door. You must try to close on every conversation to move forward.

Theoretically at least, you are not giving someone the option to ramble on and make excuses—or avoid the question—and you are compelling them to answer in a way that already leads them in a certain direction. Personally, such heavy-handed language at the initial point of contact always seems a bit obvious to me, but given you might be using this in a cold calling context, you only have a very short window of interaction, so your choice of words needs to be efficient and productive if you are to get anywhere.

I am still of the opinion if someone is not interested it does not really matter how you frame it. The answer to the Monday/Tuesday question can equally be, "Neither! Not interested, mate!". Nonetheless, carefully scripted approaches should ensnare a higher return, so we are told, as always a few unsuspecting individuals are caught off guard by targeted dialogue.

Assuming we do get the opportunity to progress, the real craft comes into play during the listing presentation itself. Having initially determined (as best you can) these owners are the real deal, and are looking to go to market, you make them feel comfortable by explaining the areas you are going to run through and by indicating you are happy to stop and take questions as you go, if they have any concerns. Just as we have laid out, you then progress through each stage: house valuation/pricing, commission, marketing and strategy (auction versus private treaty, etc.).

If you run through this blindly without pause, there could a barrage of questions or underlying concerns at the end of your presentation, making things very difficult to conclude. Hence, as each topic is covered, you obtain closure on that area before moving to the next. Even if nothing has been raised, you pause and clearly ask the owners if they understand and are happy with what you have just explained. Essentially getting their consent to move on and, by agreeing, you can effectively eliminate sudden objections at the end based around any earlier topics. When questions or concerns are raised, you ensure you deal with them directly at that point—and assuming you can satisfy the issue—again confirm that topic has been successfully covered and you can move on.

There will be the very typical objections such as commission rate and marketing fees, which will have tried and trusted stock responses to justify and manage. Sometimes there may be some curveball concerns raised and you will need to think on your feet, to a degree. It is important to listen in these situations and display empathy and understanding of the issue where needed. Experienced agents will be able to cope with this better and will try to reference a relevant example of a similar situation from a previous listing in their back catalogue, and how it was handled with a positive outcome. Depending on each owner's circumstances, their degree of anxiety, and previous selling experiences, etc., this process can take some time, but if conducted well it sets up the end game perfectly for the best chance of success.

You see, unless you are extremely lucky, the highly predictable conclusion will now happen if you allow it. The owners will thank you for your in-depth and thorough presentation, but then probably comment along the lines of, "It has given them a lot to think about," and they will definitely, "Be in touch shortly with a decision,". As already highlighted, this a common fall-back tactic to try and extract you from the house without commitment, allowing further pointless deliberation time or (worse still, from your perspective) a window to call in other agents to compare their offerings.

By applying the ongoing closure technique, you have the opportunity to politely (perhaps!) question this position. "Just let me confirm, you have advised me you are needing to sell the house and you are entirely happy with everything I have explained and the package I have presented?" Difficult to suddenly say no, when each aspect has already been 'signed off' as you go, so comes the punchline: "Therefore, can I ask what exactly you need more time to think about?" Effectively there is no answer to this, so instead comes some uncomfortable waffle about just needing a bit more time to be 'sure'.

Again, you can push, "Do you have any other concerns that we haven't already covered? If not, why wait and need me to come back again and take up more of your time, let's get things moving now, shall we?". Now, I'm not suggesting this works every single time as some people will dig their heals in regardless, but for the good operators this process and final closure can persuade people, who are otherwise '50/50', over the line to sign there and then. It's win-win as this is the most efficient use of your time, but more importantly—even if they are not quite ready for photos/inspections for a few days—secures the listing, so no other agents can come into the picture in the interim.

There are a couple of standard backups for this position as well. If some resistance is still there, the next question is, "So tell me, what do I need to do to secure your signature today?" This throws the ball back in their court. Some may still hold firm, but others who are already wavering may wilt and come up with something as a token defence. "Well, if you could do anything to help reduce the advertising figure." You may or may not have left 'something in the tank' as to any concessions, but if the request is not too unreasonable you may be prepared to take a small reduction in proposed advertising revenue or commission on the chin to close the deal.

By throwing this request out there, the owners have inadvertently given you the green light for a potential close. "So just to be clear, if I speak to my principal now and we can reduce an aspect of the advertising costs, you are ready to sign today?" One corner *your new clients* have just painted themselves into! Your seniority, experience and marketing package flexibility will determine whether you are making a pretend call or actually speaking to the principal for approval, but the answer will miraculously be the same. "Great news, we can adjust the internet costs in return for your signature today." You can throw some cheese on the top if you wish to make them feel better. "Wow, great deal, wasn't sure the principal would run with it. Congratulations!"

Alternatively, if the owners do not have a lot of imagination and are not forthcoming—but you still feel they are close to capitulation—then you can reverse the above conversation and introduce something yourself, unsolicited. "Look, I am very keen to be your agent and market this wonderful home of yours. We do a have a limited promotion running at present for a few, very select, new clients. I may be able to get you a reduced commission rate if we were to move forward now. Would this be of interest?" Money generally talks, as does the notion of getting a 'win' against the big bad agent (later they can relate to all their friends how they pushed this agent for such a great deal), so this again may be enough. "Well, yes, we would be interested if you could." Done! Thank you and good night!

Okay, so far so good. Whilst these might all seem a little staged, all are generally tried and trusted industry-wide techniques and dialogues. If practised and executed well by an experienced professional who retains warmth and good communication, they are not overly burdensome for the client and are a reasonable way for the agent to conduct the most efficient and successful business they can. However, there are always those wishing to smash-and-grab a quick close without the finesse, patience, or particular interest in the client's circumstances. With stock supplies dwindling over the last few years, this has become more acute, as have the methods to get the listing signed.

Here is an interesting paradox. If you are confident and good at what you do, you should prefer to be first in the door as, after all, once they speak to you they will be signing there and then! The standard question from the above position is, "If I have answered everything and you are completely satisfied, why do you need to waste time calling someone else in?" Again, a strong argument that often works. Yet despite a clear and present danger this could happen, for the less confident or more shifty operators, 'last man standing' is perhaps a better option.

In this scenario, someone calls you in and you immediately enquire as to whether they are seeing any other agents. If so, you attempt to find out when they will be visiting and ensure you are booked in after everyone else (you are conveniently busy prior to then). The premise is twofold. Psychologically, being last makes you the easier option to go with if the owners are a little jaded from several presentations and are not really wanting to endure getting anyone back for another round and signing. That aside, you have a good chance of finding out the best package they have been offered so far, and then you simply better it! Typically, still linking this to signing immediately, thus cutting out anyone else being given a second chance to revise their offering or come back to the house.

It is not guaranteed, particularly if the owners like one of the other agents who has already presented. But in many instances the combination of being offered the best deal, and general fatigue with the whole process, makes for easier capture. This suits the quick and dirty, as they can just undercut as required at the end without the same degree of time and detailed input to get there.

I certainly admit to having had instances where an initial appraisal went very well and, although I was still unable to close immediately, felt I had created a good rapport with the owners

SOLD On The Dream

and was in the box seat. Then only to lose out to a surprisingly low-brow choice at the last minute who had undercut, thrown in some freebies and promised the world. The only solid defence against this scenario is, indeed, to secure the listing at first visit. Failing that, your only option is stating something along the lines of, "Please come back to me, if you receive anything you feel preferable. I just ask for the opportunity to fight for the business, as I really would like to assist you," etc.

This can occasionally work, but it is more in hope than expectation as the aforementioned fatigue and urgency to sign a 'limited offer' discount will almost always preclude the call coming, as it may be all too hard for the seller at that point. During COVID-19, with commission rates on a downward slide and stock in truly short supply, it almost became a given the last man would just undercut all before. Of course, when all before had already sold out in anticipation of this (and through very real need) it's a messy race to the bottom, much to the seller's delight, no doubt.

Another very questionable technique—which ties in nicely with being last man in—is to blanket bomb the opposition and openly deride them. Now this is entirely frowned upon under the industry Code of Conduct, but as luck would have it most clients would not have a clue about that. So, for some it is open season to blatantly bad-mouth anyone and everyone to make them look like the only viable alternative to go with. In fairness, we only must look at the world of politics at election time to see this method in action. Why explain what you can achieve when it is easier to run down the opposition and advise what they can't do?! I accept some of this will always go on, of course, and we are all grownups, but the nature of such conversations being behind closed doors seems to give free license to some in

120

crossing the line and getting quite personal and quite nasty. "Oh them, they are really struggling, haven't sold much this year and *I hear* they upset quite a few people." "That office is probably going to close, from what *I understand,* small time operation and not making any money." "They have had issues recently, not good." You get the idea!

Those with the most overblown egos, and somewhat disreputable demeanour to match, tend to like this approach, belittling any competition as simply not up to the job (as compared to them). Does it work? Sometimes for sure, but you will probably earn somewhat of a 'reputation' in the process. Not all potential clients are impressed by this behaviour or, indeed, keep quiet after the event. Inevitably, if this is your *modus operandi,* it will leak out into the public domain, and you will probably then become a target for unfavourable comment yourself!

Another alternative closure technique employed over many years has been the good old 'I have a buyer' ploy. At the point of appraisal—or even before, if you are targeting a specific house— you inform the owner you have a hot buyer who has either identified their house specifically as ideal for their needs or that you just know it would be perfect for. You suggest they come through as a one-off inspection first before the owner decides on going to open market, with the allure of nothing to lose and the potential of a quick and painless sale combined with no expensive marketing costs being subsequently required.

This can indeed be a tempting proposition to the owners and there is nothing inherently wrong in suggesting such an approach as long as—and call me Mr Picky here—the buyer *actually* exists, and you offer an appropriate short-term listing mechanism to support a genuine one-off inspection (for example, a seven-day open list). Indeed, as mentioned, many sales have resulted from this method, more so in COVID-19 times, and one of my ex-colleagues was very good at this process. Critically, however, only when he had a genuinely matched buyer and with a minimal-commitment initial listing to allow the one-off inspection (thus keeping the seller's further options open until the outcome of the off-market inspection).

The problem is, in many instances, the alleged buyer is just a hook designed to engage the owner first, ahead of anyone else. They either are not really qualified, so not a particularly close match or—at worst—are non-existent (in which case your mate takes on the leading role in exchange for a slab). As long as you get some sort of 'buyer' through, the owner is none the wiser. You just come up with : a plausible excuse as to why, after all, it didn't quite match their exact requirements *(Really? Who knew?)* or 'something' has inexplicably cropped up which has stopped them from being able to purchase for the next couple of weeks (by which time they will have been forgotten about, hopefully).

Now for this to work, it must be a pincer movement. In getting this person through you must get the owner to sign a listing authority that just happens to be a 90-day exclusive (oh sorry, didn't I mention that *small* detail?). Slam dunk, the mysterious original buyer has dissolved away but, hey, who cares? The owner is now locked in with you and, therefore, the marketing and normal sale processes are guaranteed to come to you, as a follow on. Some more astute people might smell a rat or read the small print, but many won't and blindly sign whatever is put in front of them. When they do realise what's taken place, it is too late, and they most likely take the route of least resistance at that stage anyway.

Give away gimmicks might do the trick as well. Offer a $500 gift card or free night away on the Gold Coast, etc., for every completed 'list and sell'. I say list *and sell*, you see if it is something of value you need to pin it to a financial outcome for you (i.e., a settlement). Accordingly, if you are offering something in exchange for only the listing, or—worse still—just a booked-in appraisal, you might need to downscale the gift accordingly otherwise you might get done over. A coffee voucher is a good starting point!

Conversely, if you are putting someone in a 'draw' you best ensure it is a rather good prize at the end of it, e.g., holiday, car, free listing(!), otherwise it's potentially of insufficient interest. That is also a punt, however, as the level of extra income generated is not known before the 'big' prize is put up. Taking a different path (almost literally) I know of one independent start-up agency, a while back, that initially grew their client base by offering free maintenance services on sign up. This was to help the owner with property presentation/landscaping, etc., for sale.

It worked quite well, and a few others tried to follow suit, even going DIY themselves and mucking in. More Bob's Mowing though, even if the agent's name *was* Jim, as a free 'handyman' is only as good as how handy they truly are! Nonetheless, free things are always worth a try as, let's face it, some people are just surprisingly shallow!

I am sure other interesting things probably go on from time to time. How about some good old-fashioned stand-over tactics with a baseball bat or exotic 'favours' (I'll leave that to your imagination). Perhaps some full-on blackmail situations or hostage taking? Alright, I am getting a bit carried away now, but the point is closure is king. Do not come back without it! Whatever it takes, people, whatever it takes!

10 | ARTISTIC LICENCE

H ooray! In the face of stiff competition, you secured the listing—by whatever means!—got some advertising paid for, and agreed the method of sale. You are good to go! Well, yes, except now you must sell the 'sizzle' and deliver on your promise of being an expert marketeer. Stunning photos, slick video and well-constructed words are all urgently needed to ensure this property pops! No pressure then.

For newbies, and indeed some more experienced exponents, who struggle for creative inspiration, this can be quite daunting. Now, admittedly in the COVID-19 market madness you could just write *'It is a house'* and it would still sell within the day, but in more normal circumstances—and certainly for higher value homes—the need for crafted wording and stunning imagery is particularly important, both for maximising the property value potential and for your own brand perception. In truth, however, many so-called 'marketeers' are really not. Hence, the inconsistent quality of advertising across the industry as a whole and the lack of good support and guidance given to many novices in this critical area.

Best to break this down into the key constituents. Words (for internet advertising narrative, brochure summaries, etc.,) and photos (again for internet advertising and for various printed media formats) are the mandatory needs, supplemented by additional, more contemporary offerings such as video profiles, drone footage, and floor plans (2D image-based or more advanced 3D and interactive). In an ideal world, the blended use of all these tools will showcase the property to the maximum audience in the best possible light.

The wording is an intriguing topic, not leastwise views genuinely differ as to how best to describe a property to engage the buyer (which is, after all, it's only purpose). Getting a consistent answer as to best practice is quite difficult. Putting aside, for a moment, the obvious problems with those who are just plain lazy or cannot be bothered with wonderful overtures, there remains an argument. Do you write a longer and detailed essay with much descriptive and emotional content, or do you cut to the chase with a relatively brief introductory description then just list bullet points for all the main features? I guess the truth is there is no entirely correct answer, as different people react to different things.

Of course, it also depends on the medium. A relatively small advertisement in a newspaper, for instance, dictates only a catchy heading and bullets points of key features. This is due to both space constraints and impact on the eye, in competition with other properties on the same page. Unless you have a full-page advertisement, of course. Well, sorry I never achieved such lofty vendor paid advertising (as you would need a second mortgage taken out against the house you were selling!). *Yes, I know, all you inner city and Gold Coast highflyers with your $10k advertising budgets do it all the time. Well done you!*

Likewise, flyers and brochures need to be reasonably concise for much the same reasons of space, and to be memorable when you have collected 15 for the day via multiple open home visits or had them stuffed in your mailbox.

Internet based applications are more diverse, however. Back in the (relatively recent) day, most viewing was via full size web pages on a desktop PC or laptop. This allows for considerably more space and, typically, if at home the user has more time, browsing through listings in more detail, studying photos, etc.

This is where, to my mind, a longer and more engaging description of the property should sit. Some will still argue short and sweet is sufficient and perhaps that's so in some cases. But if we are just bulleting some generic points in a sterile and clinical fashion then surely the owner can do that (and hasten our demise?)! The agent should use this space to demonstrate they fully 'get' the property and the owner's vision, not just technically, but also emotionally. If you—as the agent and marketeer—cannot convey any sense of real enthusiasm or wonder in your listing, why should you expect anyone else to get excited!

For me this is a way of showing the owner you really do appreciate their property individually, and are not just 'going through the motions'. By listening to their own impressions and images of their home, including features that attracted them initially or have since been added, you can incorporate aspects of this, combined with your own take, to create something that is both reflective and refreshing. In addition, it simply shows effort and professional input for the commission you wish to charge.

I guess, by the very fact I am writing all this guff, you would expect I am in the longer narrative camp, but I accept there are others who will always feel this is overly elaborate and that people switch off before completion. I would certainly accept the world is changing and probably the art of creating a storyline is diminishing, both in the exponents and those who can be bothered to subsequently appreciate it!

Therefore, given the length and content of narrative can vary, one important constant is the heading. A simple one liner, right? Well, this can be as challenging as anything else. The first dilemma is which route do you go? *Factual:* A plain heading detailing the one or two attributes that will sell the house. *Whimsical/Romantic:* A fluffy heading that says nothing specific about the property but grabs the attention through pure word craft (well perhaps, but please remember we are not comics, or poets!). *Aspirational:* Feed the greed, something that suggests money is to be made here! Unfortunately, as much as you might like to, it's very difficult to incorporate all approaches in a few short words.

Let's take an example:

A four bed, two bath, two car, low-set home, located on a hillside (with great rear vista):

- Factual: *'Family Four Bed with Great Views'*
- Whimsical: *'King of the Hill!'*
- Romantic: *'Sunsets & Champagne'*
- Aspirational: *'Prime Location! Reap Future Rewards'*

You get the idea. What is best? Well again, different people react to different things so there is probably no right answer. Surprisingly—given my allegiance to longer narrative—I am slightly more in the factual camp on this one, certainly with relatively generic homes anyway.

If an estate house has a great two-bay shed that sets it apart from the next one, put it in the title, plain and simple! Don't make a cryptic or jokey reference, however clever you think you are, that half the punters won't get. Call a spade a spade! Going the 'creative' route on every single listing makes for very confusing deciphering of what is on offer. Perhaps a little indulgent, so you need to be clear, otherwise nobody has a clue what you are on about! Ultimately, it's horses for courses, once more.

If a property has character and is surrounded by lush vegetation in a tranquil setting, then the likely buyer is going to be someone more interested in this aspect than the number of bedrooms, and is probably a more emotional or romantic person to boot. So, 'Your Green & Peaceful Oasis Awaits' or 'Be At One With Nature' is better than a clinical roll call of house particulars. To a degree, headings online are less important. With some online real estate portals, they do not appear in the search results, so are only seen once you have selected the specific property (by which time you have made the initial conscious decision and are probably looking at the detail and photos). For static newsprint advertising it is still very important, to hopefully draw the eye to a particular property on a page.

Headings can also be used to convey an urgent message or for promotion purposes. 'Contract Crashed! New Opportunity. Be Quick!', or similar, is a common one to try to urgently re-engage with the target audience if things go wrong at the last minute (although see notes below, don't leave this up for three months!). A growing trend online—once the property has gone under contract—is to replace your carefully worded killer property tag line with the slightly less witty and original, 'Under Contract with Bob'.

In fairness, in COVID-19 times this was also the quickest and easiest way to kill the constant and unrelenting incoming bombardment of buyer enquiries. Once prospective buyers see it has gone, the phone will go silent. Like all good things, with direct agent access, this can be used and abused with headings blatantly being used for the furtherment of the brand rather than the property.

The listing portals can take a dim view of this, hence, one of the reasons headings do not appear in some searches anymore, as already mentioned. On a side note, even closing that loophole isn't watertight. The price field—which does appear in the search summaries—has a free format option for the all-important 'Inviting Offers' reference, or the like, in these days of no fixed price. In other words, a space in which you can write text rather than just input numbers. Hence, the price will also become 'Under Contract with Bob' at the very first opportunity!

What I would say is, both narrative and headings—certainly in terms of electronic presence—should always be a work in progress and reviewed on a regular basis if the property hasn't already sold, to ensure freshness. Changing something to reflect feedback, or an angle not originally considered, shows flexibility and ongoing commitment as opposed to a 'set and forget' mentality. Not good to see, as I have genuinely done, a house still advertised in February with, 'Move in For Christmas' as the heading! It might as well read, 'House Has Problems and Agent is Slack'. This recent, highly active market had excused such poor efforts, as nothing had remained around long enough for wording to become stale. In slower times, however, I review and tweak the heading, lead photo and introductory narrative at least every two to three weeks if no offers have been forthcoming.

Which leads us nicely into the most critical area: photography. You can throw in all the bells and whistles, but for me a property needs a simply well-written narrative combined with high quality photos to do the heavy lifting. I really believe it to be a non-negotiable area to get crisp, stunning visuals from a professional source. By professional, I mean a qualified independent photographer who runs a business and earns their living from it (as opposed to an agent who simply owns the infamous 'good camera' and fancies themselves as a part-time creative resource). For the purposes of charging the owner money, 'professional' should mean a little more than, "I won't use my phone this time". First impressions count and the best house in the world photographed poorly can create a misleading and underwhelming impression. Quick and free to capture yourself they may be, but dark, blurred, or badly composed photos are a false economy to both the property you are representing and your brand perception.

I have used the same professional photographer for many years with excellent results. To my mind, he—as most others in the profession should do—offers three key areas of value add. First and foremost, he is trained and highly experienced so he can determine optimum composition structure, positioning for lighting, etc. Secondly, he uses high-end equipment; not just for the camera body, but for multiple lens options, synchronised remote flash units, and aerial drones, etc. Finally, he has superior post-photography editing skills and software to maximise and enhance the final imagery (adjusting lighting and exposure levels where needed, dropping in clear skies on dull, overcast days, etc.).

Now I quite like taking photos myself, but would not pretend to get anywhere near this level of return, hence, why I use him to photograph all properties, even if I pay myself. Some agents may not agree with that last statement, but I see the constant standard of photography output as much a self-marketing tool as anything else. The internet is our big window to showcase what we do to the wider world, so why not make sure everything you put out there looks excellent and reflects well on you? Would-be sellers are looking at these images as well and are more likely to contact an agent who presents other homes immaculately than someone with a set of dark, lopsided phone photos with finger smudges still on the lens. Yes, I know, phone cameras are 'Hollywood' grade these days, but most of their users are not! Therefore, I see it as a self-investment in promotion, as good, if not better, than anything else you would routinely spend money on.

In the same way poor efforts will be a deterrent, well executed and produced photographs can give even a modest house extra presence on the internet and encourage onsite inspections. Sometimes buyers will even remark at an open home, "Looked much better in the photos," inferring, amongst other things, we have perhaps been a little deceptive. As marketeers, working for the seller, I take that as a compliment. We should be making our product look as good as possible in the photography; that is our job! If said photos are relatively contemporary—more on that in a minute—and have not been doctored to physically remove or hide issues, then I see no problem.

Things have moved a long way in recent years, and now the routine use of twilight shoots and aerial photography can produce some truly stunning results. The other benefit with professional photos is the element of self-discipline and governance by the photographer themselves. They know what works and the best way to convey things in the appropriate manner.

By contrast, there are a few agents, somewhat out there on the fringe, who are a little looser in approach. Let's have the owners pets in the photos, better still, let's have the owner in the photos pottering in the garden. The tenant still sitting on the lounge in shot because he couldn't be bothered to move out the way and—for some strange reason—you couldn't be bothered to ask him either. If you are up yourself, get out the selfie stick and join in the fun, who wouldn't want to see the wacky, grinning agent!

Alternatively, just have no new photos at all! You may get a tenanted property that is very messy or in poorly maintained condition, or the tenant refuses internet photography—which is within their rights—if you get them offside. So, instead you trawl through any previous property management photos that might be available within the office, from either routine rental inspections or when it was last advertised for rent.

All well and good to a point if it solves a practical problem. However, these photos still need to have some relatable connection to the *current* look of the property. If you are using photos from 10 years ago, and since then all the colours have changed and other features removed or added, it is a misrepresentation, and prospective buyers will become very frustrated upon arrival to find something that does not resemble what is online. Most people's reasonable assumption is that marketing photos are current, or at least close to current.

The other issue is that property managers (sorry) are even less photographically dynamic than their sales agent counterparts. Photos for routine inspections are intended for internal reference only and will often be rushed, dark and generally unsuited to a starring role on the big screen. Furthermore, these are often focused on specific items within the property (who wouldn't want their sales portfolio to include a prominent close-up of the laundry room sink?). There may be times when new photos are a challenge, but it is generally still a cop-out to put these quick, free, and 'non-confrontational' photos online. If the resulting display clearly screams out to the public that is exactly what you have done, then there is little benefit for you or your seller.

Another variation on this theme is when the owner (bless them) gives you a set of their own precious photos to use. You see, they are keen amateur photographers themselves, and know *exactly* what the key selling points of their home are and how to capture them. That's fine, but amateur is still the key word in that last sentence and, unfortunately, more often than not what they see through their rose-tinted spectacles isn't quite up to muster (still I am sure they will understand when you tell them).

They are also not bound by any silly restrictions of good practice either, so if the photos are out of date or they have 'photoshopped' all of the cracks in the walls, that's all good, right? If all else fails, you can 'steal' any previous photos by trying to download those already associated with the property via one of the real estate industry portals. A few problems here, however, not least the resolution will be poor (and even worse once you have cropped them further to remove the inconvenient watermark logo from the previous agent!). Depending on the last time the property was advertised, these can again be quite dated. If you are lucky and they are more recent, then expect an irate previous selling agent—or owner for that matter, recognising their furniture—to call you and demand they are not reused. Ownership rights will theoretically exist with the photographer and whoever purchased them (certainly not you!).

Luckily and by contrast, existing videos are generally not lurking in the rental department or available by the owners own hand, and must be produced at the point of any new marketing. That is where the good news tends to stop, however, as it also provides a much broader base for agent 'interpretation' than still photos alone.

Your first decision is: paying for a professional product (quite costly) *or* creating your own little production. Unfortunately, the gap between qualified and amateur widens here to a gaping chasm. Videographers—commonly an additional skill set now offered by the same professional photographers—have high-quality motion smoothing gimbals, independent microphones and recording equipment, and dedicated aerial drones. Not to mention the time and experience to provide guidance on pieces to camera (and correspondingly re-shoot those scenes as necessary until right).

The alternative? Me with that damn phone again! The obvious pitfalls with that interlink with the next major decision, do you appear in your own video in person, voice it over or just go pictures and music. On the theme of pictures and music, again, I digress here a minute. A property 'video' should contain separately filmed *moving* images. Recycling your still photographic images, just stitched together with some questionable presentation/slideshow animations and transitions, set to a cheery, but bland, non-copyrighted soundtrack *is a not a video!* It's called the *motion* picture industry for a reason.

Right, got that off my chest ... now where were we? Ah yes, appearing in your own video. Well again, no set answer. If the video is short (time is money!) then perhaps better to concentrate entirely on the property rather than burning up valuable seconds massaging your ego. Once you have 60 to 90 seconds to play with most opt for a short introductory piece to camera, the remainder given over to the property. I think this is a good balance and typically the approach I have used. You need to appear well dressed and professional, whilst demonstrating enthusiasm and knowledge of the key aspects of the property. With longer timeslots some become a little more self-indulgent and shoot an intro, outro and multiple interim pieces to camera in the house. If you are a sharp dresser and good orator this might still work, but it is already starting to border on the annoying for buyers watching, who are really only interested in the property itself (but of course you don't care about them, you are doing this for the would-be sellers who may also be watching).

Beyond this we delve into the dark realms already touched on of the comedy and 'alternative' approaches as a point of difference—well they are certainly different, but not in a good way most of the time—or trademark approach. Personally, I find there is a reflex cringe reaction to any agent trying to be funny on screen (and thinking they are) or 'acting' out some stage-managed scene with an assistant stooge for our 'entertainment'. Never mind, as long as the participants themselves are amused by their own antics—and the client is paying—where's the harm? *Lights, camera, action!*

With no one paying, the alternative cheap-and-nasty for social media channels is an agent with hand-held mobile just talking to camera. Droning on for couple of minutes about the great new listing they have or first open home they are about to do, *describing* the features (how about just show us?)! But no, all you can see of this wonderful property, past their head and shoulders, is a vague picture on the wall and perhaps a small section of window—*brilliant*!

I will come clean. We are none of us immune and I admit I was guilty of a blatant (upon reflection) rookie error with the use of photos when I started out. Suitably excited at getting my first decent house—with good vendor paid advertising to match—I duly created my picture signboard for the front of the property. I had been a good boy and got professional photos, so put the best four into the edit for the sign—perfect! Almost, except for the fact that one of those aforementioned shots was the impressive photo of the *front* of the house. Out of context the proof looked great and was ordered and installed. It was only when I turned up to show off my new listing to all my esteemed colleagues on the next stock run that the obvious truth hit me.

Here was a picture signboard with a very large lead photo of the front of the house directly behind which was, of course, the front of the house (just in case you missed it the first time!). Suffice to say, there was much amusement amongst my colleagues, who were so grateful I had re-confirmed what the property looked like that was just 10 feet behind the sign! Luckily the owner didn't seem too bothered, but you learn quickly, and internal/rear shots were certainly the go from then on!

Some prime examples of various 'artists' at work creating many of the above disasters, include: an agent in the majority of photos at a very average rental property wearing a Superman costume (no context that I could discern!), an agent sitting by the seller's pool having cocktails in shot, a reclined tenant smoking on the sofa in a lounge shot, and various pets that couldn't be controlled (apparently) hogging the limelight. A shaky handheld video walk through with the agent stopping to flick his hair and admire himself in the bathroom mirror on camera, "Who's that good looking rooster?"—good question! There are plenty of examples of talking-head to camera 'selfie' videos with very limited footage of the actual property. Lastly, there are the occasional photos that still somehow get through 'rigorous' vetting processes with perfectly formed fingerprints on them (at least clean the phone first!).

For all your excellent (or indifferent) efforts with whatever narrative style and photographic package you choose, it is probably worth mentioning, at this stage, there are those who simply will not bother to read or register any of it. Unfortunately, this is a growing percentage I fear, so perhaps any attention to detail or care ultimately might be superfluous anyway.

I recently had a small acreage property adjacent to a wildlife reserve with a lake. Beautiful setting with a low-set four-bedroom home. The only slight limitation (at least in these modern times) was a lack of ensuite, as it only had one bathroom. Now, this was mentioned in the text, the icons at the top showed 'four bed, one bath' and we had a floor plan on the internet as well. At least three clear touchpoints defining the property configuration, and yet, 75% of the onsite inspectors at open homes would turn up, get excited about the location, but then ask where the ensuite was! When advised there wasn't one, the usual response would be, "It's a nice position, but we won't look at anything without two bathrooms".

They had all seen the property online first, which begged the obvious question, why are you here then? Just on the off chance the owner had built one this morning as a value add, perhaps?! I have also had properties with swimming pools, where they are clearly shown in the lead photo online. Yet still people come to viewings (who have apparently shortlisted already) only to stop dead in their tracks as they will, "Not even consider a home with a pool!". Go figure.

As you were then, perhaps. Continue with your gags, gimmicks and half-baked wording after all. Comical enough, until your owner remembers they are paying for a professional! Oh well, you got the listing now regardless, so doesn't really matter, hey?

11 | Low-Hanging Fruit

Your gleaming new listing is now finally ready to hit the market with its eye-catching internet presentation and expertly crafted write up. At last, plain sailing from here to payday!

Well maybe, but that depends on several factors including the state of the market, what actions you perform in the next few weeks, and the mindset of your vendors. Unfortunately, quite often—although not in COVID-19 times!—'first in, best dressed' isn't always the case. Human nature dictates that many (well, most) sellers have an unrealistic initial price expectation of their beloved home. Thus, just as you think you are in the clear, new challenges emerge almost immediately. In simple and blunt terms, you will not sell something that is not priced correctly, no matter how much you or the seller would wish. Assuming you have identified this potential problem (and haven't got your head in the same clouds as the vendor) you now have to subtly, but firmly, highlight their misguided valuation reasonably quickly through structured buyer feedback. In doing so, however, you must skilfully eliminate all *other* possible reasons for lack of immediate contract at their dream figure (e.g., poor marketing, your lack of experience or general all-round incompetence!).

In an ideal world you will have sellers whom you have already formed a good rapport with, so they will have a degree of trust and understanding with you. If they are motivated to sell, they are also more likely to be open to genuine feedback during the process. If you have managed to go the auction route, with its more intense price commentary, this will help further (if it is run properly, of course!). If you cover all marketing bases and undertake your duties diligently, with regular and informed feedback, there is every chance you will position the house correctly and achieve a sale comfortably within your listing agreement term (typically 90 days).

The stark reality—again in non-pandemic times—nonetheless, is this scenario probably only happens in perhaps 50% of all new listing cases. This is due to the agent either being too timid or not experienced/confident enough to educate on price effectively and move the property into the active selling zone. Alternatively, the sellers may simply be very obstinate—or not overly motivated—and will not move on their rigid price requirement even in the face of well delivered feedback.

Unfortunately, in this case, it is almost a given they will then look to the agent as the reason (excuse) as to why the property has not yet achieved what *they* want. Rather than climb down and admit the property perhaps is not quite as valuable as they thought, they will cling to the notion that a better price is still out there and will come with a different agent on board. As will be seen, this somewhat optimistic hope can be very easily upheld and fuelled by other hungry agents in their ear, with positive confirmation telling them *exactly* what they want to hear!

Sure as night follows day, agents know only too well the above situation exists so any current listings on the market, that are not already under contract/sold after 30 days or more, start to become potential targets to lift. *'Sign jumping'* as it is known, has a twofold benefit. For the generally lazy or quick and dirty agent, why waste endless time and effort prospecting the unwashed masses to find one potential new vendor (aka a needle in a haystack), when here is a concise set of people already on the market and openly advertising themselves as active sellers!

Secondly, if they haven't seen the light by now, they are probably already at the point where they are only going to accept the price truth *after* changing agents—and that final 'excuse' is thereby removed—so you get the inherited benefit of reaching the sell zone (even if the first agent has tried to educate them already).

Theoretically, you should not openly or directly approach other agent's vendors for the same business, but the reality is everyone does, some subtly and others blatantly with no shame! Officially not best practice—as stipulated the industry's Code of Conduct—yet actually viewed as a bread-and-butter activity to the point that, if you have any moral dilemma with it, you are routinely told you should 'probably not be in the business'. This, then, is the delicious low-hanging fruit that is just too tempting not to pick, and so it begins.

First, you might drive your patch and do a visual 'sign count'. Essentially you note all the homes for sale with other agents that don't already have a 'Sold' sticker on them. Better still, just download an electronic list from an in-house industry database of current 'on the markets'. Often this list is not entirely accurate—as various properties haven't been updated from being withdrawn or going under contract—but that won't bother most going down this route. A few dud calls versus having to go out and spend time researching properly—no contest!

The best, and most switched-on, agents are monitoring things constantly and being already highly active in their area, will pretty much know exactly which properties the opposition has, how long they have been on the market, and whether they are priced well, etc., and this continually evolves as a work in progress. Of course, that is how everyone should be across it, but for many it is a full reset every two or three months because you have lost track (again!).

Depending on your mentality and approach, you can do some useful background research first via the real estate databases. Is it owner-occupied or rented—not much point talking to a tenant about selling their house—where is it priced, and how long has it been sitting there, etc.? The counter 'hard man' argument is that's simply 'fluffing round', putting off getting down and dirty, just hammer them all regardless! Shake the tree and see what falls. However you do it, with a degree of research or blind scattergun, having assembled your list of targets, hit the phone (or door knock, if you really want that personal touch of slight menace).

Contact the sellers on some flimsy associated pretext, "I see you're on the market, are you looking to buy again in the area? I might be able to help you with your *purchasing* requirements,". Wow, how helpful—yeah right. If they don't see through that BS immediately, then with minimum further small talk, casually ask them how things are going with selling their place. Act very surprised when they say no, they haven't got a contract yet. "Really? It seems such a wonderful house from the photos, and *priced well*. I can't believe it hasn't sold."

Of course, if you have done your homework already, you know exactly why it hasn't sold—good photos and write up—it's simply too dear! Not that you will ever tell them that ... YET. Plant the landmines that it *may* be their current agent's inability, perhaps? In short, the complete reverse logic of the incumbent's approach, i.e., frame the existing agent as the *only* reason (excuse) for not achieving their aspirational price! If they are already heading that way, works almost every time! If you are trying to convince yourself of something and others are apparently justifying it, all the better. A second opinion? Well, yes, but one that will only ever agree with you!

The general theory goes if you are doing a great job and your sellers are entirely happy and engaged, then you are surely bombproof from such blatant destabilisation. They will simply tell any would-be new suitors that they are extremely satisfied with their current agent and have absolutely no intention to change. True to a point, but when it comes to money people can still behave in unexpected ways, so never be too sure of yourself. Conversely if you are doing a poor job—either in truth, or just through denial in the seller's minds—then they will very likely spill the beans all too easily and pour their hearts out to any sympathetic agent who wants to listen (not that you are very sympathetic, but you will put up with the usual self-inflicted sob story for 10 minutes on the phone in order to advance to the end game).

As mentioned, some are subtle, crafted and tease out the situation, whilst some go in all guns blazing! I worked with one guy who would just phone directly without any pretence whatsoever. "Hey mate, why haven't you sold your place yet? What's your agent playing at? Mate, give me a go, I get results and have buyers waiting." Back to our blunt instruments again and whilst these individuals are full-on and arguably crossing the line, they are always secretly relished by the principal (over those 'weaker' agents who worry too much about silly things like reputation and consequences!).

Mind you, the scenario can be somewhat like Mission Impossible: *The mission in question Jim, should you choose to accept it, is to convert as many competitor's signs as possible to the house colours by whatever means necessary. However, should you or any of your like-minded attack dogs be caught, management will disavow all knowledge of your actions. This furtive endorsement will self-destruct in five seconds.*

As you can probably gather by now, I have never quite been in the seek and destroy gang. I would tend to make direct contact via open homes—with inspectors—or inbound enquiries on properties for sale (many selling are already looking elsewhere). The general conversation will come onto their current status and the discussion can go from there. I am inclined to use my sign lists in my area for softer initial contact by letter (still under a pretext of another service). Okay, frankly a more futile exercise, but there you go. That's why I am writing this and not lording it up as a highflyer on the coast, perhaps.

Undoubtably some very good listings can be picked up by sign jumping. Not least because—in fairness—some agents will simply be doing a poor job and those owners will genuinely need to change direction, ultimately. If you have already established contact, you have a good chance of success. Equally, there will be many instances where the current agent is doing a perfectly good job, but the owners are simply not receptive to the reality of their situation. These cases can be a double-edged sword, as they are legitimate targets, but will still need some work to get them in the right place, and they probably have no new/additional budget for advertising, etc.

There can be other complications. All incoming agents want a clean and full takeover. That is, to remove the old agent completely and install themselves instead with a new exclusive agreement. First and foremost, if the existing agent has an exclusive listing already, you cannot do anything until that agreement runs out (90 days maximum in Queensland). Furthermore, most exclusive agreements then default to an open agreement, meaning the owner must still formally terminate the other agent for you to put your own exclusive agreement into play.

Just as there are standard plays to try and attack a listing, so there are predictable counter-measures deployed in defence. The usual one is the existing agent—if they have an inkling about what the owner is about to do—will miraculously get a new 'very interested' party the day before the exclusive listing expires. This party (your mum, mate or completely unsuitable buyer you somehow duped into inspecting) will either come through, but then need 'a few days' to make a decision or will only be able to inspect in a week or so's time. The owner then has a dilemma and generally hangs on for a few more days hoping this will result in an outcome, thus buying the current agent some more time (to find a real buyer!).

Other delaying tactics can include the miraculously timed offer of some new cheap/free marketing or even a general guilt trip play on the amount of work put in so far. If the owner is already a little uneasy making a change, this may be enough to create a stay of execution or change their stance slightly and suggest only an open listing to the new agent instead, so that both agents can run in parallel. This will put most of the circling vultures off—for a short while at least—as they are not prepared to do an open list (considerable work is still required with limited/no new budget and there is no guarantee of an outcome, should the original agent get lucky with a previous buyer coming back).

Sometimes it may be worth taking on the property as a shared listing—depending what else you have on—and attempting an 'open conversion'. Despite the temptation to do otherwise, you provide a high level of service regardless of the listing status and effectively look to show the other agent up in comparison, thereby generating the opportunity to push for an exclusive listing at the second time of asking (with tangible evidence now demonstrated of why you should warrant it).

In the hierarchy of smugness, a listing gained from sign jumping always carries the highest kudos and is most definitely one to slap on the table in the weekly sales meeting (making sure everyone knows how you got it). One of those rare weeks when you relish the looming team gathering as you will be top dog. It makes you look tough and dynamic, plus the principal will massage the ego and praise you big time as this advances their own agenda of getting the entire blob to act in the same, more aggressive, manner (ah yes, if only). "See everyone, the rewards of having no fear!" A double golf clap from everyone for that, followed by a lecture on how, if one person can do it, we all can. As with most things, tracking from there onwards tends to go quiet depending on whether a resulting sale is forthcoming from this second-hand property or it turns out the owner is just a bit of a dick after all—with any agent!

12 | WHEN'S GOOD FOR YOU?

Now, let's assume by either sheer luck or expert judgement you do happen to get a listing in the sell zone early on, hopefully offers may be forthcoming very quickly. As explained, given the real possibility of an extended listing becoming a target, surely that is only good news, right?

It should be, but timing of offers is one of the thorniest issues for an agent and one that most sellers generally get far too hung up on. Bring an offer to the seller too quickly and you have not 'earnt' your bloated commission; yet bring an offer too slowly and you are useless! This may be an oversimplification, but the point is timing—to a certain degree—is irrelevant to the specific result and the means of creating it.

The seller is not paying for an agent by the hour (otherwise this client would be on the clock!). The seller is paying for the agent's experience, network, and marketing skill to deliver the best financial outcome possible—that is it.

You may have heard the phrase, *'the first offer is the best one'*. Well not always, but certainly it quite often is, and for a good reason. The property is new to the market and the agent has launched it well. It has good quality photos and a well written narrative ensuring competition has been created in the first few days, coupled with easy accessibility via open homes, and the agent potentially contacting their existing buyer database. *This* is what the seller pays for. All these things working together, along with the agent's knowhow and negotiation skills to foster activity and competition, producing the best price outcome. If that comes day one or two, so what? Take it!

I cannot understand sellers who do not want to go to auction—which has a defined timescale and structure—but then still prefer to wait a few weeks before accepting any offer under private treaty. To somehow feel satisfied the agent has now justified their commission with a certain number of days on the job (and in doing so, take $10,000 less for the house because the sweet spot has been missed!). As covered earlier, the commission fee in isolation means little, as it is all about your walkaway figure (price minus commission). If a good agent achieves an excellent offer price very quickly, the value in the service is already there and the maximum outcome delivered. You can wait until more hours are on the clock if that makes you feel better, but if the subsequent walkaway figure drops, you have not utilised the agent efficiently.

Increasingly, in this world of instant gratification and online accessibly, the point of listing is when maximum potential exists. This is further heightened in a seller's market, such as we saw recently during the pandemic period (where stock was short, but buyer demand remained strong). What are the key factors at play?

Firstly, general buyer behaviour and activity. At any one time there are a pool of buyers looking in a certain area/price bracket, etc. Most are fully up-to-speed on existing listings via their electronic platform/app of choice and often know a particular local market space better than some of the agents! Many will have alerts set up for an area or simply trawl through relevant listings at least a couple of times a day to ensure nothing new has popped up. When something does appear, it is initially new to this *entire* buyer pool and will attract the maximum number of initial enquiries. In a fast-moving market—where potentially some or many of these buyers may have previously missed out on other homes—if they like what they see they will react very quickly and want to inspect the property immediately for fear of loss. This creates genuine and tangible competition, which frankly is absolute gold and exceedingly difficult to artificially induce later.

The second aspect is: who has the balance of power? With a priced property (as opposed to auction) it is at the very beginning of the process when the seller has most control. With a newly listed property it is impossible for the buyer to push back on the price in those first few days, purely based on time on market. This means they must make a true value determination centred on their desire and any immediate competition, typically resulting in higher offers. Again, fear of loss is vital. If it looks good and is likely to sell quickly, you simply don't have the luxury of starting low and playing games as someone else will beat you to the punch.

These are very positive elements to harness, but beware, as before too long they will also work against you! Should a property remain on the market for some time—for whatever reason—then the buyer pool will by now already be fully aware of it (or have seen it) and will continue to search elsewhere. This inevitably and unavoidably reduces activity significantly to just new buyers entering the existing pool on a weekly basis.

The only option to re-engage the entire pool, at this point, is to fundamentally change something—typically list price, as in a *reduction!*—to renew the perception of the property to the wider audience. By now you are already chasing your tail.

Likewise, the very benefit created by a fast-paced market forcing people to make good early offers, through the experience of missing out, is negated once a property has been listed for a while. Now, reverse psychology comes in to play and buyers— knowing 'good' homes are selling very quickly—start to question why this one is still available? Either it has something wrong with it or, *surprise, surprise*, it must be priced too high (neither opinion being good!). What's more, even if they like it, that offer is now going to be lower and more considered than others would have been initially.

It is not just the commission justification, of course, there are other reasons for some seller's lack of decisive action when it counts. Selling a home, after all, is a big decision and some people are not actually ready, or emotionally prepared, to confront the reality of it, when the crunch comes so quickly. The biggest influence, however, is (once again) when the price expectation of the seller is a little too high. It is bad enough trying to work on this when you have time in hand, but if you land an excellent offer on day one, yet it is slightly below their perfect price, then it is almost impossible to get a subsequent contract over the line!

Another more curious aspect around price is the *moving goalposts effect* if things appear to be all too easy. At listing, the owners indicate they would be absolutely stoked if they could walk away with $500,000. Two early offers come in close to this and suddenly they now want $520,000 in hand, as a minimum! The notion is that as we are getting this demand already, we don't want to rush, as clearly there could be a lot more money out there. Possibly, but equally for the reasons already given, this could be as good as it gets, and their original—more realistic— price expectation was correct all along.

The trouble is, you can only prove this the hard way! Believe me, it is amazing how quickly you can go from king one week, with the seeming luxury of very keen interest and multiple initial approaches, to nothing new to work with the following week! The final problem is often self-inflicted as your job becomes even harder if you have 'bought' the listing (by knowingly appraising it too high in the first place to beat the competition). This will still be fresh in the seller's mind—and be repeated back in defence of their actions—as it will appear that this offer should *clearly* not be accepted, by your own assessment!

"It's only early days," "It's only the first offer," or (the cracker) "We're not in a hurry," are all classic responses from the seller in this scenario. And, too often, make an agent groan because they will already know in their heart of hearts it is a *genuinely* good offer that the sellers really should be taking (because it will most likely be downhill from here). In this situation the only remaining option is to implement the good old 'take it away from them' strategy.

Just before the offer dies a natural death, that is, when the frustrated buyers give up and move on to something else, you effectively tell the owner that has already happened, and they have lost the offer completely (and the potential of a quick sale has gone with it). This will invoke one of two responses. They either won't care as they really are set on what they want. In which case you haven't lost anything and will have at least confirmed what you are now up against!

Alternatively, they might mildly panic as in truth they had—just quietly—got quite used to the idea, over the last 24 hours, that they were about to sell the house and be on their merry way nice and quickly. Realising the buyers have gone cold—and that the sellers cannot completely dictate the price outcome—tends to concentrate the mind somewhat and they may throw out a revised, final counter-offer, which could just be enough to hold things together. White lies? Tough love? Call it what you like, but sometimes you must help people despite themselves!

They say you never forget your first love, or in this case, offer! Hence, although they rejected that perfectly decent $500,000 approach at the outset as simply not good enough, six weeks later your sellers will now be clinging on to its cherished memory and throwing it back in your face every time you bring them something else that just never seems to quite measure up. Why on earth would they take $485,000 when someone has *already* offered $500,000? Well, because that was then, and this is now (and next month the figure will be $475,000!).

Frankly, from an agent's perspective, the only *good* offer is one that is accepted (and so becomes a good contract!). If rejected, it is just a thorn in your side that will quickly become the elephant in the room for all subsequent approaches to be compared to. This is bad enough with a bona fide formal offer that has been subsequently burnt, but some less experienced agents fall into the trap of excitedly presenting their sellers with expressions of interest, or worse still, verbal offers (before qualifying and committing the buyer properly).

This is often at the beginning of the process because they have got carried away with an indicated interest that has come in early and is higher than expected (so they can look good if they pass this figure on). Talk is cheap and often throw-away figures are put out by some casual buyers only to be withdrawn soon afterwards when they change their mind, admit they do not really have the money, or things start to look more serious.

Unfortunately, your average seller does not differentiate between a formal written offer and a verbal soundbite, particularly if it appears to uphold their price thinking. Hence, the agent torpedoes themselves introducing the notion of an (unsubstantiated) high offer price, that is now firmly lodged in the owners mind, by which to judge all future genuine approaches. Often, during conversations on taking over a listing—*yes, I have picked the occasional ripe fruit myself!*—I have been told, "We already had an offer of $... with the last agent." When asked if they saw this 'offer', nine times out of ten they were just 'told' about it, but, "They were *genuine*, just apparently the mother got sick, and they had to pull out,". Okay then. *(Pull out? They hadn't even put in!)*

As an agent you can be beaten around the head all day long with this constant reflection on past glory, but you are not the purchaser. In a slower market, previous indications count for very little. You might say to a buyer, "We already had a $500,000 offer, actually," to which the likely response is, "Well, they should have taken it then, my offer is $470,000." Yep, ain't that the truth!

Now, this is not to say that you never benefit from waiting. Sometimes quirky or character homes with unique 'attractions' do need that elusive right buyer to come along, and this isn't always in the first week. I think common sense needs to prevail, however, and if an early offer is genuinely low, compared to the honest assessment of the property, then of course you push on for better. Nonetheless, when we have a clearly excellent opportunity created by early strong competition—that will inevitably dissipate—then it's time to act!

Market conditions have a significant bearing. In the pandemic-fuelled wild market it was almost impossible *not* to sell within a short timescale, as the initial offers were so strong under frenzied competition. In a slower buyer's market it may still be patience is a virtue, to a degree (although best competition remains at time of listing for the reasons previously mentioned).

I do love this whole notion of sellers suddenly not being in a hurry or, "Not needing to sell," the moment offers don't go quite as perfectly hoped for price-wise. Yeah right, you are only doing this because you love having to constantly keep your house tidy and have random strangers walking through it at all times of the day making rude comments about your choice of internal styling! Furthermore, you are excited having this new friend, called the listing agent, who you must listen to (well okay, if you're lucky!) all the time. They are just dandy and will be your buddy for life (or least until you get their cheesy settlement gift anyway).

Sorry, but actions do always speak louder than words. Unless you are a masochist, if you—as the seller—have listed the house for sale and are going through all this disruption it's probably because (guess what) you *do* need to sell. To do so, however, you'll have to address the market price truth, and right now you aren't ready for that so let's pretend we're indifferent to the whole process! Fingers in ears now and start humming.

13 | Snake Oil

L et's take a well-earned breather at this stage. We have already covered considerable ground as to what is needed for your fledging career to move forward. With a lot to take in, are you getting a bit overwhelmed? Relax, count to 10 and fear not, for help is at hand (endlessly)!

These days for almost every struggling agent, it seems there is an ex 'super-agent' who is now a real estate mentor or coach— or indeed 'non-selling' principal for that matter!—who will tell you exactly what you are doing wrong and how to fix it so you can be (almost) as good as they once were (allegedly, but please do not fact check). Well, perhaps not quite a 1:1 ratio—yet!— but certainly in an industry racked by self-doubt and underachievement there are plenty on board the gravy train of endless money to be made from hapless souls clinging to a promise of better things to come (if only they just follow the foolproof wonder plan).

Now should any of the notable 'big guns'—you know who you are and, gee, so do we!—in this field lower them themselves and be reading these humble scribblings from a 'no name' they would tell you I was clearly just another also-ran that didn't get it or make the grade for disciplined self-improvement. They would probably take offence at anyone daring to question any pearls of wisdom passed on from such wise sages, and they would cite the handful of multimillion dollar superstars they have successfully nurtured. Let us be clear, I fully acknowledge there are a few very distinguished and respected ex-performers operating in this environment who can indeed add the, not insignificant, value of their experience, systematic processes, and motivation to aid those who—and this is key—already possess a natural talent coupled to a desire to push themselves further. Therefore, to a degree, I do get it as there must always be a space for good advice, personal development and coaching (as in any profession).

However—and it is a big 'however'—the bread-and-butter of this profitable little industry-within-an-industry is not so much the occasional success story, it is the blatant feeding from the bottom of the food chain. There is a constant supply of those who are doomed to never succeed in reaching the mythical levels of performance that is suggested *everyone* must obtain to have any self-respect. In short, the relentless stream of ill-fated hopefuls is where the true dollars lie! By their very experience and understanding of the industry, these people know fully well, statistically, most of the people they are 'inspiring' are not going to re-invent the wheel any time soon. Don't tell them that of course—*everyone* can earn easy triple-figures in this industry!

Another highly annoying recent development is over-proliferation. Yes, there are a few astute gurus out there, but also an ever-growing band of other smug know-it-all's and chancers. It's not just the full-time mentors anymore—who at least had the confidence and belief to make it a career path—now we have a veritable selection of current principals, auctioneers and even gun agents all imparting their priceless knowledge and *roadmap to success* to anyone who will listen. The problem is, I simply cannot take all this self-importance and imaginary solutions quite as seriously as they all do.

Admittedly, there is a lot to unpack here. My biggest general criticism of this field—yes, I know, looking from the bottom up!—is the unrealistic (and unrepresentative) premise of the industry from which most training and coaching is based, virtually ensuring 90% of participants will fail to live up to expectations. This pervades all the way down from the top mentors, through corporate training, and on to many 'motivating' principals.

As mentioned previously, the stark reality of the real estate industry is an average of around 11 sales per year per agent (or slightly under one per month). Yet that admission is no good if you want to engage most of the workforce in lucrative additional training, so instead you push the myth that everyone needs to earn $300,000-plus a year to be credible and worthy (and that's what most 'successful' agents are doing). Of course, we should all look to set targets to better ourselves and achieve more, but they need to remain realistic and relevant.

The theory goes if you aim high then hopefully (when you only do half as well) you have still improved. However, for many people coming into the industry these goals can seem just too far removed from what is initially possible and they quickly feel the weight of failure to live up to supposed levels of 'general' performance. I have always personally believed there is a place for an honest and genuine agent who just wants to earn a reasonable living each year with a good work/life balance, doing so in such a way that suits their style and personality. I believe there is no shame in simply doing a good job, while having time to treat clients well, and making a comfortable income.

As with anything in life, not everyone can be a gold-plated superstar, but this doesn't mean you can't still make a worthwhile contribution. Indeed, this is exactly the balance of individuals in most offices, as not all are multimillion-dollar elites. I think many people who have some potential are lost because either the pressure is too great, or they are convinced anecdotally before starting that these high incomes are the norm (and soon realise they are not).

A good manifestation of this is the much cliched 'picture wall' on a lot of agents' desks. At training they say put up an image of something expensive you desire and then look at it every day as your motivation to earn the big dollars. Great, a 17-year-old spotty trainee and a 55-year-old tired 'life changer' both sitting there gazing at a Ferrari! Perhaps a moped is a more realistic aspiration (but there I go again, Mr Negative, not getting it!).

Hopefuls are also often put on the spot, asked to name a dream figure they would like to earn (and egged on to think big), err $250,000 (as we all do when starting out, right?). This is seized upon then reverse-engineered as to how many sales that requires, how many listings and, therefore, how many appraisals. Bang! Unwittingly, the albatross of expectation is immediately placed around your neck. Oh dear, you need a minimum ten solid appraisals a week from now on. "Agreed? Then best listen to me very carefully!"

I never had a wonder picture on the wall or head-in-clouds income figure (and yes, I know, that might very well prove a point!). My base target was always very simple and never changed: to try to consistently list and sell two properties per month. Now that would be deemed—and sneered at—as thinking small, yet it is still higher than the true market average *and* potentially still realistic to achieve. The key here is consistency, something that is the biggest challenge for anyone.

For those who have been around for a while, underperforming, the mood is often quite depressing and aggressive (if you don't do this now loser, you won't eat at Christmas). The argument being this is needed to shake you up and change your old lazy habits. Perhaps, but my suspicion is also some simply get off on this hardened approach and develop it as part of their mentor 'brand'. Tough love for success.

The scepticism is always this: if many of these individuals were *so* damn good, why did they give it all away in order to have to deal with the rest of us unworthy non-achievers! Perhaps it is a divine calling to help others? Yeah, right! Perhaps it is an easier and less stressful way to make good money at someone else's expense. It is truly win-win as well. If your 'disciple' improves you have worked wonders and if they don't—as is more likely—it is because they didn't listen, are simply incapable of comprehending or are too lazy to execute your finely wrought plans. Not your problem. They are not up to the grade, and you just move on to the next batch (or sting them for repeat business!).

Yes, repetition is also a big winner as many agents who are still underperforming will elect to cop another dose of the same training if that gets them off the hook for another three months without intense scrutiny, while they are still trying to 'embrace change'. Equally, it quite often suits the principals as they can farm off any upskilling to head office, or a third party, and not waste their own valuable time, whilst reminding the blob how lucky they are to have been given the opportunity of structured professional development.

As a rule, they will not attend themselves—heard it all before, boring!—but will make it mandatory for everyone else. All well and good but you do need to ensure everyone is at least on the same page afterwards. I have experienced quite comical situations where the team has attended corporate training and been drilled (sorry, enlightened) on one certain aspect of prospecting, for example, only for this to appear to be at odds with the principal's directive at the next sales meeting. Worse still, at the same sales meeting you will be asked in front of the class—just to ensure you were not asleep—"So, what did you learn from the training and what did you take away from it?". Erm, for the former, that three hours is indeed a LONG time and for the latter, a lukewarm coffee that tasted like battery acid, and a stolen branded company pen.

As mentioned, there are the top dogs who have been around for some time and are ever-present with their undisputable truths on everything, brought to you in print, online and the razzmatazz of their live stage shows! All the better when they can command some celebrity speaker to do their bidding as well and pretend they are best buddies (as long as the appearance fee goes through first).

We once even had Arnie in town to deliver a real Hollywood-style pep talk. If you could afford the fee, it was great for a possible selfie at the end and some 'A list' name dropping. But if, perhaps, you were genuinely relying on this to revive you career, it might ironically need terminating (sorry, but I had to get the obvious pun in somewhere). At least the main movers and shakers have created a complete package, and this does represent their vocation in life.

Unfortunately, also as already mentioned, this fashionable desire to tell other people what to do has mushroomed to epidemic proportions with the rise of social media. Now it seems every Tom, Dick and sales manager must do a video blog of what works for them and where we are all going wrong (and not just one mind, but typically a whole series for our delight and entertainment—*dear God!*). "Hey guys, this is what you need to do get your year on track!", yada, yada, yada. I'll tell you what you need to do, stop wasting endless time listening to the same basic concepts re-packaged 25 times over! Not sure who woke up and made all these random people 'experts', but apparently that doesn't matter, their 'numbers' speak for themselves (if only that were true, then we wouldn't have to listen to their drivel instead!).

Live interactive sessions are the absolute best, as mentors can give real time shout outs to—and name drop—all their luminary (that's a stretch) buddies who have tuned in, to the wonderment and excitement of the lesser mortals watching. "Hi Steve at Surfers, glad you could join us,"... *yeah, whatever.* Even better if you do them from your bedroom, the beach or some equally arbitrary location that looks like you are just so giving of your free time (this is a 24/7 business after all). 'In car' is also popular, squeezing a quick two-minute blog for our salvation, in between your hectic schedule of appointments—thanks mate, legend!

Annually, there are small number of big production stage conferences that stretch over a couple of days with multiple power-speakers, including the odd c-lister (with tenuous link) and various uber-successful agents and principals all imparting vital guidance for success. Typically, these showcase events will have catchy—and somewhat predictable—names like 'Succeed' or 'Power' (although never 'Piss Up' or 'Ego Trip' as I can recall, which might be more relevant).

Pay the big fee and go along to be seen. Look at me, I am prepared to invest heavily in my future, mixing with the very best. Obviously, all the after-show cocktails, general showboating and two-nights fun away from the home in a swanky hotel are nothing to do with it. Only recently, my current agency was contacted and offered the *exceptional* opportunity of 'free' tickets to a two-hour session with a motivational speaker well known on the circuit. The original face value of these tickets was very expensive—certainly for two hours!—and although most of the places were 'sold out' we were highly privileged to be able join for nothing, should we wish (just ensuring a full room, I assume).

They sent a link with the promo video for the event, which centred around establishing your correct state of mind (usual gear: the main man driving a sports car, in the gym, meeting world leaders, etc., with suitable movie style voiceover and soundtrack). The choice of words was interesting, however, as he declared he was not there to push you—as only *you* could do that—he was there to empower you to push yourself. Spot on! Entirely correct, no question. There, in plain sight, was the almost mocking admission upfront it wasn't going to be his fault if you didn't improve after paying for your enlightenment. Set up for success alright! I didn't go, by the way, I had seen him once before and already concluded I clearly had the wrong mindset!

As if all this is not enough, if you work for one of the bigger national franchises, chances are you will be forced to endure endless corporate training as well. This will repackage the same content again, but with a company badge on it. Of course, you do it all for a quiet life, come away from each session 'energised' and ready to up your game, then do exactly what you did last week. Repeat, repeat.

There is plenty of further diversification on offer as well. Why stop at being trained in the fundamentals of prospecting *(well, in fairness, because that's already information overload and you can't do that properly!)* when you can waste further time and money on auction training, social media strategies, obtaining vendor paid advertising, etc. The list goes on, as does the endless number of experts who can give you the *definitive* methodology for success in your business. Perhaps it would not be so bad if the message was entirely consistent, however, depending on what underlying course or methodology system someone is ultimately trying to flog you, it appears some of the solutions can adjust accordingly.

> *"The undeniable basics will always remain call, call, call the farm area."*

> *"Cold calling is dead; it is all about consistent and immersive social media presence."*

> *"Flyers are a complete waste of time, don't bother."*

> *"Flyers are still vitally important as part of ongoing brand awareness."*

Some will offer insights into highly professional marketing and a managed image alongside others encouraging raw communications, warts and all, with spelling mistakes and bad punctation because that will make you stand out—and you are too busy getting that extra $20,000 for your vendors to worry about proofreading—that's the way you roll, baby! *Note: If there are any typos in this book they are not mistakes, I have subscribed to the above ...*

Still confused? Perhaps you need a one-on-one mentor to keep you on track and navigate through all this! This is even better if you can set some personal KPIs with your guru of choice and be made 'accountable' on a daily/weekly basis. In fairness, this aspect will work well with some suitable candidates and that is the nub of it. There are a few individuals with natural ability and drive, who will sacrifice anything to rise to the very top. They will be the ones truly benefitting from all this—and continually showcased accordingly—but they were probably on that path already. The majority will, at best, take some ideas or concepts away to try and improve their humble business, but the temperament of those individuals and their immediate environment, coupled with unrealistic expectations will ultimately limit the value add.

Another great avenue of (highly questionable) benefit in exchange for your money is in 'lead generation'. Again, tempting for those struggling for listings, there are a number of companies offering sure-fire systems for magically capturing all those people in your area who are about to sell. Why waste time tracking them down yourself, when you can waste your money instead and have them all fall into your lap—guaranteed*. (*Well, according to the sales blurb anyway).

Many will have some 'clever' software for identifying potential vendors. Usually this is no more than yet another 'Free Online Appraisal' website where unsuspecting punters get their key details sucked out and spat at some desperate local agent in their area. Problem is that most people using these types of websites are not really sellers (otherwise they would probably have contacted some agents in the flesh). They are just mildly curious—and never read the small print—and do not even realise they have unwittingly flagged themselves up to be contacted by an agent, once they have their very generic online appraisal figure (which is usually crap anyway).

It is always the same angle from the company, even for agents, "We can give you exclusive rights for your suburb if you act now." Really? One agent subscription per suburb only, and you still happen to have my suburb available—gee must be my lucky day, where do I sign?

Unfortunately for a battling agent any electronic carrots might sound tempting, but the quality of supposed 'leads' will ultimately dictate any return on investment. In many ways, we are like the people we represent. We complain about them chasing an unrealistic price for what their property offers and yet we chase unrealistic expectations of listings and sales volume, based on what others want us to believe.

Internet solutions sound great because they appear to deliver opportunities seamlessly, without the grunt of footwork and cold calling. Just depends on your definition of opportunity. Trying to contact essentially unsuspecting members of the public who really have absolutely no intention of selling is not much of an income silver bullet. Again, the clever bit is: the failure to convert these 'strong' prospects is clearly *your* fault in execution of a successful closure, not the fact there was nothing to close in the first place.

Slightly more old-school, but much the same concept are the professional cold call companies. Yep, outsource those dire calls to someone else to do on your behalf, who will 'represent' you for a decent fee. Again, wonderous openings will come your way, but they will primarily consist of those bamboozled on the phone, by carefully worded scripts, into agreeing to an appraisal they did not want. Nonetheless, the ball is now in your court—do not blow it, Sunshine!

Why stop there? The truth is you can have exclusive rights to beer mats and coasters in the local tavern—so drunken hoons can call you at all hours for a giggle—shopper dockets at your local supermarket, and all manner of social media targeting by suburb or demographic. You name it, there is someone ready to sell you *the* method for endless leads and ultimate nirvana. Sounds all too good to be true? Well, you guessed the answer to that. Damn, back to the phones again.

14 | PHONE A FRIEND

Guess what? The relentless advice does not stop with all the professional mentors or consultants either! When was the last time you were on a plane and went up to question the pilot as to whether he was sure he had the wing flaps extended far enough for landing? Or asked to be awake in the middle of surgery so you could advise the surgeon what to do or where he might be going wrong?

Real estate, by comparison, is one of those wonderfully blessed professions where *everyone* believes they have a divine right to be a bloody expert as well. By expert, of course, I mean they have looked at some houses for sale online or in the paper—or have a relative who once did real estate 'for a living' for six months in the middle of Woop Woop—so they now have a dreaded 'opinion'. Views that can be quite forthright, at times, and yet many who hold them have never had the nerve or depth of knowledge to take this on as a career themselves (too scary and a bit of a mug's game). No, as the agent, you are the only mug in this equation who has made that big commitment, but that will not stop everyone else believing they can still 'add value' to the process.

Frustrating as it is, and indeed whether it be a superficial understanding or not, it is still important to be mindful of the seller's potential input—and questionable 'advice' from others—both at the point of listing and subsequently. Things may generally go well enough at the start. "You're the expert," says the excited vendor as you detail what you will be doing once you list the house. However, frame that statement because it will not last very long if you don't get some activity happening! Most will (at least) initially sit back and run with whatever you explain will be the process, so important to enjoy the warm fuzziness of this limited honeymoon period while you can!

Now, admittedly some owners can be painful from day one and want to micromanage every piece of wording, every photo, etc., but that is probably more to do with their personality traits. Not much you can do about that other than, to a degree, go with the flow. If there is a particular photo or feature they clearly want highlighted, because they think (or have been told by wise Uncle Bob) that it is a point of difference, just try to incorporate that without impacting your overall approach too much.

This keeps them onside and demonstrates you are listening and hopefully buys some trust and a little flexibility. I always talk about the house during a listing presentation and often the owners remark in general conversation about a feature they are particularly proud of and have put a lot of effort into like a landscaped terrace or new driveway, etc. I ensure I then incorporate a strong reference to this in the narrative (with a tag like 'enjoy the benefits of the owner's hard work') and it is always well received and, hopefully, the sellers then let you do your thing for a while.

As touched on before, at the outset many owners do not want to appear they have any urgency, for fear of getting ambushed with lower offers. *No rush, happy to wait, things will happen when they are meant to*—all common sentiments expressed at the outset to suggest your vendors are very relaxed but, in truth, once the property is live most are immediately anxious for results. Things can turn very quickly, as it is not just about receiving offers or contracts.

For example, the owner is pumped for the first open home and worked hard to get everything presented perfectly during the preceding few days. They are brand new to the market and the house over the road had eight groups for their first open last month (and *this* property is way better). They rush back with nervous excitement as you are closing up to discover—what?! No one through! And so, the inquest immediately starts. Did you have the times on the internet all week? (Yes - *tick*) Did you have enough directional signs out? (Yes - *tick*) Did you email people to tell them? (Yes - *tick*) This does not make any sense. Well, it does, because the house is currently advertised $30,000 over true market value and today's savvy buyers have—temporarily— voted with their feet (but the seller doesn't want to hear that yet). Perhaps the one over the road was just better value from day one.

In a slow market, 'no show' phobia is quite real for many agents, particularly those who put all their eggs in the one basket of a Saturday open home only. Great when there is good activity, but if the seller is hanging out all week for this one event and it falls flat, the pressure is truly on. Now, the confident and experienced agent will embrace this fully and turn it straight around on the owners as proof the house is too expensive. If your marketing is strong and you know your market, you have the conviction to do this and may well get the desired result (i.e., a price reduction).

Unfortunately, initially many agents are not so blunt through being slightly unsure of themselves—or more often not wanting to upset the owner too quickly—and, therefore, feel somehow obligated to apologise for, or explain away, the lack of bodies.

This unwittingly lets the owner off the hook, instead inferring all will be good next week (honest). There is an extensive library of comical and well-worn explanations wheeled out. "Well, it was raining heavily today, no one was out." "Well, it is school holidays, they are all up the coast." "Well, Grand Final weekend ... everyone's on the beer already." "Well, it is a solar eclipse," etc., etc. Priceless, except I have used a few in my time!

If you really cannot pin it on any act of nature, time of year or random astrological event then you default to the backstop position. "Strange, but I have called a couple of my colleagues and they have had low numbers as well this morning, so just *one of those days* when not many are about." About as bland as you can get, but if it gives you an exit strategy until next week, use it! The irony here is the committed buyer will turn up come hell, high water (or solar eclipse), if it is the one for them and it's priced right.

As the rosy glow of a new listing starts to fade, so the suspicion and hunt for excuses will escalate if suitable activity doesn't follow. Old Uncle Bob will no doubt wade again in with some further expert advice for the sellers based on when he auctioned cattle back in the 1970s. You will be asked to change the photo order or wording in some way (you didn't mention the new washing line?). Put some extra directional signs on the main road. A host of highly superficial acts that usually will not change much at all, but you go along with this, to some degree, to keep the vendor on side until you can start to work them over (hopefully) on the only thing in need of real change, the price!

The problem is, as with many things in life, the longer you put that off the harder it becomes. In the early stages you have the strongest position to push on price as the property *should* be attracting interest as a new debutant on the market. If you chicken out and dodge the thorny issue here, opting to wait (and hope) the problem will solve itself, by the time you have no choice but to speak about it, a degree of trust and patience will probably already have waned, and it will look increasingly like you are seeking an excuse for your own shortcomings. You will also now have strayed into the time zone where unwanted additional advice is very much on the horizon.

As we have already seen, the lurking danger in the shadows is when circling opposition agents—who have previously noted your new sign—also start calling and lending their agenda-laden opinion to your increasingly frustrated owners (again ensuring they *never* suggest a pricing issue). A classic giveaway when this happens is when the vendor suddenly smartens up. For the first few weeks they couldn't even be bothered to read the weekly activity report you diligently send them *(well, assuming you do send one, written reports—another massive urban myth!)*.

For arguments sake let us say you do, yet the sellers will probably have absolutely no grasp of the detailed information contained within. Then suddenly, like a conversion on the road to Damascus, the next week they have learnt big new words, coupled with newfound powers of insightful observation. "Do you think the ratio of online views to enquiries is low, this would suggest the photos aren't selling it enough?!" Pow! What the? Where did that come from? Funny, it is *almost* as if someone has suddenly educated them on all that is wrong and why they should be dissatisfied. "Someone's in their bloody ear!", is the familiar cry from an exasperated agent who now cannot seem to get his message across anymore to his previously accommodating owners. You bet!

This is often put up as a form of flimsy self-defence in the sales meeting, when under heavy cross-examination as to why you haven't got that price reduction yet and, thereby, moved this piece of stock on. A sort of third-party blame, not my fault as I am saying all the right things, but another is influencing them from the sidelines. Not much of a defence, unfortunately, as all this does is alert the principal to a potential inbound listing loss and increase the pressure on you further! They will know that if you have a reduced degree of response, and it appears there are other conversations going on behind the scenes, the stark truth is you may have already 'lost the dressing room' and it is only a matter of time. This invokes a couple of possible responses. Either this suggests it is all too hard, even now, and the white flag is soon to be unfurled and waved or, if there is realistically nothing to lose at this point, just hit them hard, regardless, prior to the listing expiration.

Sometimes this alternative advice will be a running commentary in the background each week. Annoying, but I guess at least it suggests some underlying motivation your sellers may appear to possess. Equally, it can be more discreet and creep up unaware. All seems fine until you dare to push back on price the first time and suggest this may need to be reviewed. Suddenly a list of (previously unmentioned) concerns with the marketing is put forward in first line defence of the beloved dream price. Prior to this it may have been a Mexican standoff: they will not go there if you do not go there on price.

Auctions can also be tricky, as again the vendor will probably sit back to a degree during the lead up—if there is good viewing activity—but be ready to hit you with both barrels if the auction itself falls flat. Not least because it is in public and, to a degree, seemingly 'shames' the property if nothing happens. The paradox here is you will indeed have failed to do your job if the big day is a dud, but probably not in the way the owner thinks. They will assume your marketing or management of potential buyers has been lacking, when potentially it may have been perfectly okay. What you have more likely failed to do is educate and position your seller correctly for auction day on price. Again, just hoping all will go right on the big day, if you haven't correctly and firmly addressed where the true range of the property is seen in the market, is just an accident waiting to happen.

If things do not improve, there is probably only one stage beyond this. The back seat driving stops, and all goes relatively quiet. If the pressure has been on, then this represents a welcome break, right? You try to convince yourself that perhaps they are happy to let you just continue, after all, and do your thing. Probably not, they have simply opted to avoid answering your calls or emails anymore. You see, at this point they have already given up on you and decided you're 'done'. No point in a revisitation of price now or engaging in new strategies when their strategy is set: your removal!

It is very much the calm before the final storm. They are moving on to the nice new guy on the phone who has highlighted all the current issues that are being done wrong and has promised to rectify everything (at no loss of listing price!). He is attentive and calls regularly—until the ink on the listing form is dry at least—and sees exactly the same value in the property as the owners do, regardless of what all those annoying recent inspectors have said—what do they know!

They are just very *slightly* uncomfortable about switching agents because—even if only subconsciously—they probably feel deep down you haven't really done that much wrong. Therefore, they do not want to confront you until they have run the clock down on the current agreement. Much easier to say nothing and try to avoid any awkward questions or conversations. Nonetheless, money is thicker than loyalty and your demise is apparently the only route to the upholding of their wants (sorry, needs) on price. Ninety days up, then a simple termination email and you are toast!

Thanks for your help.

15 | Is There Anybody There?

U nfortunately, it's not just wavering sellers on a faltering listing that can suddenly run for cover and fall off the radar. Essentially, it is anyone and everyone. Feast or famine, all or nothing, however you describe it, always be prepared for rapidly moving sands beneath your feet.

You're up, you're down! Fundamentally that is the simple cycle of real estate and, as such, you should never get too carried away. "My phone is ringing constantly; I have really made it!" Nope, you have finally got a half-decent listing that—for at least a few days—means people will overcome their basic dislike and guarded wariness of you as an untrustworthy individual to risk calling you for an inspection. Ah yes, for a fleeting second, we are suddenly extremely important to someone as we hold the key to what they want, literally! To the uninitiated this can make you feel like you have conquered 'breaking through' and the world is now at your feet, but beware, it may be fool's gold.

Indeed, when I say it is a 'cycle', that's probably the wrong description and overly flattering, as this suggests a process that changes over a degree of time with some form of predictable and graduated sequence. Perhaps the heartbeat on a hospital monitor is a better visual interpretation as there is no middle ground. You are either the single most important person on the planet (and must be available instantaneously 24/7) or you can just sit back and watch those tumbleweeds roll by.

We have evolved into the *now* society, particularly in the Millennial generation, so it stands to reason if someone decides they want to do something, it requires instant attention and gratification. Buyers, bless them, try to play it all very casual, but the truth is when most people come across a property that is exactly right for them and fall in love with it, no matter how hard they try to resist, fear of loss creeps in. In one way this is very good for the agent because the signs are obvious and you tend to know you have a genuine prospect, however, the flip side is they will now be on your back constantly. "We want to put an offer in *now* (on Sunday—at 5 in the morning!) and we want it presented *immediately,* etc., etc. How long will it take? Have you told the sellers yet?" Calm down!

Recent stock shortages and high demand have exacerbated the situation, so with a new listing, when you're on, you're on! Do not plan any other superfluous activities like sleeping or eating until you have answered every last 3 a.m. online real estate portal enquiry and that sucker is locked in with its new desperate owner-in-waiting.

Even simple viewings often fall into this category. Someone sees a new listing pop up on the internet that they somehow missed on the Saturday morning, so they are frantically calling that night or Sunday morning to get through it as soon as possible. If you diligently answer the call, you sometimes get the mock apology intro, "Oh, sorry we didn't think you would answer on a Sunday and we would leave a message," still followed by a requirement for immediate viewing and with the moral justification: "This is our *only* day off," (yeah, tell me about it!). In truth, it is not entirely bad as most agents are prepared to arrange things, where practically possible, for a genuine buyer—anything for a chance of a sale!—and it goes with the territory. However, the annoying thing is when this situation suddenly reverses without warning.

See, your newly acquired best buddies, who cannot live without you, frequently have a rethink!

i. Perhaps this isn't *the* property after all (i.e., a better one has just appeared on the internet this morning!), or
ii. After checking with the finance broker it is actually *just* out of their reach, or
iii. (Classic!) Mum and Dad have pointed out some issues they didn't see, etc., etc.

When this occurs, we go from white-hot to stone-cold in the blink of an eye. Once the property we hold is no longer deemed of special interest, the associated listing agent instantly becomes completely irrelevant again (so irrelevant in fact, they don't even bother to call to let you know you have just become irrelevant!).

Thus, the poor misguided agent is still under the impression 'we have a live one' and all is good. Indeed, they are getting a little bit excited and drawing up draft offer paperwork in preparation. They have also probably let slip to the owners something might be in the offing (BIG mistake, now *their* expectation is up as well). Okay, everything is ready, let's call the buyers back and set a time. That's funny—heart already sinking as the ugly truth starts to dawn, because you have been here many times before—they're not answering now and it's just going to message bank. Optimistically, let's message and email them as well, just to be on the safe side ... three days later ...

As agents we know this happens constantly, but we still get suckered in all the time because we desperately want to have something positive happening around a property, so we cling on to every suggested interest.

Online enquires are a classic example. We get a property-specific enquiry from a buyer via one of the online real estate portals and foolishly assume they may have singled out our wonderous new listing, so might be keen. This is backed up by the ticked pre-selections: 'would like to inspect' and 'make an offer'. Great! I normally do belt-and-braces at this point and email a reply straight away, but also call as a follow up. So, the fun begins.

If (big if) they answer the phone, the usual response is along the lines of, "Sorry mate, what property? I have sent so many enquiries off this morning, lost track—can you describe it?" Not exactly shortlisted yet! If you are lucky, there is about a 25% chance of getting a response to your reply email. It seems people are happy to send an electronic enquiry—saves 50c on a call and you don't have to socially interact—yet are completely incapable (apparently) of stringing together a coherent follow-up communication. Many times, I have emailed that I am happy to arrange an inspection, if they can just indicate times they are available, and there is no reply whatsoever! Didn't realise I had posed such a difficult question that made it impossible for them to continue! Ticking a box is workable (just), but composing a 'free format' sentence independently? Wow, next we'll be asking for a quill pen-and-ink reply on parchment. All *so* 20th century!

When you have a good, well-priced listing, new to the market the enquiries can come thick and fast from the online portals. Look how in demand I am, suddenly! Yep, then watch once you have a contract on it and show it as 'Under Offer' on the internet.

You will be wondering whether your internet connection has suddenly dropped out. Not so popular now, *are* you?

Hence, you can combine all the excitement of a random *specific* buyer disappearance, with the certainty they will *all* evaporate once you have a contract in place and advertised as such. Now, some agents are very happy with this. Contract signed, move on! Why waste time dealing with further enquires when you do not have to (same logic, as now *you* don't need the buyers anymore)? Perhaps, if you are extremely busy. But, certainly up until your contract is unconditional, you should continue to generate backup interest, and this is a form of prospecting (if by talking to people you generate some additional leads). Typically, I will not show the property as *under offer/contract* until unconditional, knowing full well the moment you do the phone—for this property at least—will fall silent.

Open home attendees are another rich source of anticlimax: *Eight groups through the house today and initial feedback seems very positive. Three groups suggest they will consider the home seriously, with one indicating—after speaking with their broker first thing Monday morning—they will be putting forward an offer.* Great! Yes, well until you start trying to recontact all these keen people.

I can just visualise Basil in one classic episode of *Fawlty Towers*, "Hello, hello can anybody hear me? Have I ceased to exist?". That's Monday morning call-backs after open homes! Yep, almost all these excited buyers have spontaneously combusted over the weekend and now can't answer their phones (ever). If I had a dollar for every vendor report with the line against an inspector's name: 'Called and left message, awaiting further feedback' ... Translation: *you will never hear from them again.* The end.

You may like to kid yourself but, by and large, initially you are nobody's friend as an agent. Certainly, as far as most would-be buyers are concerned more just an unavoidable annoying middleman standing between them and their dream home. When needs must, buddy up to get a result, but otherwise to avoid contact at all costs!

Unfortunately, it is not always the waning interest in a property that dictates the sudden sound of crickets. Potential listings are also cause of similar heartache. You've conducted a great presentation; the owners seem very keen on what you have discussed and indicate you're their agent once they get the house ready in a week or so. You think this one is in the bag, smugly note the address on your 'pipeline' board in the office and tell everyone at the sales meeting that you've got a good one signing up next week.

Only problem is, in the meantime, some other cut-price joker has got into their ear at the eleventh hour and—although they were genuinely going with you for a while—they have now been offered cheaper commission *and* free marketing if they sign straight away. Oh dear, money talks again (which is more than they will do from this point onwards, when you start nervously following them up because you haven't heard from them as planned). Once the contrary decision is made, there is no further need to talk with you and probably the owner is a little embarrassed at a last-minute change so just hopes you'll suffer amnesia and forget they ever existed (fat chance!).

It's bad enough when you get an inkling and heads-up before anything becomes public knowledge, but the worst feeling of all is when this new property you've been telling everyone about pops up unannounced on the internet with your direct opposition as their new listing. Time for a trip to the principal's office to explain yourself (just should have kept your mouth shut in the first place and they would be none the wiser!).

Some agents just won't accept the obvious staring them in the face. "I called the buyers *16 times* this week and left messages, but they still haven't got back to me yet." Yet!? Buddy, that ship has well and truly sailed! I know one agent, who in certain instances, would then go around and camp on the doorstep until he could apprehend them in person if they weren't returning his calls. In addition to this being a somewhat menacing approach, the words *flogging* and *dead horse* spring to mind. Personally, I can never get that excited. A call back and message, possibly a second call if I really deem them important, but—as I will openly say to vendors—if I am chasing a would-be buyer for a third time of asking about your house then you already have their feedback: "It's a 'no' from me!"

Likewise, the genuine 'A buyer' who is keen on the house will most likely be chasing you well before you even make the first call back, either directly at the house or very quickly afterwards. Essentially, chasing up buyers after the event is much more to do with just getting some credible feedback for the owner and (surprise, surprise) chasing down new business. Yes, who would have guessed—other than perhaps getting a low-price opinion you can beat up your sellers with—you don't really give that much concern as to what they think of your listing. If they were interested, you would already know by now, but they may be about to sell, so the follow up call is just an excuse to drill them for the outside chance of a spin-off listing.

SOLD On The Dream

This does occasionally bear fruit, as potential sellers do go to open homes to see how certain agents behave or to judge their property 'competition' in the local area. Only problem is if they have been to a few—and the listing agents are doing their jobs— they will have received several calls, all with the same agenda and likely questions. If their initial opinion of you was positive, you might be in with a shout ... but don't hold your breath.

I have had many instances of the last minute let-down and there is no future in this industry if you cannot accept this basic constant. That said, the breathtaking ease with which some people change their tune is still frustrating in the extreme, and many a time I have sat back and just thought, "Really?"!

- Contract negotiations are in full swing and then the buyer pulls out with no warning.
- Red hot buyers are locked in for a private Sunday inspection on a rented property they desperately want to see above all others—with special arrangements made with the tenant on their behalf—only for them to have bought something else Saturday evening and deliver a no-show (much to the tenant's amusement, of course).
- People hounding you for a randomly timed, urgent mid-week inspection, only to not show up because it is raining, etc.

The demand levels during the pandemic also led to the increase in throwaway offers on properties. Emails would constantly arrive in my inbox with sight-unseen offers on newly listed properties. Little or no detail on conditions, no requests for inspection, just a seemingly good figure and something—and if you were lucky it had an accompanying message—along the lines of *'please advise if the owners will take this'*.

184

Of course, this was catfishing for a response from agents and typically they had sent out several similar—and likely simultaneous—emails for any property in their target area that looked half-decent (and a fair few that did not) in the vague hope of snagging some attention. The thinking being that *'the agent will come straight back to me first, if he thinks I am putting an offer in'*. The problem (for them), however, was at the height of the activity many others were also putting *real* offers in immediately, and the more experienced eye had seen this all before.

I would always respond, but I would ask that a basic offer form be completed first with all conditions, timelines, etc., (including finance status) specified, and whether any viewing was intended as part of their final determination. Once I had this, I would then discuss it with the owner. In most instances you wouldn't ever get a further response and it filtered out the chancers from the real deal quite quickly.

Of course, for all that, we do not help ourselves. If we have a property with limited activity, the whole anxiety thing is going, and we often tend to overplay a suggested interest to make the seller feel we have something happening and are creating opportunities. Trouble is, that makes them as delusional as you about the likelihood of an outcome, so they become the obsessed ones chasing. "Have you phoned that buyer again from Saturday, who you said was keen?" "Yes, for the sixth time ... with no reply." Funny that.

16 | THE INBETWEENERS

As we move into this new age of digital disruption, it is suggested that agents can ultimately be dispensed with. Certainly, property pricing and awareness of the market, in general, are far more empowered directly with buyers and sellers these days, due to the easy availability of good quality data and statistics online. This aspect is potentially a good thing, as people should be more informed when it comes to making very big financial decisions that could impact their lives over many years.

However, I personally believe the suggestion that an agent is somehow becoming completely redundant in the process or is some sort of outdated anachronism misses a key point. It is precisely this individual interpretation and interaction that is key in most transactions to ensure they occur in the first place, and then reach conclusion. That is, settlement, through the potential minefield of building and pest inspections, finance, and other 'special' conditions. The agent's greatest service is to act as the punch bag or 'meat in the sandwich' between the buyer and the seller. Why? Human nature! Left to correspond directly, many stressed, and overly emotional buyers and sellers would be having a fight before the first day was done!

At the core of this we are *not* selling a cheap, sterile product with a set unit cost and complete uniformity with the next one, like a tin of baked beans (well, unless it's some questionable 'investment club' townhouses off the plan to interstate investors—but that's another story). In the main, we are offering a highly individual product with a variable price outcome (and an emotive element to arriving at exactly what that is). There are typically many questions and nuances to be covered as part of making a very big decision. To transact this entirely automatically, or worse, allow the end users involved to manage the process directly is fraught with difficulties, I believe.

In classic real estate training mode (yawn), let's indulge in some 'role play'. Below is a set of supposed exchanges which are not intended by any means to be exhaustive or comprehensive—in reality, negotiations are often long, complex and involve many aspects—but in essence simply attempt to demonstrate the agent's impact in the art of conversation and reconciliation during typical negotiations.

Buyer to agent: "We will offer $330k, but tell the seller that's it. It needs a lot of work, the current colours are awful, and it isn't worth any more than that. If they don't like that, we will go elsewhere!"

Agent translation to seller: "Great news, the buyers are really keen and have made an initial commitment to show you they are very serious. They have come in at $330k, but are happy to see where this goes."

Seller to agent: "Tell them that's a crap offer. Either they pay $350k or they can shove their bloody low-ball offer and I'll wait for another buyer!"

Agent translation to buyer: "Firstly, the sellers thank you so much for your commitment, and are quite excited to work towards a conclusion, as they are motivated at this point. They want to take this further, but the $330k is just a little too low for their agreement. They have countered at $350k but are certainly open to further discussions."

Buyer to agent: "$350k! Not a chance! But look, we do like the place. Okay, not happy, but we'll go to $335k. That is it this time. Tell them, 'They can forget it otherwise'."

Agent translation to seller: "Fantastic, the buyers are keen to make this happen! They haven't quite come up to the $350k, but—great news—they have thrown in another $5k straight away as a show of real intent. I think they want it, we might just need to give a small bit of encouragement at this stage, if possible."

Seller to agent: "It's still nowhere near, don't they get it? Look I'll go to $345k, but that's it. These people either want it or they don't. Tell them, 'Don't waste my time'."

Agent translation to buyer: "The seller thanks you for the improvement and we are very close now. They have reduced down to $345k as a sign of really wanting this done today."

Buyer to agent: "We are not paying $345k! Still too high. If that's the best they can do, we're moving on."

Agent translation to buyer: "I am certain the seller wants to retain your interest. Suggestion—if they could meet you in the middle to get this done today, would you be prepared go to $340k? I can't promise anything, but I know these guys want to deal with you."

Buyer to agent: "Look, I am not going to be mucked around by these guys anymore. I don't really want to go that high, but I guess if they are actually prepared to do that we would agree, but I want an answer now and there's no further discussions."

Agent translation to seller: "These buyers are still very keen, but are pretty much at their limit on the money, so may have to (very reluctantly) start considering other options if we can't agree. However, they really want the house and appreciate you have moved on your position. They have offered to meet you halfway as a sign of good faith at $340k."

Seller to agent: "Cheapskates! They're getting a bloody bargain, but okay, if they will sign off $340k today they've got a deal. No more mucking around."

Agent translation to buyer: "Congratulations, the seller has agreed to $340k, if we can sign off today. They thank you for your patience and are sure you will enjoy the house as they have".

Agent translation to seller: "Congratulations. All agreed. They are very happy, thank you for your consideration and are looking forward to moving in a few weeks' time."

What usually happens next? At the point both parties agree, all the stress, emotion and angst disappears, and almost immediately, they both sit back, have a wine and realise they are actually quite happy and satisfied with the outcome. In most instances, had these discussions not had the agent in the middle, I suggest they would not have progressed past a flat rejection of the initial offer accompanied by a recommendation to: "Bugger off if they don't like the colour of the walls!" (which the buyers would have duly obliged!). Game over. Emotion gets in the way of clear thinking almost every time. It is not so much the price negotiation itself, as management of the stress and reaction around it.

It is ironic that sometimes a buyer might pull out of a negotiation because they don't like the seller or get an emotional hang-up with their behaviour, when it is the house they are buying—not the occupants! Grin and bear it and they will (by definition) be gone by the time it settles. Simple concept, but many struggle to see past it in the heat of battle. In the first instance, sellers are always defensive of their price and treasured home, whilst buyers always want a bargain. If both parties are willing, usually common ground can be reached, but the success ratio would be far lower without the 'pressure release valve' of the agent (and the third-party advice they can provide).

It is not just contract negotiations either (oh, if only!). There are still ample other chances before settlement for a confrontation! The nature of contracts in Queensland, for instance, with binding agreements up front, means several clauses—or 'special conditions'—have to be incorporated to allow for subsequent checks and balances before the property is deemed finally sold (or 'unconditional'). The most common special conditions are related to checking the condition of the building and allowing for completion of loan approvals against the specific property. There is a myriad of other possible clauses that can be inserted to make life interesting, and all have the potential to represent further pinch points where there could be disagreement.

Sellers keeping quiet about undisclosed termite damage, or no council approvals on structures, are a couple of common ones. They blindly hope that the building and pest inspector will not pick up past problems or bodgie repairs thereof—err hello, that's their job!—or, magically, the buyer's council searches won't reveal their questionably built shed, patio, etc., isn't registered.

Council searches are a particular drama as many buyers, at the time of contract, do not request a specific special condition relating to conducting such investigations, yet their solicitors will always do them (quite often *after* the property is unconditional, to save the buyer initial cost outlay). There is a potential fight on, if the buyers still try to raise a *lack of approval* late in the day and the seller's solicitor (rightly) argues they have no legal grounds on which to contest. Blame inevitably swings back around on the agent at some point, "I bet he knew all along," say the annoyed buyers (a reputable agent will have asked this at listing and disclosed accordingly at time of contract, but some owners can still be a little vague or deceptive with their answers).

On the buyer's side, dragging out finance approval with extension requests and citing niggling problems under the building and pest inspection can all lead to major arguments that the agent must try to contain. During early COVID-19, finance processing times for resource-strapped banks and other lenders extended—they were still happy to take on the business, mind you—and regular discussions around the viability of granting more time to a buyer were commonplace. In this instance, all the agent can really do is attempt to get an honest assessment of where the buyer is at, and how likely a positive outcome is (contacting the relevant finance broker directly for an overview, if possible).

The frustration with industry-wide longer processing times was that the seller might get restless after the usual 21 days and chop the existing buyer—who might be about to come good—only to go with someone else in the same boat. That is where, hopefully, the agent can give the benefit of their experience, and picture of the wider market at large, to give greater perspective for the owner.

I can hear them groaning, but many solicitors really do not help much in this process either, especially when dealing with first time or inexperienced buyers. Often there is no precursor, no prior discussion, just a barren email with a major request sprung on the opposing party without warning. Often done 30 minutes before a deadline is due, either for maximum impact and decision-making pressure or—more often than not—because the diary note only popped up to chase their client for an update 30 minutes prior to that! Proactive and heading things off at the pass? Well, not really. With respect to a building and pest report, a buyer might be persuaded that—acting in their 'best' interests—the solicitor will raise a multitude of minor issues with the seller. This scattergun approach is in the hope a few things stick, but is always guaranteed to prompt a royal bust up.

Normally, the best path to steer people down is somewhere in the middle and get common sense to prevail—which it normally does, if both parties can just be refocussed on the end game of still wanting to sell/buy—but this must be done by the trusty middleman, as solicitors (and to some extent their clients) see things pretty much in black or white. A good agent deals in 50 shades of grey!

In fairness, the legal profession is no different to any other, with varied characteristics and approaches. I have worked with some excellent solicitors and conveyancers who are relatively open with agents, helpful, and want to work in collaboration to reach the best result possible for all parties. Yet I have also experienced those who look down their noses at agents and do not wish to engage with them at all, even when there are disputes to resolve. Well, of course, after all *we* are only after the dollars and will give biased advice and pressurise the clients just to hold a deal together at any price, right? No, most agents just want to try and resolve issues as best as possible to everyone's benefit. Ironically if a deal crashes, buyers, sellers and agents all miss out, but some solicitors will still have an invoice ready to go for all their precious time already expended (yeah, tell me about it!).

You would think having navigated the deal negotiations and any subsequent dramas with associated conditions, at least you can finally breathe easily once the contract is unconditional, and the SOLD sticker is in place. After all, there's no turning back now for any of the parties involved, so just hand over the keys on settlement day! Sometimes it is that simple, but nonetheless settlement brings its own unique headaches. This is primarily because, whilst it represents the last step of the extended legal process, it is only *now* reaching the point at which the owner must have the house ready to hand over!

Great if your seller is caring, fastidious and vacates on time leaving the property clean, tidy and completely empty. Not so good if your departing owner is lazy, untidy, has unwanted crap everywhere and/or a chip on their shoulder about something the buyer has already done during the purchase process. Pretty grim trying to hand keys over for something that is dirty and overgrown with three dump runs of rubbish still dotted around the place.

With a rental property, the holding of a bond payment, coupled to an exit inspection (and associated terms of the lease) tends to keep most tenants on the straight and narrow when they leave, with respect to cleaning and clearing.

With an owner-occupied home, often no such pre-determined financial structure/penalty system—or contract clause—exists so the owner is assumed to do the right thing and 'leave the house as they would wish to find it'. In effect, a gentleman's agreement of mutual respect. Contracts do allow for a 'pre-settlement' inspection which is typically done a day or so before settlement itself to satisfy the buyer that the owner has indeed prepared the property. Whilst the sale is already unconditional at this stage and cannot be revoked, if the condition is highly unsatisfactory the buyer can, in theory, request some form of compensation figure on settlement (to cover cleaning costs, etc.,) or threaten a delay until resolved.

All well and good, except there is no pre-determined scale or default figures for this and it requires the agreement of both sides, based on their own interpretation and emotions, often thrashing things out via the hapless agent once again. Furthermore, some buyers do not even bother with a pre-settlement inspection if busy, assuming the agent will have 'everything sorted' for them on the day. No doubt we would if it were our own personal property, but the crucial variable in the equation is: we are asking someone else to meet those standards for a property we represent, but cannot easily control ourselves.

To further complicate matters, where there is a chain of linked purchases, the incumbent owner might not be moving out until the morning of settlement itself so the house might legitimately still look like a bombsite the day before. In this situation they ensure us everything will be good on the day (and we cross our fingers and pray). How often doesn't this happen you may ask? Well, often enough that most seasoned agents don't get too carried away until the property has finally settled, and certainly often enough that I have a few experiences to share.

I can only speak from personal encounters, but there have been plenty of times when I have jumped in and performed last minute tasks—as the unsung middleman—to ease things home and across the finishing line. Now, as already documented, I was never really some high-flying elite agent with more contracts than I knew what to do with at any one time, so I admit some of the things I have done probably wouldn't be condoned—much less contemplated—by the big guns. However, in my travels us average guys, with a little bit more time on our hands and the practical need to get every 'done deal' concluded to be paid, more often than not go 'above and beyond' simply because it is the quickest and easiest route to payday.

Once again, leave things to buyers, sellers and solicitors only at your peril! Cleaning is probably the biggest single issue. On houses that I had my suspicions on, I would do my own private pre-settlement (if possible) to judge the handover condition. This was both good *and* bad. It meant you weren't blindsided at settlement, but it opened a Pandora's Box if there were obvious problems. In an ideal world you put all this back on the sellers, but if there are only a few hours left on the clock, and they have already left Dodge City, then you know you are up against it. This has resulted in regular last-minute vacuums (easier now with a cordless lightweight Dyson on call!), bench/bath/toilet cleaning, and on a couple of occasions oven cleaning. These are in no way full bond cleans, but if you can eliminate the worst, glaring issues of indifference there is a good chance the buyer will suck it up.

Grass cutting is another favourite *("Sorry, didn't have time"*— what in the last four weeks?!) and I have had the mower out from home on tour on numerous occasions just to smarten up an appearance for handover. Indeed, for my next career as a *handyman-for-hire* I have developed many DIY 'skills' including— but not limited to!—repairing cracked downpipes, filling and painting damaged walls, re-seating and lubricating sliding doors, replacing garage remotes (and recoding them) and so on, all in the name of an on-time settlement.

I am no stranger to the local dump either, doing last minute runs with unwanted items left abandoned (*"Sorry, didn't have space,"*). One of the more random times involved removing bark mulch from around some front yard tree trunks at one property. The buyers had asked to have it removed, by settlement, as they felt it might encourage termite activity. The sellers had agreed, but then, due to other issues during the process, didn't bother (on purpose) for settlement. A potential petty argument over nothing looming, so two hours prior—in the rain—there I am shovel in hand, mulch in boot and off to the dump (again). Settled on time and buyers were satisfied.

Ultimately, all things we shouldn't need to do, as agents, but throw back some trivial unresolved issue to the solicitors and who knows when the end might be in sight. In truth, by this point—if it has been one of *those* contracts—we are probably somewhat tired of both parties involved and it is less painful to just do the outstanding dirty work yourself and be done with it.

A beneficial by-product is that the buyers—who could be your future sellers—often realise if you have resolved something yourself (having already clocked the seller's attitude and realising it would have been out of character!). This, hopefully, stands you in good stead later as they appreciate you have made an extra effort to assist them and ensure settlement is the exciting and happy experience it should be. Of course, the attack dogs would disagree, but I feel this type of assistance is just as much valuable prospecting work as any cold calls or sign jumps (and to that extent is not wasted time or effort).

Experience generally provides a sixth sense for pending problems, however, sometimes it is just too late to influence a positive outcome due to last-minute curveballs. Where the property is only being vacated on the morning of settlement, there is always scope for unfolding drama. This can be either delayed removalists (broken down truck, last job overrun, etc.,) or worse, *no* removal company at all with the owner, instead, doing it 'on the cheap' with a self-hire truck and—if they are lucky—a couple of mates on a slab-of-beer-promise. Always the truck is too small, and always the time calculated for each run is woefully underestimated.

The worst example of this I had was a family moving from a residential block out to a small acreage on the same day with simultaneous settlement. They had chosen the 'self-removal with hire-truck option', which I was aware of, but had emphasised the need to be fully clear by the settlement time of their existing property. They seemed to get this—or so I thought—so I assumed they would get a reasonably sized vehicle and, perhaps, some friends with additional cars and move everything out in the morning, and then be 'on the road' in readiness for the settlement of their new property (or indeed negotiate some early access).

In the event, it appears they did neither and waited until the acreage settled (which was *after* their existing home) to make the first run with, yes, too small of a truck. I had a slight nagging worry, but had not heard anything adverse and settlement went through around 3 p.m. The buyer called me and asked I meet him at his new house at around 5 p.m. to hand over the keys. I called the sellers to congratulate them on settlement, only to then be told they had fitted less than half the furniture onto the truck— and being acreage, their new home was a 40-minute drive away—so they were running behind and were not sure if they would be clear at 5 p.m. Concerned, I reminded them it was no longer legally their house and they needed to make every effort to remove the remaining items as quickly as possible. I blindly hoped this would be by 5 p.m., but in the pit of my stomach I already knew that was unlikely. I headed down a little early, around 4:45 p.m., hoping to quickly assess the situation before the buyer arrived (and have a suitable story if needed).

Unfortunately, the understandably keen buyer had also finished work earlier and got there simultaneously, turning into the cul-de-sac just ahead of me. As we both pulled up, we were greeted by the site of the front yard of his new house absolutely full of furniture and all manner of other items scattered around. In addition, the owner's teenage daughters were still there—minding the possessions—along with their two large dogs bounding up and down (the ex-owners were still driving back from their *first* run).

As I sheepishly got out of my car, the buyer looked at me with a face like thunder, "What the hell is going on?". Needless to say, very unimpressed. Luckily, he was not moving anything in until the following day, but nonetheless, this soured the whole experience as there was his house with someone's kids, pets and furniture still in residence! I tried to play things down as best I could. Apologising on the seller's behalf saying they had experienced 'unexpected'—yet in truth, totally and utterly expected—delays, and were 'rushing' back to retrieve the remaining items.

I had managed to, somewhat, calm the buyer down, just as the sellers returned in their 'truck' (well, van). Of course, this now meant the very thing you never want, was about to play out. Buyer and seller interacting directly when emotions are already running very high on both sides. I, at least, hoped the sellers would see the stressful predicament—however unfortunate—

was primarily theirs of the making, and be suitably apologetic (as I had suggested in their absence).

Instead, already being anxious, they felt they were now being hounded by the new owner. He fired first, "You know you should be out, this is my house now". This was met with, "Mate, we are doing the best we can, *what is your problem?*". Oh dear. "My problem? Are you serious?" Both then squared up to each other on the drive and I had to physically stand between them to stop an altercation. I expressed my understanding that everyone was upset, and the situation was not ideal, but I would stay, help the ex-owners load up their remaining things as soon as practical and within a couple of hours we would be okay. Touch and go at this point, but thankfully both parties backed off. I had a further quiet word with the buyer and apologised again, asked for his patience and assured him I was not going anywhere until everything was sorted. I then rolled up my sleeves and got on with loading the van.

Now once again, a funny thing happened. From the brink of a fight, everyone stood down and as things progressed, the buyer could see the sellers were genuinely trying to get everything finished, and he could also see the agent was not going into hiding, but actively helping to get things resolved as soon as possible. His demeanour changed and by the time we were loading on the last few items—around 7 p.m. by now—the buyer was actually helping us!

When all was done, both apologised to each other, shook hands and the buyer wished the sellers well in their new property. He thanked me for staying behind and getting things to a conclusion. Once again, left to their devices who knows what would have unfolded, probably an assault charge! Stressful, but diffused and ultimately resolved. He duly moved in, as planned, the following day and we kept in touch subsequently.

Things can always be a bit dicey when you have owners leaving relatively close to settlement, as you simply do not have any time to determine the vacated condition until it is too late. On one or two occasions I have been so embarrassed by the filthy state of a house I am handing over that I have offered the buyers to arrange a cleaner (at my expense). Again, "not my problem" many would say, but I still believe the agent's true value should be as the fixer, the middleman who makes things better.

Moreover, if that results in a favourable impression to clients, then I believe the chance of repeat or referral business is much higher. Only recently I had a property that, due to difficult circumstances for the owner, was vacated in a relatively poor condition. The young, first home buyers taking it over were a little deflated at handover, so I arranged for all the windows to be cleaned along, with the kitchen and bathroom, before they moved in. A couple of months later I got an appraisal request from the lady's mother—who had also been at the handover—presumably happy with the extra efforts I had gone to on her daughter's behalf. At times I have had—apparently superior—colleagues laugh and sneer at such actions as being beneath them, yet if they offer the opportunity to cultivate some future leads, it's justification enough in my book.

Occasionally, there isn't even an issue to resolve yet somehow you are still caught up in the middle. Only recently I sold a quite modern property that—unusually for this day and age—didn't have a dishwasher installed. There was just a space in the kitchen where one could easily be located. No big deal, obvious and simply no reference made in the advertising, and no inclusion on the contract (usually noted if present).

I had some lovely first-time buyers who looked through—as did their parents separately—and they decided to put forward an offer, which was subsequently accepted. We went through the entire contract period very smoothly and, even at settlement and handover, everything was rosy. Settlement gift greatly received and plaudits all round. The following day, however, I got a call from the new owners concerned that the ex-seller had removed the dishwasher at the last minute, and did I know about it?

I explained there never was a dishwasher and perhaps they just didn't notice the big space! Interestingly, I was then instantly quizzed on why it was 'in the advertisement' and—presumably—noted on the contract (neither of which were the case). As nice as this couple were, their default reaction was still deflection. No initial admission on their part—or the parents—for missing something relatively apparent, but instead assuming any misunderstanding lay with the agent and that I must have surely indicated in black and white a dishwasher was installed (which was why they didn't look?)! The inference being, if I had made such an oversight—in particular—on the default inclusions on the contract, some recompense would need to be sorted.

They rechecked the contract and advertisement and soon realised I had not done anything untoward, and things ultimately remained amicable. They bought a cheap dishwasher themselves and all was good. Nonetheless, it still highlights the precarious position we agents are generally held in during any transactions and, when there are genuine issues, the need to provide clear, unemotional solutions.

Most recently, I had a settlement where it was not a problem of people coming together, quite the reverse in fact: nobody in sight! I had a small one-bedroom Brisbane unit for sale that was being rented out by an absent overseas-based owner, who on a practical level was only contactable by email. We secured a contract with an owner-occupier who was prepared to offer a long three-month settlement to give time for the existing lease to end and the tenant to move out, for vacant possession. All well and good, except this owner was randomly (well not so randomly, as they were dirt cheap) using a Sydney-based property manager for his Brisbane property. The concept was they were primarily online-based and utilised 'local' agents when needed for things like rental entrance and exit inspections, etc.

The unit was in a very tired condition and the owner had agreed to fix a few items under the sales contract prior to settlement. Now call it intuition but—despite the long contract—I had a nagging feeling this was going to cause drama. Perhaps this was fuelled by my initial convoluted experience getting spare keys for access when listed. The Sydney property managers could also only be contacted by email and then supplied a secret code for key pickup from their Brisbane agent (I say agent, actually a convenience store in the city with a dodgy key safe—*would you like a slushy with that?*).

Furthermore, the tenant, who was quite helpful, also revealed he had outstanding maintenance requests unfulfilled and had never seen any local agent/rep doing routine inspections or checking on the property. The tenant vacated on time, around eight days prior to settlement, and to his credit had cleaned the unit well on exit. Some of the repairs I had already arranged directly on the seller's behalf with a plumber I knew, and these had been rectified many weeks prior. Nonetheless, I had left a couple of other items with the owner to arrange remotely through his property managers.

Most notable of these was the replacement of a missing laundry door. Now you would think with three months' notice, and with over a week of the property being completely empty prior to settlement, arranging this repair would not be too difficult. I had returned my access key to the convenience store some weeks prior also, to ensure easy access for any other trades. I had emailed the owner on an almost weekly basis, as time ticked down, to keep on his property managers and ensure the work was done. As we entered the last week, he advised me they had not done the work still, as the door had been 'on order', but was now due in a few days prior to settlement.

I urged to him that the turnaround must be quick so the property would be ready for its long-booked pre-settlement inspection with the tolerant buyer. I was advised this would most definitely be done. Again feeling somewhat uneasy, on the day of pre-settlement I headed up to the city early to get the keys back from my man at the corner shop (the access key was now joined by all the main keys, recently handed back by the tenant). I wanted to check over the keys and the unit well in advance of the buyer turning up, just to ensure all was in order.

I had my latest secret code for the key release from the property managers, only to find there were no keys whatsoever at the convenience store as the allocated hook was empty. The man behind the counter could advise me on their fresh sandwich selection for the day, but unfortunately not where the keys were. I had to urgently email the property managers in Sydney— I tried their one 'contact' number which went straight to voicemail—meanwhile, the scheduled inspection time was drawing closer. After 30 minutes I finally got a reply, with a different code to try. I went back and same story, no keys under that code.

This time I had at least been given a direct contact number, so I called it and explained the situation. After a further delay I was given my third code for the day, which would surely work—but no! At this point the property managers said they would have to investigate further and get back to me. I had to call the buyer at this point and put the pre-settlement on hold temporarily until I had the keys.

Finally, I got a call back from the property managers who explained the keys were not there at all as they were still with their Brisbane 'agent'. He had done the exit inspection after the tenant left some days before and had 'forgotten' to return them. To compound the problem, he was already away for the weekend and could return them only when he got back. Now this was a Friday and settlement was on the Monday following, so being told I might get the keys by Tuesday was not an option. After a blunt explanation of why I needed the keys immediately, I was then sent his contact details to try and arrange something directly (nice side-step, guys).

On calling this 'agent'—a building services/maintenance manager, again probably employed on the cheap—he revealed he was down on the Gold Coast (a 90-minute drive away) with his family for a long weekend and had no chance of returning the keys until next week, sorry. Two choices emerge at this stage. Either tap out and throw it back to the overseas owner as 'too hard basket' and let him deal with the consequences—delayed settlement, penalty fees, etc.,—plus disrupting the buyer's plans (having already waited 90-plus days for settlement) or simply try to fix the problem myself for all parties. In the car I jumped, and drove down to the coast where the 'agent' *(very generously)* took a whole two minutes out of his holiday schedule to get the keys out of his car and hand them over. I say keys, actually it was *a* key—singular!

Yes, the next twist was the ex-tenant's main key set was still nowhere to be seen, along with the security fobs that give access to the secure parking areas, and so on. Another 90-minute drive back with a next-to-useless key that would allow basic access only and was certainly not sufficient for handover. Further messages enroute to the property managers, to that effect, "Please track down where the hell these other keys are!". All the time copying in the owner, but with little or no practical input that he could add.

I updated the buyer and we decided to go ahead with the pre-settlement inspection late that afternoon now that I at least had *some* access. I rocked up about 20 minutes ahead of time, went inside and surprise, surprise no laundry repair, just a gaping ugly hole! More frustrated emails to the missing-in-action property managers finally brought about a vaguely encouraging, but unsubstantiated, response that this had now been escalated and the trades would come in over the weekend to ensure completion before settlement.

Furthermore, it *appeared* they had the other keys as the job was not done yet and they still needed access. They would leave the keys at the property after the weekend work was complete. The buyer, whilst not entirely happy with this, could thankfully see the unit was at least clean and presentable (courtesy of the tenant) and that I had spent most of the day running around to ensure we could do an inspection. She also knew the other elements of repair work I had directly co-ordinated had been done many weeks before. To this end she was happy to continue, based on the assurances indicated.

Sensing the inevitable, that the drama was not done, I took time out of my Sunday afternoon to go back to the unit to see if indeed the 'weekend work' had been completed. It came as really no surprise to find nothing changed from my Friday departure. I sent pre-emptive emails off Sunday evening, but still returned early Monday morning in the vain hope, perhaps, they were turning up first thing instead to complete the work. Of course, this was a hollow expectation and the status quo of complete inaction remained in play on my arrival.

It was now settlement day, so trouble was looming! Frantic emails to the owner and calls to the property managers initially got me nowhere. I had to advise the buyer of the status and she consulted her solicitor as to her options. After much pushing, I finally got out of the property managers that, *apparently*, the trades were still waiting on the delivery of the replacement door which is why they hadn't installed it yet. The weekend work suggestion was therefore somewhat spurious from the outset!

The work was not done, but also—more urgently—I still did not have all the keys. The property managers initially suggested they would stay with the trades until done, but I explained this was not an option as the property needed to settle and I had to have a full set of keys. They investigated things further and then (surprise, surprise) discovered the trades *didn't* have them after all. They were, in fact, still at the original convenience store I had visited on the Friday morning! Just on a different hook under a different security code (having been handed in by the tenant separately and not put together after all). Back in the car and back to my friend at the shop (I did buy a fresh sandwich this time as it was lunch by now!). Lo and behold, there were the rest of the keys and security fobs. One problem solved.

I then hounded the property managers for the contact details of the company doing the repair work. They reluctantly gave the information, and I contacted them directly. I got straight through, and the gentleman explained the door was on order from a certain big-box hardware store, but had been delayed and was now due on the Tuesday, after which they could install asap. I explained the back story and asked he deal with me for access as the keys would no longer be at the convenience store, but potentially with the new owner (if we settled on time!).

Not entirely satisfactory, but I felt back in control, at least. I finally had all the keys (with associated access to underground parking, etc.,) for the buyer and now had a direct communication with the trade company, with a credible update. I explained the situation to the buyer, and she decided to settle on time, without penalties and in good faith, on the basis the door could be completed within the following couple of days. I had also re-checked with the property managers that they had written authorisation from the owner and had issued a works order—so he would still be picking up the bill regardless.

Just time to buy a settlement gift and be ready onsite to hand over the keys on time to the—generally—still happy and somewhat relieved buyer. Despite the settlement having occurred, I still followed up the next day with the trades, the door duly arrived in stock, and I coordinated an installation time with the new owner, so all was ultimately resolved.

Would the property have still settled without all my extra intervention? Yes, probably, because ultimately the buyer needed to move in regardless, but almost certainly there would have been delays, penalties charged and significant disruption for the buyer, in particular.

Ironically, for the financial year, this was my cheapest sale, with least commission. And yet it required almost two full days of running around to ensure an on-time settlement and a satisfactory outcome for all parties, despite the fact the property had been unconditional for weeks (so technically my job of selling the unit was long since done). Not every agent would have done all this, and I was quite lucky it coincided with a couple of relatively quiet days where I didn't have similar commitments elsewhere. Yet this is a perfect example of what most punters do not see or appreciate in terms of the extra value many diligent agents do add through a variety of unsung actions. Of course, to some degree that is the point. Like the duck serenely progressing, with legs frantically kicking below the water, so we try to arrive at the finish line having dealt (relatively!) calmly with all those little dramas and diversions along the way.

There then, is the case for the defence in terms of why an agent is still relevant. Perhaps our overall brief will be trimmed over the coming years, but I will be surprised if it completely disappears. Conceivably the jury is out for some people, but I wish them well if they go it alone. Walk in our footsteps at your peril!

17 | Fairy Dust and Drama Queens

N ow, I can already hear the disquiet from many hard-working elite agents who have forged their careers through consistent application and quality of service, to this next suggestion. No issue with that at all, but sorry, I am still going to run with this because I believe it to be true! You see, there are just some chosen individuals who are simply born to be in real estate via some God-given gift at birth. Chip on my shoulder? Jealous? Perhaps, but more bemused wonderment than anything else!

These people possess strange mystical powers, and the normal rules of bad luck and missed opportunity the rest of us underlings are dealt, seemingly do not apply to them. What goes around, comes around? Not in their case! Most of us toil away with an honest week's legwork trying to fashion any small glimmers of opportunity here and there to work with. Yet these 'gifted' individuals can appear for just one hour of reluctant floor roster, the magic fairy dust lands upon them and bang, they pick up two 'walk in' listings!

It is difficult to fully define really, just about being in the right place at the right time, and somehow having more 50/50 situations go your way. Again, I fully get that you create your own luck in this world and, of course, it helps if you have the gift of self-confidence and a force of personality into the bargain—but this is something more, something different. Many a time I have been in an office where I have been diligently, but fruitlessly, on station with other colleagues, when one of the less reliable team members finally rocks up and puts in a guest appearance (they have been 'busy' for the last two days 'out & about'). Land line rings, they pick it up and it is—randomly—Joe Blow, who bought through the office many years ago, wanting to speak with someone who can sell his house, *immediately*. No problem, be with you shortly and off they go again! Strange, but at the end of the week this will probably be their one new listing, not anything from the other days out of the office.

Now I accept there are a few factors at play. As mentioned, these individuals are typically pushier and more confident to start with, so are more likely to convert an opportunity. They will also be quite self-obsessed and selfish, so have no hang-ups with taking an opportunity from under the noses of others, when they have minimum prior input. Indeed, this will almost act as a positive reinforcement of their abilities and, therefore entitlement to take leads.

In their head (or out loud!) the thought process is along the lines of, *good job I was here now, otherwise you lot would have probably lost the chance*. The ruthless will also fully recognise in this dog-eat-dog arena, just capture the flag and worry about any ill feeling or fallout later. After all, he who holds the listing can do no wrong, and anyone who complains just needs to do better and stop with the whinging routine. All acknowledged, but we all need something to work with and the number of times random leads pop up and go the way of the chosen few is quite surprising and frustrating!

The interesting thing is such divine talent (or luck) can be utilised in one of two ways. Some will sense they have a natural propensity to attract opportunities, but will still strive to combine this with hard work, constant improvement and learning to be become the very best in the business (and they deserve all that comes with it). However, there are others who sense that this means they can put their feet up for three weeks every month and then get by with a week of 'quick & dirty' activity (that still yields a higher return than your average plodder).

Choosing this route for their 'talents' means ultimately they will never rise to the top of the industry because they are way too inconsistent (and yet they will still be able to earn a reasonable income, simply with less input than most). For those of you who know your footballers—soccer that is!—it's a bit like a Cristiano Ronaldo or a David Beckham (further honing their obvious natural abilities through hard work and rigorous training to maximise their career longevity and success) versus a George Best (undeniably gifted, but wasteful and inconsistent with ultimately a disappointing truncated career for such an innate talent).

If you fall into the second—and far more interesting—category it helps if you can cover your tracks, so to speak. If you can put on a bit of a show around anything you can be bothered to do or follow up, it tends to elongate the sense of activity. Essentially, never admit something just came your way relatively easily. Instead, devise exciting narratives around how this resulted from your dynamic door knocking or sign jumping and then how you fought off other cut-price agents and won the business against all the odds, etc. Such high theatre is what we want in the sales meeting! Bloated egos generally assist this process nicely and always ensure there are a few drama queens around putting in a 'performance' for every relatively mundane action undertaken.

There we all sit in the meeting room, clock watching and wishing the weekly ordeal was over as soon as possible, but now we have to listen to a 10-minute rundown of how a listing was won, and the unique particulars of the property. Perhaps there was a run in with a competing agent or opposing principal to add spice to the story, or it was stolen away from the opposition at the eleventh hour, etc., etc. The principal (or sales manager) running the meeting will, to a degree put up with these overly embellished and long-winded monologues—generally from the same usual suspects—if they think it will encourage the rest of the blob into action or seemingly set an example of achievement.

To be fair, this talking it up ploy is useful for anyone really, as it creates a sense of endless effort and endeavour, regardless of actual outcome *(although that sales board don't lie!)*. In saying that, it probably needs to be underpinned every so often with some tangible results. If you just try to make endless prolonged anecdotes about flyer dropping or sign jumping—without outcomes—purely to make some noise, this will wear thin over time and eventually you will be asked to pipe down or keep to the point. Nonetheless, most will go into the sales meeting prepared with a least one backup story they can pad out to make it look like they are doing something, if put on the spot.

The level of performance put on, and underlying waffle, can change exponentially depending on what you have accomplished recently. By some miracle, if you had a banger week with a couple of sales and three new listings, then less becomes more. You recount these achievements in a more succinct manner as (after all) you have so much happening *it would take all meeting to go into the detail*. Conversely, no listings or sales again this week, better drone on for five minutes about this new prospecting initiative you are doing and all the leads you are now working on as result. You even detail particulars of the properties involved as if they were already listings, except of course they are not—*just a little more time*. If that is too hard, perhaps recount how colourful your new flyers are and just hope that carries you through.

There is another dynamic at play here as well. Sometimes those with biggest presence and need to be heard are secretly the most insecure. By creating noise, they create attention, and this forms some sort of reassurance. They feel the constant need to talk big, as much to convince *themselves* how good they are, as anyone else. Yet others are quite content to call a quiet week exactly that, a quiet week, confident enough in their overall abilities that any short-term drop off is not a problem in the medium term.

Indeed, I worked with a great agent for many years who was a strong and consistent performer, yet was straight down the line and detested the 'show pony' antics of the sales meeting. If he had a slow week, he would deadpan call it out for what it was. "Nothing to report this week, so guess I did bugger all then!" The principal would never know quite how to take such remarks because it wasn't really the 'right stuff' or 'on topic' messaging for the team. But equally, they knew fully well he was having a little light entertainment and was a way better performer than most of the other hot air regulars around the table. Perhaps what was even more amusing is while most of the assembled got his sardonic humour, others still merrily ploughed on with fluffing up their own week of underachievement.

Often at the conclusion of the sales meeting, we then have the exciting prospect of the follow on 'stock run'. We all jump into our assorted vehicles and undertake a road trip to view the (hopefully) various new listings of that week. On paper this is so we can demonstrate to our relevant new sellers how our wonderful office works as a fully integrated team with everyone taking a keen collective interest in their property to understand it thoroughly (and determine if they have any buyers it might suit). Superficially yes, but given—as already mentioned—there isn't that much teamwork going on, and the listing agent really does not want to give any commission away immediately on his hard-fought new listing anyway, this is often more about going through the motions.

However, it does provide another great space for the prima donnas to indulge themselves and give a far too in-depth viewing of their new prize, along with a *meet & greet* of the owners, relating half their life story in the process. That's fine, if there is only one property on today's run sheet, but if there are several, geographically spaced out, it is time for the packed lunches and survival gear, as this will quickly turn into a long expedition!

Typically, the rules for a stock run are: exclusive listings only, and only those properties within the main farming areas of the office. For the most part this would be followed, but if you had just come off a lean run and hadn't been able to do a *'show & tell'* for a while in front of class, the occasional open list—or one further afield—is attempted to be slipped in unnoticed. And if sprung, "I have already promised the owner the team will inspect,". Really? Unlucky! Occasionally, I have even experienced a couple of agents trying to slip properties not yet formally listed on to the list, just to keep the momentum going. That is quite a high stakes move though, as it's very unlikely it won't be rumbled by somebody.

The stock run would usually finish with a team coffee at some café along the route. This would be a weekly bonding session where everyone could interact away from the office and the constraints of the sales meeting. A pleasant enough concept, but even this would highlight those who were quite relaxed and would therefore *not* endlessly talk shop—or about themselves— over their cuppa; instead engaging in wider conversation and some good-humoured banter. By contrast, others couldn't switch off 'show mode' and would still be banging on to anyone who wanted to listen—normally whoever was trapped next to them—about what they were doing next and how great those new properties were.

Those with big personalities, and big insecurities to match, tend to go beyond the public arena as well. 'Behind the scenes' queens are the worst! Constantly on secretive, hushed phone calls to the principal, either brown-nosing by giving an embroidered running commentary of what they did that was *so* wonderful today—nothing much usually—or complaining about some form of perceived unfair treatment—given their status— that has taken place and how they feel they deserve to be treated a little better (than the rest). Their numbers for the last quarter might determine whether the response to the latter is either *'suck it up, Princess'* or *'just humour them for a quiet life'* (and massage that ego as usual!).

Why put up with all these theatrics then? Simply because it is *not* the journey in this case, but most definitely the destination. As abrasive and annoying as some of these individuals may be, whilst they are ultimately producing similar (or better) dollars than the calmer and more professional—but slightly underachieving—alternatives, they will be tolerated. The dreaded sales board is indeed the *only* measurement that counts.

This is an industry where it is easy to get bogged down with being busy, yet achieving nothing. You can graft away all week dropping flyers in 40°C heat, cold calling disinterested people, diligently doing floor duty, and more than your fair share to 'front' the business, but if you don't have a listing or sale to show for it at the end, your week just became invisible. Alternatively, you can be missing in action for days, not do your roster times, only to come in for an hour and jag a slightly dodgy sign jump; the fairy dust falls and, hey presto, you have a listing, which in turn you can talk up. Who's achieved more in quantifiable (profit) terms? Quick & dirty (with exciting added narrative) wins—no questions asked!

18 | FRIENDS REUNITED

W hat else do we need to know at this point? Many things perhaps, but another major one is real estate is very, very incestuous. You should never entirely burn your bridges with anyone, be it employer or client because, rest assured, today's sworn enemy is tomorrow's next opportunity ... again.

In terms of agents and agencies there are only so many fish in the pond, and you will keep bumping into the same characters, like it or not. Generally, offices and their key players will have set geographical areas in which most of their business activity will be undertaken. It is, therefore, inevitable if you are working the same areas that you will regularly encounter familiar faces. Likewise, if you are doing a half-decent job, you will also be known to others and on their local radar. Whilst most of these people and their companies will represent the direct opposition, you never know when you might need alternative employment options or perhaps a conjunction opportunity on a slow-moving property. So, in general it pays to keep a—superficially at least—cordial relationship whenever you come into contact. Moreover, that is probably the best tactical move anyway: keep your enemies closer and all that!

There might be a lot more of them, but even with buyers and sellers if you predominantly work the same core area all the time—and manage to stay in the business longer than six months! —you will quite often start to see some of the same customers coming across your path again. Investors potentially acquiring another property for their portfolio, unsuccessful buyers from last year trying again, or (the best ones) past purchasers who are re-selling within a relatively short time frame. There are a multitude of reasons why people may come back into your world.

Play this phenomenon right and it can have obvious benefits in terms of repeat business with the same client and/or referrals with their family and friends. Many people change properties with a surprising regularity due to many reasons, some planned and others unexpected. As you slowly build your back catalogue of contacts, this can be a strong potential source of future leads and listings, if you have cultivated positive experiences along the way. Personalities differ and some may still chase whoever the 'agent of the week' is in their locality if they feel that will net a few extra dollars. Equally, I have always been heartened by a good deal of other people who respond to friendly and professional service, and who will track you down for additional business and advice at a later stage.

However, if you are more of a 'churn and burn' merchant with little or no regard for excellent customer service, you really have to keep your new client volumes up because there might be a much lower level of repeat business coming back (i.e., there is a need to hit up everyone else that *doesn't* already know you instead!). Cut and run to the next mug and don't look back! Mind you, in saying all that, when money dictates actions, literally anything can eventuate!

I had a glaring example of this in the fledging days of my new career path. I well remember when I started at my first office, I was immediately handed a property to take over because another high-profile agent in the company had just left the previous Friday. Great, given a listing straight off the bat, that will help with experience and profile building. However, clearly the agent in question had been running the clock down on this property, and a few others, for a while (pending departure). Now the owner was extremely angry having been left in the lurch with no warning and little activity or feedback in the preceding couple of weeks. He ultimately withdrew the house from sale with our office, but initially demanded his spare keys were returned immediately as proof they were not still with this rogue agent otherwise, he "would have the police involved". He no longer trusted this character, who had effectively blindsided him leaving his house sale stalled with no one at the helm.

A damning judgement and rightfully so, perhaps. Imagine my surprise then—although, with subsequent experience, not these days—when a few months later the same owner finally sold his house through the original discredited agent (at his new agency). The owners initial distain for the agent's actions and extreme reaction following his departure was slowly and surely overcome as he struggled to achieve a credible sale, in the interim, with a couple of other alternative agencies.

Upon reflection, perhaps he might still be able to supply a buyer at the price the owner always wanted. After all (with self-justification mode on) he did always have good contacts, was knowledgeable on the local area and, more importantly, this unique and wonderful property. Anger soon subsided, replaced by need, so all bets off and pretend nothing happened! A price was achieved that was reasonably close to what he originally wanted—close enough to swallow his pride for a second time in short succession—so smiles all around for the photos in front of the big red sold sticker!

The moral of this tale? Only a select few become your true friends (or indeed enemies!) in this business. For the majority it is simply what you have to offer at a particular point in time. When dollars are involved, motives and memories can become highly selective!

There is a further interesting caveat to this story, which I will grudgingly admit to. You see, in the immediate aftermath of his departure, trying to salvage this unstable listing I had inherited, I offered to pay for some additional marketing myself. Trying to anchor the situation back down, and being new to it all, I thought this would be a sign of good faith to the owner and would endear me to him, having put in such a commitment. He readily took it (of course) and I did get to work on the property for a few more weeks, but he still withdrew it from sale with us a little later, regardless.

I had managed to present a couple of offers in that time, but they were some way below his happy price so, sorry buddy, your time is up. Tough lesson learned. The mistake was thinking this gesture would automatically secure some form of renewed and elongated loyalty from the owner. In fact, the reverse was true. You see, it was *my* hurt money not his, so it made it easier for him to withdraw as he owed nothing financially (and who cares about morals, right?). Without any outstanding advertising costs, there was no Sword of Damocles hanging over him, so move on. No skin in the game, no worries!

There was effectively a readymade excuse available for use at any stage, once the original agent had departed, along the lines of: never really being happy with the agency since then in terms of how they let the situation arise in the first place and damage the selling campaign of his property. I should have seen it coming but in my 'fresher' naivety and excitement I made a one-sided commitment that, unless it was backed up quickly with unachievably priced offers, was doomed to failure from the outset. We live and learn. Looking at the overall situation, the guy that took over and put time, effort and some money into the process (but couldn't quite get the desired sale price) got nothing, and the guy that blatantly shafted him originally got the sale in the end. More karma, of sorts, just real estate style!

Many a time you might be speaking with a seller who is already listed, but deeply unhappy with their current agent through lack of service, etc. They made a mistake, desperately want out and are ready to sign with you as soon as the existing agreement expires. In truth, they really don't like the current incumbent or their attitude. Great, this one is in the bag! Almost, but hang on, at the last possible minute old mate only goes and jags a potential buyer. They beg the sellers for a couple more days extension to see if they can get an offer as (surprise, surprise) this buyer is talking good money and seems keen. What does the seller do? Nothing! Chance of some bucks after all, so sit tight and wait and see.

Now, this buyer might be a ringer to stretch the listing out or it might just be legitimate (timing is everything). If it is the latter and an offer is forthcoming, chances are the deal will be done and you will never get your chance. The owner has just sold with someone they openly disliked and wanted to remove, but, hey presto, money talks so 'as we were'. Indeed, some sellers will select an agent they do not even like right from the outset, but if they think their arrogant or overbearing manner has occasioned better results—either in truth or just because that is what they are being told—they sign up regardless. (And then complain about their agent's behaviour, but hopefully still pocket a whole $10 more at the end!)

This erratic behaviour is by no means restricted to customers. Indeed, it is rife within real estate offices! Agents leaving the trusty blob for pastures new, often only to reappear 18 months later. This could be simply because things did not go quite as planned elsewhere or the original office is regretting their departure, income is down, and the principal has swallowed their pride and lured them back onto the fold.

In short, it goes something like this. Agent A leaves Company A to go and work for Company B. Principal (inevitably) initially bad-mouths them in the next sales meeting at Company A. "Wasn't pulling their weight. Needed to go anyway. Didn't like their attitude," etc., etc. Fast-forward 12-18 months. Agent A returns to Company A (didn't work out at Company B and Company A is now struggling a bit and needs to fatten the blob again). Next Company A sales meeting, amnesia settings to high, "Let's welcome Agent A, great to have you back, proven performer,". We are happy families all over again.

It really is quite comical, as you can virtually track this process unfolding. Departing agent initially derided or (worse still) never mentioned again in a *'he-who-must-not-be-named'* type scenario. The odd barbed reference may follow over the next few months. Then as the thaw starts—when needs must—their name begins to be mentioned occasionally (in reference to what they are doing elsewhere). These references increase in regularity and then suddenly the principal 'bumps' into the old employee by accident at a bar, posts a Facebook picture "Never guess who I ran into this evening?", etc. This is the softener, as at this point everyone is already thinking, *'Okay, so when are they coming back?'*. Lo and behold, normally within two or three weeks of said social media exposure, guess who walks in the door? Ah, the games we play.

I think it is assumed we all have very short memories, but I can remember being told, in no uncertain terms, by a principal about a high profile *(if they did say so themselves)* agent who had recently departed being spent, "over dealing with buyers" and generally "tired of real estate". No big loss then? Apparently not, for the next couple of years at least, until they were then miraculously welcomed back to the same office—by the same principal—like the proverbial prodigal son with a big fanfare and a (paid for) personal marketing 'launch' to match. I guess they must have had a nice little rest at the other agency and were not so tired anymore! Perhaps we are all just too insecure in our own positions to call out such blatant hypocrisy to the boss, after all, our desk might measure up quite well for the newly reinstalled headline act!

To be fair, the agent in question above was a bit of a player and very well skilled in becoming your best friend when required. Here is the thing, if an individual can get success by being all things to all clients and making them feel like they are their best mates, they can easily apply this same talent to a principal or sales manager as well, to gain an advantage or route into an organisation. The employer simply becomes the next 'end user' you need to make feel warm and fuzzy. Quite often works a treat: *tell them what they need to hear (just as you would a seller) and all is sweet.* We all know they are doing a number, but again needs must, so even though my suspicion is that these principals know they are being worked over, they will go along with it if current circumstances dictate blob fattening and more inbound dollars (assuming the agent is half-decent). Indeed, like the numerous 'companions' on Doctor Who, it would appear many principals need to have their constant 'buddy of the moment' to hang with. Never hard to tell who it is at any point in time: social media posts of shared drinks, outings, and even little holidays together! Ah, how nice. Well for six months yes, until there is the predictable fall out over some work-related issue and this close, inseparable new 'friendship' will evaporate as quickly as it was formed. Time for the agent to move on and select a new target for bestie and the principal to find their next companion. Yes, I know, how very cynical of me, but it happens. Business is business and everyone expediently does what is needed at any given point in time.

Over the many years, I have witnessed several agents returning to a past office, for a second tour of duty. As we will see next, this is fuelled by an almost endless desire to keep moving on (hence, the exit the first time around). Ultimately, I get that people change positions regularly in this industry and that is fine. Also, sometimes it's *better the devil you know* when things do not work out perfectly elsewhere. I just laugh at all the associated hypocrisy and back tracking that goes with it!

19 | MAN THE LIFEBOATS

Right, you've been in the game for a whole 10 minutes by now and already learned so much! Obviously, time for a change?! As I have just highlighted, this industry is relatively insular, and most agents (and agencies) are fully aware of each other and what they are up to. This, coupled with the constant pressure to perform, leads to the very real temptation to throw in the towel at one company and move to another—seemingly more attractive—one if things are not quite going as well as planned (or the blunt instrument is heading your way). Real estate has constant staff turnover, and average employment terms are quite short by other industry standards, so what are the factors at play?

Ironically, most agents are no different in mentality to some of those annoying sellers they must deal with, who are in denial about their price expectation (and start searching for another agency in the hope this will change the outcome). We are quite often in denial about what we are doing, or rather *not* doing, to achieve our—usually overestimated—business objectives (and start searching for another agency in the hope this will change the outcome—*didn't I just say that?*). Similarities continue, as there is a comparable honeymoon period at the beginning of an employment contract which, just as with a listing, can start to dissolve relatively quickly if no results or significant constructive activity is forthcoming.

The culture of different agencies can vary considerably and sometimes an agent may (upon reflection) just not be the right fit. There are the relatively aggressive franchises and principals who demand constant 'attack dog' activities in a rigid style of micro-accountability. Some hardnosed individuals may prosper in this environment whilst others will soon buckle under the unrelenting pressure. Equally, there are more laid-back environments where a degree of lateral movement in how you operate is given (especially if you already have a track record). Experienced agents with good morals and strong self-discipline will work well here, but those with limited self-control or imagination will drift and achieve much less. As with anything in life, different individuals respond and thrive in different circumstances.

Within an established office any number of things can conspire to upset the apple cart. A change of line management or principal, re-branding to a new franchise or even perceived preferential treatment of 'selected' colleagues, can all be factors that can influence an agent to promptly review their situation and abandon ship. Changes to the amount of self-marketing a company may be doing—and thereby the amount of 'walk in' business it is attracting—can also be another potential trigger (and we will cover this separately). Essentially anything that impacts a perceived cosy status quo can have dramatic effects. The problem is, by its very nature, real estate is dynamic and constantly evolving, so I have never known of any office where things have remained in equilibrium for too long.

By and large, whatever the apparent reasoning, things will generally fall back on the agent simply not doing well enough, and hoping a change will magically resolve the problem or simply fire them up again. 'Fight or flight' reactions generally result in the latter! For some this can become a semi-regular occurrence and whenever one of these *serial jumpers* turn up they still have a good reason for their latest move: their last principal "changed" (translation—wised up!), they didn't want to be "micro-managed" (translation—they don't want to be managed *at all)* or the more in-depth analysis for leaving, "They're all just wankers there!". Okay then, fair enough!

Perhaps slightly more prevalent a few years back, another occasional, but dramatic, happening is the exit *en masse*. If there is (for a change) a relatively close-knit sales team that has perhaps bonded well under a particular sales manager or team leader, should said manager become disillusioned by a sudden directional change or takeover, then there is a chance the team will be influenced and consider defecting with them. Sometimes a good team may also be targeted, and headhunted by another agency. The sales manager may be offered a bonus for each team member they can bring along with them. The advantage for the recruiting agency is quick growth with an 'instant' proven sales team created, that has already worked well together. This maximises the likely returns and (theatrically) minimises the risk of petty agent rivalries or a single disruptive individual coming in. The only problem with this blanket bombing approach is if the whole team moves, to remain together, you then need to ensure you can keep the entire roster happy to avoid a similar group transfer in the future! As much as it is a big coup at the time, 12 months is an eternity in real estate.

My first real estate office had been through that exact process not long before I arrived. As I discovered, virtually the whole team I was now working alongside had moved over together (with their relatively young sales manager) from a well-known rival in the same suburb. At the time this had been a major success story for my principal, and expanded his team substantially overnight to become a major force in the area. The previous company, whilst high profile and well established, had gone through a change of long-standing management and a few feathers had been ruffled in the process. A degree of discontentment had set in and before long conditions were right for an audacious raid. The team already knew each other well and the 'collective' continued to work as before, simply under another brand name. Great, what could go wrong?

Well, not too much for the first few months I was there, but then the inevitable cracks started to slowly appear. Whilst the public awareness of the office had been undeniably raised with this new team transfer, it was still not quite at a level enjoyed by their old office. The degree of commitment to news media advertising (then still a key component) for ongoing profile building was not as high and transaction volumes, whilst good, were not at the levels some had previously enjoyed.

Slowly but surely things began to unravel. Of a group of 10 or so who originally moved, a couple broke ranks and decided to move on independently. A few of the others began to question the level of backing. Then the gentleman who had showed me the *Dark Side* on my first day was finally called out for what he was (lazy and slacking off!) leading to a confrontation and mutual parting of the ways. It appears the sales manager, who was the original catalyst for the move, had also not quite lived up to billing—be that of his own making and some pre-determined KPIs—and dramatically became another casualty following a particular incident where he got a bit mouthy and unprofessional with a client. He was indeed one of the aforementioned number put to the sword on the shop floor in front of me as I sat at my own desk, somewhat stunned and bemused whilst trying to keep a (very) low profile. It was only a matter of time from there.

The remaining group dwindled quite quickly, hastened by the hiring of a replacement (and very different) sales manager who immediately decided—due to reducing income—to chop the debit/credit salary scheme for some of those who had moved over, and forced them on to commission-only remuneration. In fairness, as all had previous experience they should have been on this already (but that must have been part of the sweetener to come onboard).

Yet making any change, however justified, causes drama, nonetheless. Within a couple of months of this decision virtually all the remaining team had gone. A classic roller-coaster ride, small team of two or three swelled instantly to 15-plus, only to be back down to the same starting numbers within a couple of years. You look so good as an office 'on the up' when the numbers rise with experienced operators, but equally questions are asked in the industry when staff members depart constantly and quickly, meaning other agents are far more wary of joining in the future. And it is almost impossible to replace the mass exodus—some post-departure bad-mouthing of the office from the occasional leaver won't help either! Being such an open book, with all your recruits constantly on public display, there is really no way to disguise such a reversal of fortunes and fall from grace.

From a perspective of balance, it all sounds like *by default* everyone has itchy feet six months in. There are operators who have remained with single offices or brands over a long period, and if the office is successful and stable there is a better chance this will happen. Also, over a longer career there are simply times when you genuinely re-assess, and I have changed companies a few times in 16 years (but never with less than two to three years minimum under my belt at any particular one).

One ex-colleague of mine, who is also now a good friend and (in my opinion) the perfect 'balanced' agent, has nonetheless moved on a few occasions himself over the years. That said, it has always been on his terms, and even at these points of self-re-evaluation he was still one of the main contributors in the relevant office (so such moves have never come from a basic lack of performance, using the office as an excuse).

On a side note, you may be wondering what a *balanced* agent is? Just the right amount of pro-active and insightful prospecting to ensure there are always consistent leads to work with—particularly referral and repeat business—without being too pushy or overbearing, coupled with a strong sense of moral values ensuring honest and fair treatment of all. Finally, a faultless commitment to the best outcome for the seller, while not being unduly influenced by the buyer's demands or a desperate need for quick sales, in this instance. Sounds simple enough, but few can tick all boxes. I freely admit my weaker area has always been that initial return on prospecting to generate enough good quality leads, and it continues to be something to work on. However, I am realistic enough to know any fault lies with me to continue to improve, not at the foot of yet another office.

One other highly amusing aspect to this never-ending switching of companies is the whole preciousness and double standards around protection of data. In most cases when an agent departs there will be some form of directive imposed from the principal or corporate management whereby they cannot pursue business with any of the recent clients they have dealt with, as these contacts—and any stock—remain the 'property' of their current employer. That's all well and good, except if that same company is employing an agent from another firm they will encourage and *expect* that agent to try and 'jump' their old clients and stock from day one. Double standards? Of course! The reality is nobody 'owns' anyone. Some people have genuine relationships with a particular agent (rather than their agency) and will follow them wherever they are. Perfectly reasonable and quite futile to try and hinder. Most agents will respect this directive, to a degree, and will not overtly chase down all their old contacts immediately (perhaps, if only for a quiet life). This might also depend on whether the departure was acrimonious or on good terms (remember, don't burn those bridges just yet!).

However, should an ex-client make contact and want to list specifically with you, it's just too good to turn down. General rule of thumb here, get them to pen a signed statement saying they contacted you first and then you are pretty much covered (for when the property goes live, and you get the obligatory toothless threat of action via a 'cease and desist' letter from your old employer!). Of course, even if you called the client initially and blatantly solicited the opportunity on purpose, still get them to say they contacted you first!

Some brave souls will go hard from day one, and the departing agent mentioned in the story in the last chapter had not only run down the clock on that property with the (initially) angry owner, but had done so on about eight other listings, under the principal's nose. He quietly let the exclusive periods run out, without being renewed, and thus turning them into open listing targets, ready to hijack once on the other side. Now, this should really have been picked up earlier with some alarm bells ringing, but for whatever reason, it wasn't.

Having clearly courted some of these owners prior to his departure—as to what was about to unfold and would they be keen to stay with him elsewhere—within a few days of leaving many had been re-signed with him at the new office as exclusive listings and terminated with the old office. This was quite high-risk, to say the least. Some unhappy owners could have spilled the beans beforehand, although he clearly knew which ones to target, who were likely to be accommodating to the idea and ignored some others who might have unpredictable reactions (old angry mate, for example). Also, there was probably an arguable case for some form of legal action in this instance given the relatively blatant nature of the exercise. A calculated gamble, but one that paid off. Bam! My principal was not best pleased, to say the least, but ultimately didn't pursue any formal action. Secretly, I think he knew they had dropped the ball and missed what was obviously going on. Court proceedings were costly and probably in the too-hard basket. Sometimes you get to just take it on the chin and move on. Life is too short.

In concluding, there are numerous reasons why changed circumstances within an office may lead to spontaneous staff turnover. However, it must be said there are times when nothing is at fault or altered with your current surroundings, yet you are personally struggling or the market is slow, and listings are difficult. It may be then the appeal of a competitor promising *money-for-nothing* and *your-listings-for-free* is too good to ignore.

20 | Feed Me, Seymour!

O h dear me, office-generated leads, the biggest single source of internal angst, mistrust and suspicion between agents. The dirty little secret many (in truth) otherwise very-average-agents need to survive on, but don't want to admit to. Quite a broad area as this can cover attraction business enquiries, landlord property sales (from a rent roll) and a juicy selection of other 'brown paper bag' gimmes and freebies.

Let us put some context around this first. If you work for an established 'bricks and mortar' franchise agency with a well-known name and office profile to go with it, there should effectively be two tiers of activity operating alongside each other. At the core there is the prospecting conducted by the individual agent to generate their own leads. This consists of a wide range of activities (well, hopefully!) including phone calls, door knocking, flyers, social media posts, and interaction through open homes, etc. Contacts and potential leads generated through this process are directly taken by the agent who created the opportunity. This typically should be the primary source of your business and theoretically is what you are judged on performance-wise.

The concept remains 'business-within-a-business' and controlling your own destiny is key to this. Nonetheless, at a secondary level, the agency (ideally!) will have an ongoing marketing budget and strategy to promote the brand/office itself, thereby creating the potential for additional attraction business (that is, people voluntarily contacting the agency to request a service through generic awareness of the brand). As touched on above, this can be further supplemented if the agency has a large rent roll—that is, properties that are managed on behalf of investment owners—as from time to time some of these landlords might need to sell and generally (although certainly not always) will go to the managing agency as the first port of call for a sales appraisal. Additionally, often an experienced and long serving principal (who will be known in the area and will have a considerable back catalogue of contacts, etc.,) will receive direct requests. Depending on their situation and workload, they will farm these leads out—particularly if they are *non-selling* themselves—to selected members of their sales team to follow up and support.

It is certainly not unreasonable to expect leads from these secondary sources. Indeed, if you are working for an office-based franchise brand (and therefore paying away a considerable lump of your gross commission) you expect to see something in return, i.e., significantly more prospects than if you were working independently. Whilst it is great when an agency is working well and generating all these extra opportunities, the problem is (by their very nature) they are generic, so must be internally allocated to a specific agent to deal with. Big trouble! In a room of needy, ego-driven individuals whose very essence is to constantly hunt down any openings, where, when, and who these go to can inevitably lead to dramas. The suspicion is there are teacher's pets—and of course there are, usually the aforementioned current 'companion' to start with—who are secretly given an unfair proportion of these leads to take on, thereby inflating their activities and (ultimately) income.

I have seen many established, supposedly self-sufficient agents up and leave in a hissy fit because they perceive someone else has come in and is suddenly getting all the best leads (I mean they *must* be, because they are doing better than them!). Part of the problem is openness, or rather lack of it. It is bad enough knowing someone in the room is getting a handout, but even worse when that individual then tries to disguise it as a lead they have worked on themselves to generate (which they will do for image and in order to 'protect their source', i.e., the principal!). Some are easier than others to camouflage, for instance, if it is off the rent roll, pretty obvious it is a handout!

Frankly, I find this all quite hilarious. Several so-called experienced operators arguing over scraps thrown at them, like seagulls on a chip! What it is to be a 'top' performer, but still be paid a retainer on the quiet (just in case of the slow month, that of course you *never* have) and be desperate for any hand-me-downs. I have utmost admiration for genuine elite performers who achieve great things through their own determination and skill without the constant need for propping up. Equally, I can empathise with those struggling to make a go of things, but are honest enough to admit it, and know their own shortcomings.

In either of these situations, I don't begrudge that additional openings may come their way as either reward or incentive to keep trying. Where things grate somewhat, however, is the middle tier of adequate enough performers who still fall back on this and then like to convince us all they are somehow greater than they really are. As already covered, there is a real need for self-promotion to the potential customer in this industry, but lording it up with your own colleagues who know better is another thing. You still can't kid that kidder, remember.

Some make a whole career of this approach. Ensuring they are always buddied up wherever they are and in a favourable 'receiving position', so to speak! Furthermore, only moving on when (invariably at some point) this cosy relationship breaks down, but not before they have ensured they have the next accommodating situation already lined up and suitably softened. Good luck, I guess. I am sure they would argue they are just maximising business, and *more fool me* for not doing the same and instead totally relying—as I now do—on my own devices (probably right!). Nonetheless, the need to constantly brown-nose and fawn undying mock devotion to the current office is a bit tedious.

The clever part (and to be fair, it is quite ingenious if you can pull it off) is to unashamedly build your reputation utilising these performance enhancing 'supplements' to bolster overall achievement. Hence, when you do need to look elsewhere you will be deemed enough of a 'catch' or trophy recruitment for a competitor, that they will chase your signature. In doing so, no doubt agree to similar provisions that have kept you where you are to date (nice little retainer with meaningless senior title to justify it, plus a nod and a wink on some of the best future leads). Sweet! The circle of life continues.

Yes, best leads. That's another issue. There's a big difference between an overpriced, poorly presented rental with long term (unhelpful) tenants in place, versus an immaculate owner-occupied home with attentive owners, who will listen on pricing and feedback. One a poisoned chalice and one a winning lottery ticket, but both could easily be leads, just from different sources (e.g., landlord's rundown property from the rent book, versus old friends of the principal). Give one each to a couple of agents and they have both had a 'feed' right? Just that one is very happy and will have a payday soon whilst the other is going to endure a few weeks of pain with no guaranteed result. Such selection will again most likely reflect on who is the flavour of the month.

Another variation here is where the principal is still selling, themselves. They will (quite rightly, as it is their name over the door) take the good ones and then potentially still farm out the duds to other people. This has a two-fold effect of still appearing to be benevolent every so often by passing on opportunities, whilst not having to deal with the obviously crappy listings yourself! A sort of 'Captain's Pick', if you will!

Now this, and indeed the last couple of chapters prior, might seem all very cynical (and they are!). Whilst I am not suggesting for one minute this applies to everyone, the percentages of jumping around and need for support is certainly greater towards the bottom end of the food chain. I know of top performers who have been with the same company for years and built an excellent reputation and great team around them. Yet equally, I have personally known agents who can tick off many of these undesirable traits.

One, for example, who shall certainly remain nameless, had fostered an image in our area as a gold standard performer. A certified six-figure earner wherever they were, with glowing testimonials to match. Yet dig a little deeper and they were still being paid a 'safety net' retainer always (when many of their lesser colleagues were paid commission-only) and were always miraculously the best friend (at that point in time) of whichever principal was employing them. Now given they had moved at least four times in less than 10 years (including one return to a previous employer) that is quite a feat.

At one company, where I knew the principal reasonably well, they had been headhunted and came in with 'companion' status from day one. Nights out, fitness classes together, all the usual stuff. How sweet, best buds for life now, regardless of work? Well, no, for a couple of years, or thereabouts until the pipeline of opportunities started to dry up and wheels had been set in motion elsewhere. Once everything was ready, off they trotted and (to my knowledge) have had no further meaningful contact with the previous principal since their day of departure. There you have it, the trifecta of office jumping—including back from where you came—buddying up and taking the goodies! Oh well, if you can live with yourself, it pays the bills nicely and maintains the legend.

I have also known of a few instances where an individual has been given the sole and specific role of selling the rent roll stock. The trick here is the principal does not have to do it themselves— far too tiresome dealing with those annoying tenants all the time—but can still keep these listings 'close', so to speak, by using one (carefully selected) agent only. The individual must be struggling enough to take the bait, and subsequent underpayment, but be reasonably trustworthy and relatively benign in nature. This agent is then guaranteed a procession of listings, but in return the principal takes an additional cut (typically 20%) as these are rental properties and are 'generated' by the office.

In one of my offices a promising young starter was selected and only paid a modest fixed fee from the commission for each sale. If you are lucky you might get a special title to go with your unique role, 'Investment Sales Consultant' or the like, but in reality it again takes a certain character to be prepared to do this. Taking reduced commission for more difficult rental listings with little to offer in imagination or flexibility just to get a steady feed. In addition, you will have to live with the slight stigma of this role (being the artificially 'kept' agent) not to mention the resentment of your colleagues who are now not getting any rental stock handouts themselves anymore! That said, most with any flair wouldn't want to be lumbered with only doing this anyway.

As the overall listing numbers have reduced in the last few years, so the focus has increased on *where* to source what dwindling stock there is. The COVID-19 period put this into even more sharp focus with a very limited stock supply for a long period. It was no surprise to me that during this period several mid-tier operators moved from their smaller independent agencies, where they were undoubtably the 'star turns' (but office-generated leads were drying up) to larger franchise agencies. In doing so, to a degree, they became slightly more anonymous as part of a bigger and already well established/successful blob.

On the surface this seems at odds with self-image promotion and almost a backwards step in terms of your individual brand and standing-out-from-the-crowd. However, the large franchise offices have the large rent rolls and higher attraction business. The payoff then for a slight loss of self-profile market share was more listings through the robust office pipeline without the hard slog and uncertainty (and a continuation of the appearance of good levels of business in a market where many were struggling to survive). The public does not understand or care where the listing came from (or that you might be getting a lower cut or sold your soul to acquire it). All they see is you are still active, so must be good at what you are doing, right? Indeed you are, perhaps just not in the sense of independent prospecting, so much as perfect positioning! Each to their own, and I certainly do not condemn it, just muse on the gap between bold rhetoric and financial reality.

The go-ahead principals of these big offices, with sizeable rent rolls and marketing budgets to match, know that this represents a big enticement to other agents, and they can use this as easy bait to bring one or more of these medium hitters across if they ever want to bolster the ranks. One large agency with extensive market share in my area had the principal openly declaring that none of his agents had to go and hunt for listings, all their leads walked in the door. No matter how good you think you are, that is a powerful drawcard in hard times (he certainly fattened his blob substantially over the COVID-19 period with some notable local 'signings').

One of the notoriously tough franchises to work for, that really pushes its staff for results on a daily basis, lost a number of agents a few years back. I worked with a couple of their ex-employees at different times who both simply had enough of the pressure cooker atmosphere and constant micro-scrutiny. They felt they were now experienced and successful enough to move to other agencies where things were less intense, and they could develop their own signature styles and further good results.

This indeed worked well enough for a while, but intriguingly both these agents (plus at least a couple of others I am aware of) have now all moved back to the dreaded company of origin during the pandemic. Why? When all had been so adamant about escaping from the previous oppressive culture and never returning! In short, because that very culture was still delivering leads in a market where they had all but dried up at their new offices where they were, to a degree, on their own. The previous employer was able to entice them back by demonstrating they could still offer listing opportunities in a tough market via the next set of underlings below them being put through the treadmill. They could find the initial leads with their hard graft, and these could be fed up the chain to the now, more highly regarded and experienced senior agents (as they would be on their return). Reality bites, and this became a proposition that might just pay the bills and keep the all-important profile alive and well.

Despite the recent challenges, I have happily remained on the more independent route, resisting any temptation to return to the franchise office arena and dine on handouts. Eyes wide open, knowing that any chance of freebies is extremely limited. At times it is tough work, and my volume numbers would be consistently lower than some others, who I genuinely don't believe are better agents, but simply have sucked it up and taken a different approach in difficult times. It suits me, I have a reasonable repeat and referral rate and I am happy not having to be a constant yes-man, whilst appreciating true value in my listings. It encourages me to foster good relationships to retain customers and business, rather than take anything for granted.

Ultimately there is no right or wrong solution for how you set up shop to get your leads and (other than by a few disgruntled colleagues) most people will not question your methods or sources. Just a little more transparency at times would be nice, but hey, this is real estate!

21 | Do Not Disturb

As the saying goes, *there is just no getting through to some people*. Absolutely, and in real estate terms that is when they have 'Do Not Call' phone numbers, 'No Junk Mail' on the letterbox and 'No Salespeople' stickers on the door! Yes, many of us, it would appear, just want to be left alone and not harassed in any way, shape or form. Fair enough I say, after all I am much the same!

This trend is growing in the digital age where more and more things can now be done online (buy a car, sell a car, arrange a loan, get insurance, etc.,) without the need to have those awkward conversations and interactions with real people. Fewer of us want to engage face-to-face and, crucially, with our busy lives many people only want to communicate at the point of requirement, not in some seemingly pointless chit-chat months or even years before they may have a specific need.

Trouble is, however, that at some point in the future these very same people will still want to sell their house and will need to select an agent. We all know this, so how do you get yourself in front of these people and in their heads when you cannot use the usual methods? Well, easy for some, just completely disrespect their *quaint* preferences and bombard them in exactly the same way as everyone else! Once again, another moral dilemma presents itself. Do you hound people regardless of what they have indicated, or do you respect their wishes and try other less intrusive avenues?

The problem here is what you are really trying to achieve ... and how you frame it in your own mind. For example, you drop 1,000 flyers out to homes in an area, 300 of which have 'no junk mail' signs (which you ignore and drop anyway). The quick and dirty agent will point out if you drop enough 'No Junk Mail' boxes regardless, *eventually* you will get one of these suckers who will respond because they just happened to be thinking about selling. And although you are annoying, you are also convenient at that precise moment in time. This one potential outcome then completely justifies the method, from their perspective.

In this same scenario, the more cautious and respectful agent may well have a greater concern with all the others that were dropped and *didn't* reply (and who are now pissed off because your office keeps ignoring their 'No Junk Mail' sign!). In short, you may have caused brand damage in 299 other homes to chase one *possible* outcome in another. Glass half empty or half full? Okay, so where does management stand on such a dilemma you may ask? Easy, if it potentially results in some business, turn a complete blind eye—indeed, unofficially encourage—but if it only results in a serious complaint, be seen to superficially throw the offending agent under the bus for not following non-existent 'company' guidelines. Plausible deniability, always. Believe me, I have seen this scenario played out a few times with lively debate as to who is in the right, with both sides of the argument justifying their stance. 'Strong' but uncaring versus 'weak' but respectful.

Cold calling 'Do Not Call' numbers employs exactly the same logic depending on your viewpoint. "Where did you get my number?" asks the irate owner, "Err, you are on our database," comes the generic fob-off answer (where 'database' means a list of downloaded numbers you obtained without the individual's consent from an internal real estate industry source or purchased from a direct marketing company). Better still, "I did an appraisal for you a long while back and I'm just catching up," even when you didn't!! Now you may think that is terrible, but I have seen it used—and work—on more than one occasion! Human nature is a funny thing, put some people on the spot and if they cannot remember (because it didn't happen!) they may still go along with it, nonetheless, not to offend just in case it did happen, and they might have simply forgotten. Fairly high-risk strategy, but the agent conducting it will have the sort of personality that will not care how many people call them out or complain in the meantime. It's just collateral damage whilst finding the next dumb punter.

Some will even wear such conflict as a badge of honour. If management gets an isolated call from a disgruntled owner about unsolicited contact—or much better still a competing agent complains about their existing vendor being tapped up— then this can be seen a positive sign of someone 'doing their job'. Of course, depends on what that job definition is: getting new business or increasing reputational risk! This may even be highlighted to the rest of the underperforming blob at the next sales meeting as an example of tenacity and dedication to the task in hand. At least until the complaints become more intense and sustained, then we are all told to mind what we are doing, as the red double decker starts heading towards the offender at some speed.

It is a little like a sports team, when they are winning fewer questions are asked of management techniques and, indeed, any cracks are easily papered over. If the results stop coming, however, and a poor spell is encountered the coach starts to feel the pressure with divisions and questions quickly following. In short, if the listings are flowing in and you are the flavour of the month, then all methods are acceptable!

It is a genuine predicament. To ignore this increasingly large section of potential customers is certainly not good business, nor equally (in my opinion) is getting a reputation as a pushy agent who blatantly disregards people's wishes. What is the solution? Well, apart from the *ignorance is bliss* approach, increasing 'attraction' business potential is probably the key. In simple terms if you cannot directly contact these people in the first instance, you need to make sure—when they do come to consider their real estate needs—there is a good chance they will contact you through general awareness of your brand and reputation in their local area.

This is where a strategy of comprehensive agent/office/brand advertising comes into play. Importantly this must be concentrated in your target area, but can take several forms, for example, billboards, bus stops, and buses themselves, company car branding, sponsorship of local organisations, and pages in local free magazines and papers. All of these methods effectively bypass direct contact whilst still placing the brand in the line of sight, albeit passively. It may sound obvious, but success also breeds success. If you have a good number of listings already in an area, then those numerous 'For Sale' boards will act as a valuable additional advertising channel. Assuming most progress to receiving a big red SOLD sticker on them, this also subconsciously signals achievement and an agent/agency that gets results.

Many of the newer, independent and boutique agencies have chosen bright and unusual colour schemes. This is very much by design, not by accident. A purple or pink sign will stand out from a distance and, if it becomes associated with a certain brand, then signage can be enormously powerful. On the other hand, using yellow as a brand colour might be less effective, as it's already associated with a couple of major franchises. Digital suburb presence is also possible, at a price, by securing the advertising banners available on the real estate portals for a specific location. Every time someone searches for properties within that area, up pops your name or company logo at the side or top of the screen, slowly but surely reinforcing your continual presence.

Sorted then? Well, that probably depends on whether you go 'all in' or not. The biggest downfall with attraction advertising is simply not doing enough of it. People's attention span and memories are limited, so for such advertising to work it must be constant, consistent, and thorough. For those who follow their Formula 1 or V8s (and apologies to those who don't, who will now be bored rigid by this analogy!) it is similar to going out with cold tyres and brakes. You must go hard to bring them up to operating temperatures when initially there is little or no responsiveness. It is, therefore, an act of faith to push through on the edge and to gain the performance window required. Drive too cautiously and you never obtain the temperatures you need, and the car will remain uncompetitive and difficult to handle.

Good attraction advertising is no different. You must have belief and go hard from the start—typically without immediate return—until the brand awareness is fully established. If you try a too conservative approach (usually budget driven) and only do selected things here and there you will never get 'up to speed' within the public consciousness. The most successful offices spend a substantial amount of money on attraction marketing, but the rewards are considerable if you get it right with a succession of people—including many of our target 'do not disturb' brigade—presenting themselves to you, unsolicited. Unfortunately, with smaller offices it is all too easy for them to try one thing (perhaps a local sponsorship or the like) not gain much traction from it in isolation, and then be hesitant to commit further big sums in this area, instead putting it back on the blob to follow up the cheap and cheerless activities of cold calling and door knocking, etc.

Providing open access opportunities for public contact without obligation is also important. Participation in local fetes or school carnivals with a stall is a popular idea. This can work well, but it is essential the primary reason for participation is not overtly real estate related. Consider a sausage sizzle, charity raffle or free goodie bags, and so on, as this allows those of a more guarded nature to decide in their own minds whether to approach and ask about any property matters in a more relaxed and less confrontational environment.

Likewise, professionalism and good presentation around open homes is paramount. Not that you tell the seller, but open homes are also a vital listing tool where you can showcase both you and your brand to potential new clients. Yes, they increase the foot traffic and exposure of the house you are selling, but equally you are conducting them to increase your own exposure and gain future contacts. Again, a cautious would-be seller can come along under the pretence of being a buyer—and they do!—and make an initial judgement on you and how you act before showing their hand as a possible vendor. They can see how you present and run an open home (as you would do for their own home).

The guideline is: always put as much information (brochures, market guides, flyers, etc.,) out on the kitchen bench as possible and create a sense of comprehensive service. Another benefit here is, because of their attendance, you will have *legitimately* captured their contact details (unless they outright lie) and can add them to your *real* database now! You also have a valid reason to call them now for feedback on the open home, with the inevitable follow-up questions about their current situation and if they are looking to sell in the future.

Some savvy agents/agencies have also created online appraisal portals that mimic those of the lead generation companies. Typically, these will be deliberately de-branded (don't show your hand yet!) and have some generic snappy title instead, such as *WhatsMyDogboxWorth.com.au*, etc.,—you get the idea. The more reserved out there may use such online sites to get an initial price indication, without the stress of speaking directly to an agent. After all, if it is online-only, and not an obvious agency, where's the harm? None ... unless the moment they submitted their details—expecting a nice, automated report back—they instead got some loud, overbearing joker on the phone trying to immediately list their house.

I have been involved with the creation of a couple sites of this nature and, fundamentally, I don't have a problem with the concept, it is how you deal with the request professionally (or not) that is the problem. If you advertise an online appraisal service then (in my opinion) that's what you must provide, not a trap to simply gain direct contact information with which to then harass the sender, without providing any value-add upfront. On the websites I was involved with, we observed a strict process whereby an initial desktop appraisal in PDF format was produced and emailed back to the recipient. We then simply offered a

SOLD On The Dream

follow up call service if required ('Soft!' I can immediately hear some battle-hardened veterans shouting). Perhaps, but I believe it comes back to trust. The public don't need any encouragement to think agents are deceitful, so if their first contact with you is via a disguised website, that hasn't delivered what it promised, it's probably not a good starting point! Equally, if you do what you say, then potentially a better chance of further communication when some degree of faith is established.

Does it work? I have certainly seen a couple of prime examples of local agencies adopting strong self-marketing techniques and substantially increasing business as a result. A few years back an existing operation in my old patch, that had been around for a considerable time as an owner-operated husband and wife team, was bought out by a new principal/owner, when they decided to retire. The office was in a good spot and had survived well enough, but had never been overly dynamic in its approach or marketing. Despite being a respected name locally, it had a reasonably modest market share given its location and potential client base of surrounding upmarket homes.

The new principal retained the underlying positives of an existing office building and agency name, but set about changing everything else. New, very distinctive (both in unique colour choice and styling) company branding, securing of 'banner' advertising for the suburb on a well-known real estate portal, local school sponsorship, and the acquisition of a couple of additional local agents with a good track record, amongst others. Offering more flexible listing packages as an independent, the combination of all these factors lead to a sharp increase in listings and sales to the point of them becoming the lead agency in the suburb within a number of months. Same office, same name, but with a complete refresh and full commitment to self-marketing. That initial year would have required a substantial investment (and faith in the outcome), but once brand perception and profile was raised, so the attraction business started to roll in.

In the suburb where I live there is another local agency, this time a recognised franchise with a reasonable market share already, that decided to go on the offensive, nonetheless. Having, perhaps, a little more resources to start with they didn't change the branding (as a franchise, they couldn't!), but instead made sure the brand was everywhere. A full fleet of local buses were all wrapped in company colours. Some were generic in design with general office advertising, and some with specific agents— even the property managers got a shout out. Quite costly, but very clever as by opting to go on multiple vehicles—many of which only operated short diagrams within the suburb—it was almost impossible not to see at least one of these mobile billboards every single time you went out on the road.

Again, they took out all the main banners for the suburb on a well-known real estate portal and ensured they had two to three pages of advertising every week in the local full-colour free magazine distributed to every house. This was in addition to extensive—professionally printed—flyer drops. They already had a sizeable rent roll, but also purchased another large chunk of properties under property management from a former rival who had traction in the area, but was now closing down. The monthly overhead for all this must have been colossal, but then again so were their results.

This coincided with the rise of the COVID-19 market, so the advertising could accentuate every record price, and every auction success in a blitz of feel-good public relations. Now this was all real information, so no problem there. Of course, the market conditions were helping these results, which some other agents/agencies may have also been achieving too, but didn't have the same platform by which to broadcast it. Hence, perfect timing to appear as *the* agency of the suburb, that was simply unstoppable and was consistently achieving extraordinary outcomes. Get this right and attraction momentum takes over.

Would-be sellers (critically including those in hiding thus far) were now all thinking to themselves, *'These guys are the ones to contact. They are killing it and are attaining excellent prices'.* It was impressive to watch, as this company became the *de facto* choice for most in the suburb. One of their young agents was propelled along on this tidal wave and became heavily in-demand. Perhaps in other circumstances his quite youthful experience and appearance would have put some off, but when the cultivated persona of constant superior monetary outcomes surrounds you, then nobody questions it. I totally congratulate him and his principal/agency because they took a big leap of faith, but by sticking to the process the influx of business came. Everyone wanted *their* sign at the front of their home when selling, as a badge of aspiration that their property was worth the best guys in town being on the case. Once people are calling you, unsolicited, as their number one—and probably only— choice, things get a whole lot easier!

Hence, there are ways to engage and tease out these reserved and elusive creatures when the time is right, but it tends to be by playing the longer game with financial resources to match. For those who cannot or will not wait, then as you were. Just dive in regardless, take the flak, and hope for the best!

22 | CAMPFIRE TALES

nevitably, working in this diverse industry (and with the public) for many years leads to some very interesting situations and meeting some unique people! It would be remiss of me not to recount a few of the more memorable 'happenings' witnessed throughout my career. Names and locations are, of course, removed to protect the innocent (or unhinged!).

In fairness, the first instance of unhinged might refer to me! Now I am a rational person, but I had one experience a few years back that somewhat spooked me. It is very rare and very sad, but we had an instance of one property with a sales contract in place where the buyer unfortunately passed away during the finalisation of the purchase process. The house had to go back on the market and, by now, was vacant (the owner having moved out in anticipation of the original contract conclusion). It was my colleague's listing, but she felt uneasy being in the house after the circumstances of her original buyer.

This was understandable and I freely offered to conduct the subsequent open homes for her in the empty house myself. The house was relatively isolated, being a seven-acre rural property. On my first Saturday as stand-in, I arrived at the house and set up in the now bare interior. It was an attractive, elevated, timber home with wide wrap-around verandas. Being morning, the day was warming up and this had a tendency for the structure to start making noises. With no punters on the scene, in this empty house things started to get a little strange. Okay, I thought, great shame about the original buyer, but nothing to see here now. *Yes,* those noises *do* bizarrely sound just like footsteps, but I know the walls and roof are just expanding with the temperature increase and heat of the direct sun, perfectly explainable (despite a slightly increased heart rate!). All good, I walked through the house a couple of times, steadied myself, no one here just natural physics on display.

Thus, things remained calm for another five minutes or so until suddenly BANG, BANG, BANG! This abrupt and deafening noise emanated from what appeared to be the main bedroom. I was momentarily frozen. This wasn't any expansion, nor was there anyone here except me. Was I going mad? BANG, BANG, BANG! Loud, unmistakable, and with a force and intermittent regularity that wasn't structural. My mind was racing ... BANG, BANG, BANG, BANG! There was no option but to investigate this unearthly noise, as surely there was a simple explanation *(or was the previous buyer now troubled by our attempts to resell the house he had already secured?).*

I edged along the hallway towards the main bedroom (yes edged, I admit it!) as the sound grew louder and more violent. I lingered slightly at the door and put my head around the corner, not sure what I was expecting to see! There, on the veranda directly outside the full-length picture window of the bedroom was the biggest black crow I had ever seen. It could see its reflection in the window, and it was hitting the glass with its large powerful beak in an uncontrolled show of aggression (I assume thinking it was another hostile bird). I went up to the window and it eventually backed off. I was relieved I had found the source of the noise and *it was only a bird.* How foolish, fancy being worried?! It was only back at the office when I relayed this tale to my somewhat freaked out colleague, we then started pondering the symbolism of a black crow wanting to enter the house. Perhaps her buyer was still wishing to take up residence after all.

Another sad, but inevitable, situation we deal with quite regularly are sales related to separations or divorce. The hope is always that these can still be executed amenably by both parties. In some positive instances this is indeed the case, but in many others there is suspicion, non-co-operation, and a great deal of heartache. Unfortunately, as agents we are often in the middle of the battleground, while just trying to pursue a fair and reasonable outcome for all parties.

I had one interesting episode of a property being sold with the ex-wife still residing in the home, while the ex-husband had since moved out. There was no formal ruling around this, plus the ex-husband still had possessions in the property, and had returned there on numerous occasions. As things progressed, however, the situation became acrimonious, and the ex-wife started refusing entry to the ex-husband (who by now had no keys to the home, himself). When the property was listed—and circumstances were slightly better—we were given his spare keys for access, and both parties signed the paperwork as the joint legal owners of the house (with no restrictions).

And so the scene was set, as one morning we took a call at the office from the lady saying her ex-husband was trying to gain entry to the house and was being threatening. She had refused him access and he was now coming to our office to demand the spare keys back, so he could get in. She was distressed and asked for us not to release them to him. This created a dilemma. He was also the legal owner of the house, and they were as much his keys as hers, so we had no formal authority to withhold them if he requested them back.

However, we also had a duty of care to our client, and after consulting with one of my colleagues we both decided there were fair and reasonable circumstances to withhold the keys. We based this on a perceived potential danger to a lone female in the house. Minutes later the ex-husband appeared at reception, and I had to try to explain to him face-to-face we were not releasing the keys to his own house. He was already fired up, so needless to say, things got interesting. He accused us of taking sides and breaking the law (this would prove a little ironic later). He said his ex-wife was trying to sell off items he owned without permission, and he simply wanted to retrieve them (perhaps this was true, as there are always two sides to an argument).

Nonetheless, I explained we had concerns for everyone's security at this stage and advised if he called his ex-wife and had further (calm) conversations, we would release the keys *only* if she instructed us to do so. At this point the gentleman informed me that if I wasn't letting him in, he would take matters into his own hands and find a way in. With that he left. That's most likely that, we thought.

A few hours later the ex-wife called and updated us on subsequent events. True to his word the ex-husband had returned to the house, climbed on the roof and started unscrewing the Colorbond panels above the garage to gain access via the roof and loft space! Wow! On seeing this unfolding drama the ex-wife had called the police, who duly arrived and took him away for a chat! Now, the *real* kicker to this story is at this stage the house was already sold (unconditional contract) and the wife was in the process of moving out for settlement, hence, she *was* selling things off.

Problem was that the people buying it were currently tenants living in a rental house across the street. They liked the location so much they decided to buy in the same spot when this house came up for sale. The one time this had to happen was the one time when our buyers coincidently had front row seats to their newly acquired home being 'deconstructed' in front of their eyes, not to mention the cops arriving and putting on a show!

I digress a little, but whilst on the subject of police intervention, the best ever 'bust' I can remember befell an unfortunate colleague of mine. He had an acreage for sale with a slightly interesting owner (however, ours is not to reason why—just to list and sell). It was in a prime location for future subdivision and had an existing house and large shed on the property. Nothing too unusual there, and my colleague took the property on in good faith, hoping to get a developer interested in the potential to create smaller residential lots. The owner wanted top dollar because of this, of course, and so the listing sat for a while.

One morning another of my colleagues was heading into the office and passed the property only to see multiple police cars on site, sniffer dogs and all manner of activity going on. When he arrived, he asked my colleague who had the listing what on earth was going on. He wasn't even aware! We all joked it must be a drug bust (well, that wasn't the half!). My colleague made some calls and tried to find out what was happening. Didn't have to wait long, just switch on the TV and look at the news! In fact, this unassuming acreage could well have been the prototype for Mr White in Breaking Bad, with a fully kitted out underground meth lab discovered beneath the shed! We were dumbfounded on many levels!

Firstly, that it existed in the first place and was actually 'a thing', and secondly, how on earth the owner was seriously trying to sell the property with this still in place!! Would have made interesting reading on the buyer's building and pest report: 'No termites in the shed, probably due to the chemicals already present below'. Needless to say, my poor colleague was given plenty of stick along the lines of, *You need to update the marketing to include the additional underground storage facility and viable ongoing home business, etc.*

Returning back to the arena of separations, I had a very different experience with one property that wasn't to do with threats or issues of access, but clever, concealed calculation and planning. The property in question was another acreage in quite a nice rural setting with rolling countryside around, and numerous sheds and pens for animals. The owning couple had split, but the gentleman was still living at the house. The ex-partner had moved out and she was living some distance away. It had already been on the market for a while when I took over and the pricing was a little high for the condition and size of the main residence.

That said, it had a lot of character, and I was happy to take it on and refresh the marketing with new photos, new write up, and the potential of some open homes. The owner was helpful—and seemingly keen—but a little cagey about inspections and what people could see (he wanted some sheds off limits for initial inspections, etc.). Quite often after inspections we would have a good chat, right the wrongs of the world, and it felt like it was a good client relationship. At the same time, I kept in contact with his ex-partner and fully updated her on inspections, buyer feedback, and so on. It was quite a specialist property and it did take a fair amount of time to get the pricing right and then locate a buyer.

But I persisted and finally we got a lovely couple looking for some rural peace and quiet with the option to keep a few hobby animals—perfect! Or so I thought, as there was a back story I was not privy to. The gentleman had tried to buy out his ex-partner at the beginning of the process, as he didn't want to move at all. However, he was not prepared to pay the initial figure the ex-partner wanted to 'walk away', and it went to market instead. Ultimately it still had to be sold for a financial settlement between the two.

The ex-partner was much happier to sell it this way and ultimately to accept a fairly determined 'market' figure. This still took some negotiations amongst all parties, but eventually we got to an agreed figure, albeit somewhat lower than their original intentions. The buyers had signed a formal offer up front, but subsequent negotiations had been verbal between all parties due to the diverse locations. Final agreement was reached on a Friday afternoon, and I verbally confirmed to the emotional and excited buyers we now had an accepted figure. The property was effectively theirs, pending the owners' signatures to formalise everything. Both owners were happy enough, having confirmed agreement over the phone.

The gentleman asked that his ex-partner sign the paperwork first (as she was remotely located) and then he would sign straight afterwards. With time always being of the essence I arranged to meet the lady on the Saturday morning, and she duly signed her side as the seller. As things turned out, this was to be the high point! I called the other owner at the house, expecting to drop around and grab the final signature Saturday afternoon. After a couple of unanswered calls, I finally got hold of him. I confirmed everyone else had now signed, just waiting on his contribution and we were good to go. He advised he was 'busy' on that afternoon and away from the house (in hindsight, red flag number one!), so could I email it over instead (red flag number two!) and he would get it back to me on Sunday.

I duly dispatched the paperwork by email, updated the buyers on progress and felt confident we would have the formal contract locked down on Sunday. Well, Sunday dragged on, no email, no call. At this point I started to get a bit anxious, *'Does he want to sell this damn place, or what?'* I thought to myself (ironically not knowing the real answer to that, as outlined above). I called a couple of times, no answer. Sent another email, no reply. Sunday rolled into Monday morning and by now, back at the office, I was really getting concerned. I made more calls, still no answer. I called the ex-partner to see if she knew anything more, no answer.

I could find no explanation for the lack of communication, but knew something needed to be resolved quickly as the buyers were still, to all intents, essentially 'hanging', despite assuming the property was already theirs. (And having had the whole weekend to get used to this idea and excitedly tell all their friends, no doubt!) I determined I would need to go to the property and see if I could track him down in person. Monday mornings are always busy in real estate, so I scheduled to do this at lunchtime (really hoping I would still have an outcome before that point). Late morning, I finally got a call back. Joy! Well ... not, as it happened.

This was the ex-partner calling. She was both upset and very apologetic. Then it all started to fall horribly into place. The gentleman (this term becomes more difficult to use as this story goes on!) had gone to his family law solicitor first thing Monday morning with the partially-signed contract I had emailed him on Saturday, deliberately ignoring me in the interim. He never had any intention of signing, but wanted written evidence of the figure she would *now* accept to sell the property—albeit not to him—which was of course lower than her original buyout figure. Deduct from this the agent's commission (as I was charging for the sale) and the net figure was lower still so, bingo, there was the real figure for a buyout.

I was not privy to what legal agreements they had pre-existing, but it appears her solicitor advised he was in a position to force her to sell to him (as first refusal) at the figure she had now agreed for the third-party sale. Boom! The whole process right from the beginning, of going to the market and then, with the unsuspecting agent's help, pushing the price down (which he was always keener to do than her, in order to 'sell it' on the market—oh dear, red flag number three!) was a complete smoke screen. It was devised simply in order to get a lower figure that she would unwittingly commit to, which he could immediately use to force through a buyout. He was never intending to sell to anyone else and just needed some dumb shmuck agent to inadvertently help him engineer the plan!

The lady herself seemed genuinely distressed at this turn of events, both because she didn't want him to remain in the house and she knew how much effort I had put in. Also, she realised we had 'sold' the house to someone already. I admit I find it hard to believe she didn't have some inkling this could happen, but at least she had the decency to contact me and explain everything.

Any initial anger and self-pity I had was soon overtaken by the dawning reality of now having to phone the buyers and advise them their dream home, all agreed on Friday, was now lost. We have to make plenty of calls letting buyers know they are unsuccessful (multiple offers or simply rejection of a final offer, etc.,) but this was different, and it was one of the hardest calls I have ever had to make. The wife was very upset and started crying on the phone, and I could offer little in consolation other than explaining that, unfortunately, nothing is legally locked in until all parties have signed off—even if all have verbally agreed. I offered—more in sympathy than hope—to try and find them a similar property (but never managed to match what had been on offer and eventually they did move on to other things).

Once the pain of that call and conversation was over, then my own feelings kicked in. I am not sure what hurt me the most, having to let down genuine buyers because someone else was deceitful, or just being used in such a cold, calculated manner to ensure a contract with a suitable price and her signature was delivered for his use elsewhere. To go from friendly conversations and banter one day to complete blanking once the requirement was achieved was unbelievable. I could have tried to pursue things further, but (as you quickly learn in real estate) what's the point? To this day I have never spoken to him again. Take out? Verbal agreements count for nothing and if you think *only* agents are deceptive, think again, once more!

Sometimes things can take quite a surprising turn, when least expected. Once, when rolling up for my first open home at a new listing, the owner warned me to look out for a man pretending to be a kangaroo! He was well known, locally, to turn up at open inspections and generally cause a bit of a nuisance. The owner preferred he did not come into the house, and he be turned away. Whilst acknowledging this somewhat unusual request, I have to say I was secretly a little bemused. I was thinking this was, perhaps, very unlikely and that the owner was being overanxious, possibly based more on an urban myth than fact. Famous last words!

As I settled down for my 30-minute stint, this gentleman appeared and approached from the road. He was decked out in safari-type clothing, a little along the lines of a Steve Irwin, but *'Everyone to their own,'* I thought. However, upon reaching the driveway he then proceeded to hop towards the house! Well, well, this is our man then—no myth! Kangaroo Man (as I immediately felt it fitting to call him) bounced all the way up to me and asked to come in. Again a slight dilemma, technically he had done nothing wrong at this point—and it was an *open* home—but I had been warned and it appeared he had 'previous form'. So, having given my assurance to the owner not five minutes before, I had to turn him away.

As some other buyers had by now also appeared behind him the trick was to do this without causing a scene. "So," I said, "Are you looking to buy today, because the owner's specific instructions for this property are they only want inspections conducted internally by people ready and serious to buy." At this point he saw through my thinly veiled put-off. "I just want to have an initial look; it is an *open* home." The conversation went backwards and forwards along these lines for a while. "You're not going to let me in then?" *Well, no, as we actually have a general policy not to let marsupials in unless by prior appointment!* He finally got the message and backed off, as I started dealing with other people.

However, rather than withdraw completely, he decided the front yard area was a perfect spot to just hop around in for a while! Needless to say, there were a few strange looks as I tried to marshal other people into the house quickly. Eccentric and harmless, rather than intimidating. I must admit I found him somewhat entertaining and amusing ... perhaps just not when trying to sell a house to make ends meet! Eventually he got bored and bounded off, without time for a psychological evaluation (of him or me!) and things returned to normality, dealing only with randoms of a human declaration!

I had another property once where the tenant would never leave while inspections or open homes were taking place. And despite politely informing him to keep out of the way, he would still try and engage with any buyers and talk them to death, as if he owned the place himself. He was a nice enough guy, but he wanted to know their business, and most buyers just want to be left in peace when inspecting, and certainly don't want to deal with the tenant. Regardless, things progressed along, and we ended up with a couple looking to purchase and live in the property. The tenant was on a flexible periodic lease so would be given an appropriate notice to vacate before they moved in.

The buyers had undertaken a couple of inspections before deciding on the property, and both times the 'helpful' tenant was there giving them advice and his view of world. When it came time for their building and pest inspection they asked me if, perhaps, I could kindly get the tenant(s) to leave while this was on, just so they could go around with the inspector in peace. After some persuading, I managed to convince the tenants to do so, and they indicated they would go to his parents' house, who lived in the next street over (one of the reasons they had chosen this house to rent in the first place).

Now, this is where it is always good to check the detail and work out your worst-case scenario in advance! As the inspection was unfolding, the buyers were out the back with me and commented that (in all honesty) it was a relief not having the tenant there wanting to be their friend and know all about their particulars. "Well," I remarked, "if all goes to plan your side, they will vacate shortly, and you won't need to deal with them again". Of course, with almost perfect theatrical timing, no sooner had I said this than the very same tenant popped his head up over the fence at the bottom of the yard and shouted, "Hello guys, any problems so far?"

Surprise! Yes, it turned out his parent's house was *right behind* the rental! Begrudgingly acknowledging him, the buyers both looked at me with furrowed brow. "What is the tenant doing in *that* house?". At this point I tried to think of a plausible explanation that didn't suggest they were lumbered with him on the fence line forever, but just had to wave the white flag, as I had nothing! "Err, I think that's his parent's house, perhaps, it is around here somewhere, I believe," I mumbled, half hoping they wouldn't hear me. "You mean he's going to be right behind us when we move in?!" they replied with some concern. "Oh no, I'm sure they will be moving to another rental elsewhere and just *occasionally* visit the parents," thinking *'I have no idea, but please God, be true'*. Turns out, luckily, it was true, and they did indeed rent some distance away. Although I am sure there were more instances of attempted over-the-fence banter on their (quite regular) trips to the parents' place!

Tenants are always good value, particularly on stock runs, as often—despite being advised—they completely forget that a bunch of agents are turning up to look at the property. This has led to finding couples still in bed, caught having some

267

(interrupted) fun! Others, thinking there was a drug bust going down, had various shady characters exiting the rear of the property and ducking for cover on our arrival, accompanied by much frantic flushing of toilets! Others are the reverse and carry on obliviously as if nobody is there. It's quite surreal walking through the middle of a household as if you were a fly-on-the-wall camera observing exciting social dysfunction or an episode of *Extreme Hoarders*.

I could go on, but perhaps it's time to give my fellow professionals the stage. It is not always the public that provide the all the entertainment, as plenty of agents can also add to the merriment.

23 | DANGEROUS LIAISONS

A t last, I hear you say, this is what we have been waiting for! Dish the dirt! Proof agents are a shoddy bunch. Well, I never said there weren't some, just not the majority (and, as already seen, balanced out by equally dubious clients). For ease of reference, I would say we can group things at this point into a few generic categories and repeat offences. The 'office *romantics'*—and that is terming things *very* graciously— the 'loose cannons' and the 'outright deceptive'!

As with any workplace, we spend a considerable amount of time with our colleagues. Throw into this mix ego, ambition, adrenaline and the relatively close proximity of other agents in a (for the most part) relatively unscrutinised daily structure and there is the basis for a few to go astray. Now again, I would say this only reflects on the innate personality traits of these individuals to start with. I am not suggesting there is some unavoidable moral decay for anyone who happens to choose this line of work.

Simply, the environment is a good catalyst for those of a slightly less virtuous nature. After all, nothing like a conveniently vacant house you have keys for that needs to be 'inspected' by two *very friendly* agents at the same time … just saying. Late night *unavoidable* contract signings, overly boozy awards evenings (with associated hotel stays) and other equally alcohol-laden social events, are all perfect opportunities for those so inclined to fly under the radar away from home, with some extra action.

Much of course is a nod and a wink, you hear the inevitable stories and hints, but there is little proof. Nonetheless these things do happen and perhaps more often than in some other lines of work. You might think the empty house reference is a bit of a clichéd suggestion, but I know of a least one competition agent who had a bit of a reputation for unnecessary house visits when out with certain female colleagues.

Interestingly, on one occasion I found myself in direct competition with him on a possible listing. It was a deceased estate and the son had asked three local agents to attend at the same time to view the property while he was there, and then provide appraisals for his consideration. Simultaneous agent viewings are never great and somewhat awkward for all involved. But a listing is a listing so you suck it up, go along and be outwardly courteous to the opposition (at least in the presence of the would-be seller anyway).

Two of us duly turned up on time and looked through the house. We both talked with the owner and things were amicable enough. He then remarked that a third agent had been due to attend but hadn't turned up. As we were finishing, the offending agent pulled up outside (a little flustered, realising he still had an audience) running some 20 minutes late, for no apparent reason. Needless to say, he had brought a female colleague along with him, again for no apparent reason. They were not a team, and he was certainly experienced enough to do the appraisal by himself. Now I may have put two and two together and made five, but it certainly fitted the profile!

Alright, that is still circumstantial at best, you want something more substantial, right? There a few good stories I have heard over the years including a discarded company tie being sent back in the post by a rival agent, allegedly left behind after a late-night liaison (which was subsequently admitted to by the offender on account of exhibit 'A'). Then there was the bombshell email sent to all the staff in one office from the partner of an offender on finding out about his *extra relations* with one of the sales team, outing them both 'live'!

There are many other 'who went home with whom' anecdotes, but the most startling realisation of an ongoing situation occurred openly in one of my past offices. We had employed a new agent from a local rival. He was a smooth operator, for sure, and had won over our principal with his spin, and promised much. He was also player, however, both workwise and with the opposite sex. Around the same time we had also taken on another female sales agent, who was relatively young, and (speaking dispassionately of course) quite attractive. We already had a similarly styled receptionist, and so the game was afoot.

Which one would our new 'slick' covertly turn his attentions to first in the hope of a clandestine liaison? Wrong question, as it turns out. Silly me, clearly *both* simultaneously—but without the other's knowledge—so the real question was, *how long before that powder keg would blow up in his face?* Juggling (it would appear) after-work trysts with one, and lunchtime rendezvous with the other, went on for a while. A shame he didn't put that much energy into prospecting for homes! But it was doomed to fail and so it did, in a very public manner! Returning from another lunchtime *missing in action*, that coincided with the receptionist's lunch break (who was now going home for lunch) it appears some barbed comment was initially fired off from the other member of the triangle. I assume the penny had finally dropped.

Whether this was meant to lead to some sort of discreet discussion I do not know, but quite the opposite transpired. It seems there was some sort of less than helpful response and before anyone quite knew what was happening there was a full-on emotional showdown happening in the main office! The female agent was terribly upset, accusing him of lying and being a rat, etc. He tried to defend himself in return, and suggested he wouldn't put up with this public intimidation. It was very raw and clearly there was some genuine hurt involved. Nonetheless, he cleverly threw it open and declared if 'nobody' trusted him, he would walk.

In hindsight that is exactly what we should have let him do, but the rest of us—including the principal—were somewhat reeling and not up to speed. So, the strategy was more to calm everyone down, separate them, and try to establish exactly what was happening. Subsequently things were diffused (to a degree) but the damage was done. There were promises on all sides to avoid further confrontations and that such 'activities' would stop as they were a clear conflict of interest. An uneasy—and frankly unworkable—truce descended for a short while, but within a couple of weeks the instigator had left, his position effectively untenable.

Now the story doesn't quite end there. As I said, he was a smooth operator and it turns out whilst he had been at our office, he had systematically ingratiated himself with the corporate team from head office and convinced them he was their man to open a new franchise office they were planning, in an adjacent suburb. He appeared to have gained a mysterious financial backer (sugar mummy, most certainly)! And, as money talks, despite the red flags that should have been heeded from the circumstances of his previous departure, he duly became principal of the new office, which opened in a flurry of optimistic marketing. Don't worry, it gets better!

In this relentlessly incestuous industry, who were his first two recruits? Yep, you guessed it, his ladies from the little *ménage à trois*! Both handed in their notice at our office and went to work with him. Now that is some recovery! Give the man some credit for how he pulled that off with *both* of them! None of us could quite believe it and we couldn't see how this could possibly work, or last, in the long term. Well, it didn't, the office folded not much more than six months after it was launched. I can only imagine the internal dramas that may have contributed to that, but it was an ego trip and ultimately you cannot fake it forever. The office simply didn't generate anywhere near enough business because the balance and team setup was completely wrong, and the principal's motivation deeply floored. Ultimately, it appears, justice was served!

It is not just inappropriate relationships that can lead to problems. Trust is at the core of effectively running your own business-within-a-business. Company guidelines are clearly laid out on commencement and the Code of Conduct (theoretically) already well known. Yet there are many hours each week where you are left to your own devices and are required to police yourself. How you deal with the public and treat your teammates internally can have a big impact on the office. Trouble is you are often trying to create business in any way possible to survive, whilst still under the umbrella of an established brand. Most get this and behave appropriately, that is, not bringing the bigger business (that you represent) into disrepute through poor behaviour.

Again, it's down to personalities, but some will ignore convention, take risks, and do whatever they think necessary regardless of potential fallout. For a principal this can be difficult, as rash or impulsive actions may only come to light after the event when damage may have already been done. That said, most in this category are serial wrongdoers, so a pattern does start to emerge. What are we talking about here then? Well, take your pick really. Lazy and inaccurate completion of formal paperwork (leading to possible legal ramifications), overly coercive behaviour towards potential clients, defamation or interference with other agent's activities, and lack of teamwork or shared responsibilities with colleagues, to name a few!

I have personally witnessed many poorly executed documents, and heard conversations on the telephone that are clearly untrue or highly exaggerated in order to gain business. Agents deliberately missing floor duty on a regular basis or not attending sales meetings on some flimsy pretext (*only* time they could do a *critical* appraisal—yeah, sure). I have known of several agents who might go directly against the Code of Conduct and specifically undermine the reputation of competition agents and companies with misleading or untrue statements just to better position themselves. In addition to our office Romeo from earlier (who will reappear before this chapter is done!) I can think of a couple of other erstwhile colleagues over the years who pushed the boundaries until it eventually caught up with them.

The first guy just did his own thing and, for the most part, couldn't be bothered with floor duty, regularly leaving other colleagues in the lurch. He was very direct and would sign jump anything and everything without any concerns or regards for consequences (as this was less time consuming than otherwise boring prospecting!). Another 'two days on and three days off' merchant who survived by doing just enough in those two days to warrant being kept on, at least for a time. You see the problems start when the other team members begin to react to constant breaches of policy by an individual. As much as there are favoured performers behind the scenes, to keep a larger team together there must be common rules which broadly apply to all.

The elites might be given a little more wriggle room, but when you have someone performing no better than the masses, clearly, they must be seen to comply—otherwise there are genuine accusations of double standards. This particular guy had been tolerated to a degree by the principal, but his continued lack of input to the floor roster was becoming a problem that couldn't be ignored. The principal started to resort to driving by the offender's house when he was meant to be on duty to see whether he was at home (and duly summoning him back if he was). Therefore, things were already coming to a head, with a couple of verbal warnings issued.

However, the icing on the cake was when he jumped a listing of one of his own colleagues! A relatively new agent in the team had gone out in the morning on an appraisal following an office call-in. It had gone well, and she came back to excitedly discuss it on the floor to get some additional input on likely pricing, as she was heading back at 5 p.m. to sign up the listing. For once, old mate was at his desk and duly gave his feedback. At this point the light must also have come on that at some stage in the distant past he had some form of conversation with the owner of this property himself. Here then, was a listing just waiting to happen with someone—regardless of whether they remembered him—that he could work a previous contact angle on.

The trusting new agent had left it hanging until 5 p.m. whilst revealing the details to her colleagues, who were all supportive, bar one. He wanted the listing himself, and I am sure felt he was the better agent to sell it, so he quietly slipped out of the office around 2 p.m., drove over to the house, and (somehow) convinced the owner to sign an exclusive listing with him first. I presume he explained he also represented the same office and was more experienced, so had been deemed a better choice, etc. The poor original agent arrived at 5 p.m. ready to sign up, only to find her own colleague had beaten her to it!

Serious double trouble. Firstly, you *never* cross your own team. If he thought he had a legitimate claim to speak with the owner as well, he should have brought it up with the principal beforehand for an independent assessment. Secondly, by the arrival of the original agent at 5 p.m., it became clear to the owner something was not right and there was (at best) no team communication, but more likely infighting going on. Hence, potential reputational damage to the office by making unethical decisions and doing your own thing, regardless of going through the correct channels. The perfect loose cannon and the perfect way (as he subsequently was) to get sacked.

The other agent (well, 'team') I encountered were husband and wife and were generally a little underhand and, again, did as they pleased. One or other, or both, would often miss sales meetings on some flimsy excuse, essentially because they couldn't be bothered. One day I got a call from an ex-colleague from my first office. He was a decent enough guy and we had remained in touch. He was somewhat perplexed as he had put a set of open home signs out in our area for one of his listings, only to find when he returned to them, they had all been mysteriously stolen. It is quite common for the odd sign to go missing, or end up in a ditch courtesy of a teenager or late-night reveller who thinks they are *so* original and the first person to ever think of kicking over a sign. Yet a full set removed is quite unusual.

The questionable couple just so happened to have a listing in the same area with an open home, at a similar time, and (with reputation preceding them) my ex-colleague was effectively enquiring as to whether I had heard them make any smug comments about removing the opposition signs. Opposition in branch only, as it was the same brand! This is completely against the Code of Conduct, as no agent can interfere with another agent's listing or signage. I hadn't heard anything, but said I would keep an ear out (having my suspicions as well). As it happened, things were coming to an inevitable head around the same time anyway. A culmination of relatively minor (in isolation) but growing number of issues, including: poorly completed and deliberately ambiguous paperwork, not declaring or entering appraisals into our in-house system, not wearing correct uniform on duty, and missing the floor roster, had finally got to the point where the principal needed to act or face a rebellion from everybody else!

On the very day there was due to be a stern discussion following on the from the latest sales meeting, there was a no-show again due to 'car trouble'. This was the final straw and instead a formal warning email was sent (which I had the joy to help word) outlining what was expected and how things had to improve from here. Within 30 minutes of being sent, back came the reply that they couldn't stand this 'intolerable' micro-management (if only) and they were leaving! The writing was on the wall, so walk before the inevitable push. There were various threats of discussions with head office and unfair treatment, to which the consensus was—go for your life!

The postscript to this? Having decided to leave the brand completely (obviously head office were no help then!) they returned on the next Saturday morning—when they knew the sales team and principal would be out and about—and dropped off at reception all the old signs they didn't want to clutter up their garage anymore. Fair enough, except the dynamic duo not only returned our signs, but amongst their hoard (you know what's coming) were four other signs that mysteriously belonged to the branch my ex-colleague worked for. Another Exhibit A, your honour!

Whilst what I have described so far may not be great, it predominantly represents internal issues of correct conduct and behaviour or, at worst, how the office is perceived by other agents or potential clients. The more serious situations can occur if specific illegal activities could expose an organisation to a genuine risk of legal or financial action, be it through fines or lawsuits. Thankfully, I have never witnessed any major deception or malpractice on a large scale, and whilst a I know there have been a few high-profile cases of very murky behaviour in the past, I will only cover what I have experienced.

One area open to potential abuse is the creation of supposed competition, through fraudulent misrepresentation of multiple buyers. This is used to 'encourage' (i.e., pressure) a would-be buyer into making a firm commitment—when perhaps they otherwise wouldn't—and possibly paying a higher figure, in order to avoid losing out to an unnamed 'rival'. When someone decides they like a particular property, that subconscious fear of loss can start to creep in. This can motivate people to make snap decisions, so if you feed this paranoia (with 'other buyers' waiting to swoop) all the better! Needless to say, there are strict guidelines around how legitimate multiple interest is handled and conveyed, given it does often happen for popular properties.

Auctions are the most common situation where you may come across competing parties. Surely all is good here, you can physically see the opposition bidding, so they must exist, right? Well, firstly there can be telephone bidders you can't see. There was at least one popular urban myth doing the rounds a few years back of an agent working a 'phone bidder' during an auction only for his phone to ring in mid conversation (perhaps silent mode may have been preferrable!). Comical, if it indeed really happened.

Not quite so funny are two auctions where I have personally witnessed dummy bidders. The first, it pains me to say, was effectively my own. At the time I was still relatively new to this method of sale and—for various reasons—had inherited an existing office listing that was culminating in an auction. Despite limited prior experience I duly ran buyers, and by the big day it appeared, miraculously, I had a couple of live ones who might stick up their hands. There was a full turnout in support from the office, including the principal, who had a friend with him who was potentially interested, but who had belatedly only come along that day to view.

Perhaps still being a little wet behind the ears, I thought nothing of it and took names and numbers as required. Things kicked off and after a slow start the principal's mate pitched in the first bid. This in turn fired up one of my other bidders. There were a couple of bids and counterbids between the two, then the first guy dropped out (still well below the reserve price). The other bidder remained and was joined by the second person I had been working with. There were a couple more bids, but we fell just short of the reserve price and the property was passed in. After further private negotiations post-auction, the highest bidder did eventually secure the property.

Overall, I was quite pleased with what had happened on the day until I commiserated with the principal regarding his friend who missed out. He laughed and advised he was just there for the show and to gee people along! My heart sank as it dawned I had been party to a bidding process that was not quite what it appeared. Not much that could be done now. In some defence, whilst this was not ideal, the 'ringer' was only used to break the ice, much like a vendor bid (no one ever wants to bid first!). As the numbers got closer to the reserve price, he was immediately withdrawn to ensure there was no impact to the final price determination or outcome. Bottom line was nobody got to the reserve price on the day, so the final outcome was effectively unaltered. Nonetheless, I still felt somewhat uneasy about the experience at the time.

I shouldn't have worried, as a few years later this was comfortably eclipsed by our old friend from earlier in this chapter. Before his dalliances got the better of him, he had a property up for auction. He had run the whole marketing program himself, but we duly all turned up on the day to add our support. It was a nice family home in a good suburb, and he was confident of a reasonable turnout and bidders. Proceedings got under way and, indeed, there were a couple of active bidders. Things went back and forwards between the two and the price edged up. The auctioneer announced we were on the market and duly closed the deal with one of the parties.

We were all quite stoked for him, as it is always nice to have an active auction with a good outcome for the owner. Both bidders had been worked well and we congratulated our colleague on a well-run auction. All good, until the following Monday morning when it became apparent, through some whispered observations and rumours, that the under-bidder had almost certainly been a plant and paid to play the counter role and push the actual (and therefore only) buyer all the way up to the full reserve price. Unlike my own experience some years before, this deception arguably had a direct material impact on how far the eventual buyer had gone with his bidding. Great for the seller, but a potential legal minefield if the real buyer had any subsequent suspicion he had been played. However, this buyer was happy with their purchase (and what they had paid) so the matter was uncomfortably left as it was, given there was no hard evidence of foul play. Like I said, he was a smooth operator.

Just for balance, the only other time I know of a dummy bidder at an auction it turned out to be a plant by the seller! Unbeknown to anyone, including the listing agent, they had sent a friend along to gee up the price on their behalf! Didn't really work that well though, as the owner wanted too much in the first place and there were no other active bidders! Still, once again, it's not just dodgy agents! I must stress, this is three isolated instances in over 16 years of attending many, many auctions, and the vast majority of auctions are run with integrity and exactly as you see them. In addition, the requirements for a clear audit trail of bidders and confirmed identification, including phone/remote bidders, etc., has been tightened over the years to make such occurrences very difficult to engineer.

Perhaps more common is when this scenario is applied to private treaty transactions. By the very definition, any negotiations here are not in the public domain and you effectively must take the agent's word there is another bidder hot on your heels. This opens the door to those who may wish to be deceptive. Again, there are rules in place to ensure (well, at least encourage) correct behaviour. Key to this, in Queensland for instance, is an 'Acknowledgement of Multiple Offers' form which should be completed by all buyers in the event of more than one formal offer being presented to the owner.

The idea is that buyers have been formally notified by means of paperwork, which leaves an audit trail, that is, (theoretically) you can't have a multiple offer form completed and not be able to demonstrate you have two formal offers on file. All well and good, but this assumes buyers are even aware of this legislation or indeed what constitutes a 'formal' offer, and is open to easy manipulation. Often an agent might gee up a buyer telling them he already has another 'offer' so they will have to act. In reality (if at all) this is probably no more than a verbal indication from another buyer which carries no weight and, indeed, in Queensland is not recognised legally.

A formal offer is just that, a proposed contract completed and signed by the buyer. Until you have two of these, you have no multiple offer. Yet it is all too easy to circumvent this requirement and just use some flimsy secondary interest to create your alternative bidder. Chances are the buyer will not realise or question this (more concerned about losing the house) and the desired effect is created. Many times I have spoken to buyers with stories of putting offers in on other properties, and being asked to pay full price, or over the odds, due to the 'other offers'. But they never signed (or were even aware of) a multiple offer form. Most agents will simply get away with the subterfuge through word of mouth and no audit trail whatsoever. But if this behaviour is detected and called out, their office may face issues and potential fines.

Bogus buyers are not just good for contract closure either, as the concept can be applied to obtaining listings. As already covered, if you have someone dithering on signing up (and perhaps still considering two or three agents) one tactic is to call them with an 'A' buyer on your books who really wants to look through their property, as it would be perfect for them. If they like it, could be a very quick and easy sale without even going to market and needing to pay advertising, etc. Just need to sign some 'authorisation' paperwork to legally allow them to come through. It happens the paperwork in question is a sneaky 90-day exclusive agreement which the owner unwittingly signs, and bingo! Once signed and locked in, either the mystery buyer cancels at the last minute or comes through briefly, but doesn't (surprisingly) like it. Oh well, never mind, we are signed up now. Let's just advertise as normal, hey?

Ironically, the exact reverse of the quaint concept of legally allowing someone through can be pushed by the unscrupulous operator, as well. If targeting an existing property on the market that may have already gone to an open listing, some agents will call the owner directly when they think they have a (legitimate) buyer and dangle them as bait. They will try to bypass the current agent and potentially suggest a one-off inspection, even without any paperwork being signed, so as not to trigger any conversations elsewhere. If the owner complies—out of the need to sell the house by any means—they can swing the buyer through undercover and, if they like it, then create the listing form and offer simultaneously, thereby executing the perfect coup!

I recently had one listing that had (for various reasons) been on the market for longer than I wanted, and another local agent tried this tactic. Luckily one of the two co-owners cottoned on that this wasn't the right way to do things and alerted me. I immediately called the offending agent and put them on the spot, and they had to back down. In the interests of the owner (with gritted teeth) I did allow their buyer to still come through, but as a conjunction inspection in my presence. Needless to say, nothing came of it and, fortunately, I managed to secure my own buyer a few days later.

The Code of Conduct stipulates we have a duty of care to advise potential clients of situations that could detrimentally impact them. Again, paperwork has been modified over the years to assist with this. One example is ensuring (if taking over a current listing) that the seller is out of the exclusive listing period with the existing agency, and indeed issues a written cancellation notice. This ensures there is no danger of two commissions being due in the event of a quick, subsequent sale. However, not every agent would push these checks that hard, too interested in signing up the client first themselves (their problem to sort, too bad, too sad). Likewise, selling properties with tenants in place requires clear and careful explanation to the buyers as to the existing lease situation and their rights for vacant position, if required, at settlement. I have seen instances where this has been fudged over to get a contract signed and left to the buyers to work out themselves when it becomes apparent the tenants can remain for longer than originally expected.

All these instances are relatively isolated, for sure, in the great number of overall transactions, but rest assured they do happen. There are those for whom the deal is king and to hell with everything and everybody else. Many of these actions could result in fines and penalties if pursued through proper channels, but all too often the disgruntled punter seems to somehow just put up with it and simply bad-mouth the industry in general instead.

Status quo maintained.

24 | PANDEMIC! (& OTHER OPPORTUNITIES)

T he old adage states *'One man's loss is another man's gain'* and never is that truer than in real estate. Now, I need to make an acknowledgement here before we go any further. The global spread of COVID-19 was a horrible event resulting in the untimely deaths of many thousands of people worldwide. Frontline health workers selflessly put themselves in harm's way to provide care and comfort to those in dire circumstances. I am in awe of these amazing people and, likewise, have sympathy for anyone impacted by the loss of loved ones and the long dark shadow cast by this unrelenting virus at its peak. In no way do I wish to belittle what many endured, nor the ongoing legacy, whether it be economic, physical, or mental wellbeing.

That all said, the introductory statement still stands, and there were many trying to 'make hay while the sun shone' during this period. With most professions it was either boom or bust through this unprecedented time and, unfortunately, your fate was determined by the industry you were in. Air travel and related business suffered, along with tourism and hospitality yet online sales and home improvement companies were laughing. I begrudge no one for trying to continue to make a living, and any company must take advantage while a situation allows them to do so, regardless of the underlying circumstances. Perhaps, somewhat unexpectedly, real estate ended up being one of the short-term lucky winners in the crazy new world of lockdowns and social distancing. If you had asked most agents as events first started to unfold (including me) as to how things were looking, I think the initial analysis then was somewhat gloomier.

Restrictions on movement and the standing down of many employees did not bode well for continued business, but the full lockdown period didn't last very long (well, in Queensland at least) and it soon became apparent JobKeeper funding was keeping many people afloat quite well. Lending rates were pegged to an all-time low and borrowing restrictions eased. The result was effectively no loss in buyer activity or demand. The retraction came only in stock, as some would-be sellers became hesitant due to future economic uncertainty or—in fairness— during the initial stages at the thought of plague-ridden hordes tromping through their sanitised homes.

The net result was effectively an increase in the ratio of buyers to homes available, and a subsequent upsurge in net demand. Prices increased and time on market reduced as purchasers increasingly desperately chased down a dwindling number of homes. In short, if you had stock it was going to sell—and you could look like a champion in the process—but getting that stock in the first place would become the challenge. Ironically this created a juxtaposition of those capitalising on COVID-19 in real estate and the underlying messages being sent out.

From an agent's perspective, suddenly most homes were selling in days or even hours, with buyer feeding-frenzies and multiple offers to match. This is that extremely rare, but *true nirvana* when buyers have genuine *fear of missing out* (FOMO), all by themselves! It is simply something you cannot manufacture or fake, but when it happens (due to market conditions) it is magical. No longer having to outwardly appease frustrating buyers who deliberately dither and take their time, then put in lowly offers. Oh no, people sticking their hand up immediately wanting to pay over full price. Well, assuming you priced it in the first place or just 'invited offers'—whoopee! They have lost out already elsewhere several times, everything is going under contract immediately and they do not want to miss out again! Gee, even a dud agent can get a result in a market like this!! *Exactly*, yes they can, so that's when all the BS starts! The pandemic and the market had created the perfect storm, not anything new or inspirational the agent had done, yet all the social media channels lit up like a Christmas tree and went into overdrive. 'SOLD in one day!', 'Multiple offers and sold $30k above list price!', 'Another gone immediately!' etc., etc. Wow, how amazing, it is almost as if *everyone* was doing it!

Suddenly the *entire* industry has become collectively excellent overnight or, perhaps, they are just the same and circumstances have come to them? No matter, Joe Public will not get that, so keep smashing out those ego posts making it sound like you are the *only* one achieving such miracles. Strange, didn't seem to see you doing that a few months ago? For a while it became relentless, all the usual suspects of course, but even people you hadn't seen for years (and thought must have long since left the industry!) were suddenly trumpeting their unbelievable successes and powers of getting the best deal. Never mind the general suffering going on around the place, this is absolute gold! Ring every last drop out of it.

Coincidence or not, this all seemed to happen around the same time as everyone suddenly woke up to the delights of those platforms offering algorithmic and AI-based services for immersive social media advertising to your specific 'target' market. Overnight, anyone who had dared to look at anything even vaguely real estate related over the previous 12 months, via a device, was bombarded in their feeds with endless 'sponsored' advertisements from agents *very* far and *very* wide telling you how bloody brilliant they were right now (and just click here for your free appraisal).

The initial self-marketing approach is always one of supposed differentiation—despite the fact, in this case, all and sundry were claiming unparalleled achievements. In good old *Matrix* fashion, you needed people to think you were the 'one', so they would call you first. In a market where everyone had suddenly fired up, however, this could be a little more difficult (although he who shouts loudest probably still wins the day). Assuming you were, indeed, believed to be Neo and were lucky enough to get the call, there may have been a subtle shift in the narrative at that point.

The seller is potentially still a little hesitant in these strange times, so then you must open things up and reveal that the market as a whole is indeed on fire, stock is moving very quickly and if they are thinking of selling *now* is the absolute time. Feed the greed! Of course, this somewhat gives the game away that perhaps it is not just you performing divine miracles, but by then you are already in the door. More importantly, the dollar signs are starting to take over in the seller's mind, so they have already lost focus as to what prompted them to specifically call you in.

As mentioned earlier, for a while prices just went through the roof. You could look like an absolute superstar just by running an open home, handing out some 'Expression of Interest' forms and watching the cash-laden offers come flowing back in. This enabled boisterous self-promotion and no fear of 'buying' a listing (when, for once, the buyer would do that for you!). The attack dogs prospered because if your strength was wrestling the listing signature at all costs, there was little or no comeback now. The house would be gone in a few days, regardless. Conversely the more cautious agents now had their work really cut out, as it became all about *getting the listing* (even more than normal, if that is possible!). Cut-price commission, free marketing, whatever price you want to try for, it is all good—just throw the kitchen sink at it! As per the Metallica classic: 'Nothing Else Matters'! As a devotee, plenty of their other tracks could be applied to this general narrative as well: 'Seek & Destroy', 'Sad But True' and most definitely, 'Master of Puppets'!

Another bonus, for those more arrogant agents who also have no real time for buyers, even in a slow market, is now you could really treat them like dirt, and they would have to put up with it in their blind pursuit of the target property. No more niceties (if indeed there ever were any) and you could really play the unsubstantiated multiple offers game with no questions asked, as everyone was suddenly pre-conditioned to certain competition! Do not get that vaccine going too quickly, we are on a roll here (as luck and incompetence would have it, the Government duly obliged on that one!).

From my earlier comment, the attentive amongst you by now may be thinking, 'So, what of the counter position from some elements of the industry you alluded to?'. Surely, all one-way traffic and the same message. Well yes, to buyers and sellers, but remember our old friends the mentors and trainers? Spare a thought for them, they still need to earn a crust! Ignore the positives of buyer demand and concentrate solely on the negatives (from an agent's perspective) of a serious lack of stock and changes to work practices. Well before the unexpected sales successes were starting to emerge, the professional development sector had already gone to DEFCON 1, sensing blood in the water.

With initial lockdowns and great uncertainty, it was obvious many agents would be anxious about their immediate future and what they needed to do. Within days of restrictions starting, so the emails and social media posts from the usual pundits began. 'How to survive COVID and still make money', 'How to weather the next 12 months in real estate', 'Hard times, new techniques—learn how to adapt and ride out the storm', etc., etc. Yep, any number of pop-up online seminars and web sessions promising to show you the light and deliver you from evil (again!). Whilst things were not as bleak as we all thought, limited stock undoubtedly meant there were going to be agents and agencies struggling, so where there is strife there is money!

Struck me as interesting that unless all these gurus were much older than they looked and were around for the Spanish flu, they had no more idea on the implications of COVID-19 than the rest of us! It was, after all, uncharted waters yet they already had all the answers for you (at a small price). Of course, a strong internet presence and certain marketing techniques, such as virtual property inspections, etc., would become very important. And these areas could be highlighted and taught along with the more general concepts of adaptability and flexibility. Fair enough, but you cannot help but feel most of it was common sense.

Moreover, as an agent if you are down to your last few commission-only dollars, do you really want to give them away in the hope of salvation? Perhaps, but that is the equivalent of putting everything on red. Hand in hand with this (as usual) where the too-good-to-be-true 'lead generator' companies still claiming—even with dwindling genuine stock—to guarantee you so many opportunities per month, and associated listings, in return for paying to become their select agent in your suburb of choice. Amazing how many 'unique and proven' formulas for success were apparently out there that none of us knew existed, despite all our intensive corporate training! The more you were struggling, the more invitations you would receive. These guys check out who has no stock and target them. 'We can partner and assist real estate failures, sorry, professionals like you!' Wow, thanks for singling out me (apparently) as there are now 50 other losers to choose from in my farm area alone!

There it was then, half the industry boasting it was one of the best times they had ever experienced, with record sales and performance, whilst the other half was advising agents would be lucky to last six months without significant support and reinvention in their 'darkest hour'. Horses for courses!

Somewhat annoyingly, it could be contended both sides of this argument were true. Some agents were, indeed, killing it with record sales and the best of times—wham bam, thank you, Wuhan! But with very limited stock it doesn't take a genius to work out that it was a relatively small percentage, certainly way smaller than the blanket bombing self-promotion would have you believe. A good colleague of mine summed it up quite nicely at the time: if you were already up and on the wave, then you could gloriously surf it all the way in. If you were still paddling around waiting for the next good break, too late!

Essentially those who already had momentum and good self-advertising coming into the pandemic benefited greatly from initial continuity, picking up listings as things first started to unfold. Then, as if by magic, everything they were selling started becoming street, estate, suburb records. With a degree of volume and existing profile to then push these (let's be frank here) unexpectedly good results, further attraction business went into overdrive and the dream of perpetual motion was momentarily realised!

One of the other surprises was just how long this situation was maintained. Most thought, initially, the end of 2020 would see some sort of stabilisation, and certainly the removal of JobKeeper support in March 2021 would have an impact. It did … even higher prices! Without getting too political, the sluggish complacency of the government in the early stages—yes, we are the "envy of the world"—coupled with the subsequent circus, otherwise known as the vaccine rollout, ensured a lockdown or two was never far away well into 2021, and the unpredictable climate remained. Yet the economy had apparently bounced back already—just like nothing had ever happened, if you ignore the billions in national debt—and everyone was being told by the media house prices would continue to rise significantly in the coming months. Do not stop, buy now (and pay later … in many ways!).

All this is nothing new, even resulting from a sudden pandemic. The fabled *Four D's* of real estate always deliver opportunity: Death, Divorce, Debt (aka 'd'bank') and Downsizing. The first two are fairly self-explanatory and provide a constant source of properties. In both instances there will most likely be a definite requirement to sell (guaranteeing an outcome). The only fly in the ointment, sometimes, being the in-fighting between siblings or ex-partners as to what constitutes a good price, typically due to conflicting motivations. Often it is money, not blood, that is thicker than water! Both these circumstances inevitably create sadness and stress for those directly involved.

Unfortunately, they also create easy wins, so that is their problem not yours! Tea and sympathy to a point, but let's crack on as I am sure you just want this resolved so you can all move forward (and someone can get paid). Death probably outranks divorce, as the owner is—well, let's be honest—out of the picture and you probably have an empty house to work with. Also, the siblings are a little more detached from the actual process and are probably focused more on the financial outcome. Although they may still disagree about figures when it comes to signing a contract. By contrast, in a situation where a couple are separating and selling, one (or both) may still be living in the house and the level of conflict is potentially higher. So, you must also ensure you are seen to be dealing with both parties equally and fairly, unless there is a court order to the contrary.

Debt is another banker (pardon the pun) at certain times. Rising interest rates normally result in mortgage stress and several associated defaults. *Hindsight spoiler alert for those who had been buying in 2021—interest rates had been low for a long time, just saying).* Very difficult for those involved, but great news for all those agents being handed juicy mortgagee-in-possession auctions with fully paid advertising, with (historically at least) not too much pressure on the final purchase price. Self-profile and a quick, cheap sale for you, probably with remaining debt for the owner as a result, but so be it. Where the bank has yet to take the reins, there are more cash-strapped owners still needing to urgently sell (at a loss) before control is taken out of their hands. Sit down with them for yet more tea and understanding, happy in the knowledge they will have to sell, come what may. Locked in payday!

Downsizing is also common. Empty nesters will inevitably look to reassess their property requirements, whether just at a practical level or to release some accrued asset value to assist in retirement, etc. You can probably throw in an extra 'D' as the odd natural disaster does not go amiss either. After the Brisbane floods of 2011, why not market heavily in the worst impacted suburbs? Surely a lot of new potential anguished sellers there, right? Their dramas may be your gains, albeit buyers might be in short supply as well. Then again you can always find some mug buyer willing to take a punt (literally in this case) in a flood zone … if the price is right. Come on down!

Now that was originally intended to be the end of this chapter, but the good old pandemic just keeps on giving and giving. When I first started collating these musings, COVID-19 was no more than a twinkle in some laboratory tester's (or bat's) eye. Since then it has overtaken the world. Writing the majority of this chapter in early 2021, it seemed we should soon be reaching some sort of conclusion and things might start to return to near normality, be it in real estate or life in general. But no, it remained a movable feast as I continued to write.

With delivery delays of 'good' vaccines and fear mongering of the alternative (AstraZeneca as the pantomime villain, altogether now—BOOO!) the inevitable relay race of *who's turn it was for a hard lockdown this week* continued. With not-fit-for-purpose hotel quarantine creaking at the seams, as an added extra. Yet apparently the economy had never been so good, things were on the up and, thus, the utter madness continued unabated.

Only now, as I start to bring things to a conclusion—in 2022—has the interest rate elephant-in-the-room finally made its presence felt. Lockdowns have ended, all except the hard-core anti-vax brigade are jabbed up, and we are all finally free of

COVID-19 *(okay, that last bit isn't true).* We now have thousands more infections than at any point previously, but not to worry, as being open, not closed, is the vote winner now! The bubble that had been riding this wave for two years finally burst around March 2022 as the federal election loomed, fuel and food prices started to skyrocket, and interest rates quickly began their inevitable climb to match. Rabid activity that still existed in January and February, dried up almost overnight as buyers cooled on the realisation and bite of higher mortgage payments.

As the previously insatiable demand dipped, guess what, supply started to increase. Those clever (I would never say greedy) sellers who had been hanging on, as month on month their asset values increased—expertly gauging the top of the market— suddenly realised they had perhaps already missed it! Hence a flurry of new listings trying to desperately chase the prices of a couple months prior, more out of hope than expectation (well, at least amongst the agents).

This subtle increase in the levels of available stock aided by knee-jerk reactions, ironically, contributed to the price cooling effect. The 'peak price' horse had bolted, but some owners were still hoping it might trot back in before they had to shut the gate. Subsequently, stock appears still in relatively short supply and prices have, perhaps, held up better than expected, given multiple interest rate rises. Yet with many on low, fixed rates that are running out, more stock is an inevitability. Unfortunately, like time and tide, no man (or agent—not even the self-proclaimed superstars) can halt basic economic cycles.

Less Demand + More Supply = Prices Drop!

Pretty simple equation, which might just stem that stream of street record 'socials' in the future!

25 | A BIT ON THE SIDE

Now this will come as a slight disappointment to some, given the click-bait nature of the heading, it might suggest more salacious revelations are about to be revealed, but alas no. The 'cheating' here is purely financial, essentially extra relationships furtively entered into with other occupations. Yes, the (not so) shocking truth is many agents cannot make enough money—despite self-promotion to the contrary—from their real estate activities alone. Hence the need to indulge with a second income source. This concept might seem a little alien for the elite earners, who would have no need for an extra revenue stream and, regardless, are certainly far too busy to branch out in other random directions. However, down at the bottom of the pyramid, it is all too common.

Of course, I must be a little careful here. *Pot calling the kettle black,* and all that. Attempting to write a book—even if the subject matter is relevant—probably falls into this category, albeit I might be the only exponent of this particular avenue due to the extended timescales involved. And this is coupled to a chance of success and financial return that is most likely much worse than said real estate career! Besides, I personally have no big issue with this. We must all make ends meet and do what we need to do. My amusement is simply the pretence of the ultra-successful sales persona compared to the reality on the ground. As I say, my chosen secondary path is a little more out there. By contrast there are some *old faithfuls* that can be relatively easily worked into a patchy real estate schedule, when listings are low.

In our modern society, top of the list—and a perfect partner in crime—is being an Uber driver. Oh yes, flexible hours you can fit in around important appointments—assuming you have some—and a relatively cheap and easy start up with no previous experience required (sounds familiar? See Chapter One!). As long as your vehicle of choice looks half reasonable and isn't about to fall apart—being a successful agent of course, this won't be a problem—and you are not well known to the local constabulary, you should be right. What is more, you are meeting and conversing with the wider public! The very thing we spend every week in our day jobs stressing about how to do successfully.

Well, well, two birds and one stone! Earn some extra dollars *and* have a captive audience for few minutes at a time, that you might be able to subtly question about their real estate status for future reference. Perfect, let them come to you! Moot point as to whether you do admit up front you have another occupation, as the clever ones might put two and two together and question why you are doing this if you are a top dog (depending on the time of day, the rest are probably too drunk to listen or care, for that matter).

Mind you, that analysis applies the other way around, so it's a bit of a giveaway when your phenomenally successful local agent turns up on your driveway to list your house with Uber and Ola stickers on display in their back window (I have seen it happen, trust me). It always starts out the same, just a little extra 'top up' a few hours a week, to take the edge off. Then the realisation sets in that this is money earned concurrently for hours worked rather than waiting for a listing, contract and (fingers crossed) settlement before any sight of a paycheque. Thus, time creep begins and, lo and behold, before too long your addiction grows, and you have a career in rideshare apps with a secondary side 'hobby' of selling the occasional house.

Let us see now, another pointless floor roster or a quick four hours in the car, earning instead! Some will need to do it in a clandestine way because the principal will simply not tolerate such distractions and will ask you to make a stark choice and apply all your energies accordingly. In tough market conditions I have witnessed a few being allowed a degree of lateral movement if it 'doesn't interfere with' their real estate job. Good luck with that approach, as it is almost impossible to determine clear use of time. One man's drive of his farm area 'checking signs' is another man's taxi ferrying local passengers! Even if you do not cross timelines, potentially being out to the small hours during the most lucrative earning window probably does not bode too well for attentiveness at the sales meeting the next day. After all, that is a challenge even for those with a solid eight hours sleep and three coffees to the good!

Next are those who might try to align similar activities to keep those 'key skills sharpened', whilst having a slightly higher chance of an earner. Hence, a part-time used car sales role is not a bad option (hey, at least you have already got some stock to sell for a change!). Same old routine with the would-be buyers, just a different product. Seen a few go this route although, generally, this must be declared, just in case the principal walks into your local yard looking for that first car for their son or daughter. In a similar vein, getting linked up with a local developer is a reasonable shout. You may offer to front their latest 'Land Sales Office'—onsite shed to you and me—for a few hours a week in return for either an ongoing pittance or (more likely) a small cut of any interested parties you can sign up on an 'Expression of Interest' for a block of dirt.

Again, the stock (in this case land being subdivided by the developer) is already there. You just need to sit there, smile at people when they come in, and fire up the tried and trusted patter. Timing is a bit more tricky here, but many offices will allow a day off in lieu during the week, due to sales agents working Saturdays (and often Sundays). This allows a non-conflicting window of opportunity to sit in your *Portakabin* in a field on a given day, no questions asked. Moreover, you can still answer your mobile and check emails, etc., in the downtime keeping both balls in the air, so to speak.

Property management certainly keeps you in the same industry, and a few sales agents have expanded into the rental arena to establish some form of fixed income whilst utilising aspects of their existing skill set. The problem here is, once there are a few properties on the rent book, things can start to get very time consuming, as this is a whole field in itself. You will either unwittingly transition into a full-time property manager—with an occasional landlord related sale remaining—or will need to take someone else on, which somewhat defeats the original purpose of expanded personal income.

I know one sales agent who successfully branched into the arena of commercial letting and building management on a controllable scale. They took responsibility for a small commercial development and managed both the lease procurement and building services on behalf of the owners. A nice by-product of that was getting a favourable deal on one of the office units for their own use, meaning they had a local presence for their sales operation (and building management) at a cost-effective rate. The building maintenance role allowed for additional services to be offered, such as carpet cleaning, etc., for which they invested in their own equipment, gaining further income from these activities.

Hospitality works quite well. Just as with ride share: flexible hours and the chance to interact with many people. Quite visible though, so if doing some bar work or table-waiting at a venue within your local farm area, be prepared to be recognised—well, if you have any profile, that is—and perhaps for some awkward questions asked, for example, "The house selling going well then, is it?!", and so on. I was quite surprised, while out with friends once, to be served at our local hotel bistro by an agent who worked for one of the bigger franchises in the area. And who, from their office's weekly advertising, you would have imagined had no need for such extra work. Mind you, that is the point of fluffy marketing!

As already covered in some detail, the burgeoning real estate coaching arena also beckons and, if you are successful enough, is probably a more suitable look than waiting tables. Imparting valuable knowledge and assistance in your primary field of activity due to your *undoubted* achievement, plays out rather more positively than scraping by behind the scenes in some other unrelated line of work. For many though, I still feel this is more ego-driven rather than by financial necessity, unless you are highly successful and are prepared to put considerable extra time into regularly appearing on 'the circuit' and building your separate mentor brand profile.

Perhaps a little more specialised for a limited few, but nonetheless a real phenomenon, is embracing the political arena. There are, after all, many parallels. Needing to have profile and exposure in your chosen local area. Needing to build as many contacts and supporters as possible—both amongst the general population and local businesses—through meeting and greeting, and the old favourites such as phone canvassing and door knocking. Also, being thick-skinned and having a certain confident—but not arrogant, mind!—manner in public certainly applies. The beauty of all this, however, is the same database of contacts is effectively good for either vocation. And often these individuals tend to move in and out of both interlinked fields on an ongoing basis, depending on how the last election went! As a political newbie, setting yourself up for canvassing and electoral consideration (be it at local council, state, or even federal level) can be done while holding down a real estate career as well. This ensures some ongoing income remains and your name is still out there if things do not go as planned.

Additionally, you can potentially leverage off your existing database of ex-clients as a handy addition to other contact generation. Should things go swimmingly, and your eager public endorses you for your nominated position, then you drop the real estate career—for the time being—and take on your new lofty role with conviction (and a salary). Now, you probably do this with the mutual understanding of your ex-principal, who you keep sweet just in case the bold political journey ends abruptly at the following election! In that scenario you can drop straight back into your old role with an even bigger database to drill down on, plus now you are a local 'identity' through your previous exposure on the electoral stage. The ex-principal will be happy enough as any agent with a good set of contacts and some local notoriety will be an asset (also looks like a happy ship if they return to their old office).

The same applies if you never get to office. Lose out in the vote and simply revert to a full-time real estate role until you decide whether to run again in the future. In one office where I worked, we lost an agent to the local council and another agent to state politics. Both won their relevant seats at the first attempt, and both were voted back for a second term during following elections, so they have yet to return to the old job (give it time).

I have seen at least a couple of—presumably suitably talented—agents run a prominent sideline in motor racing, allowing them to appear dynamic and exciting whilst plastering their vehicles with easily visible 'sponsorship' from their own real estate office. Lower and specialist divisions in the main, not quite F1 or V8s—with more of an outgoing than additional income, I would have thought—but, nevertheless, an interesting diversion. Serious involvement in sport is somewhat limited by your ability (or lack of it) so most of the activity here tends to be in the other direction, that is, retired sports men and women coming into real estate. Ex-rugby players of both codes seem to be a favourite, although there is at least one ex-AFL player now in real estate, I know of.

Again, the draw is the same as with the ex-pollies, already well known and with many existing contacts. I wonder on the level of suitable experience and market expertise on offer sometimes, but perhaps this is the ultimate pitching of the two modern fixations of money and 15 minutes of fame against each other. Do you pick this ex-legend to sell your house because you can impress your sporty mates with name dropping, but in doing so risk not getting the absolute highest price that you might from an alternative seasoned professional who has always been in the business, or does this last dollar win the day instead? If they have a natural talent for their new calling, rather than just being a figurehead, you may get lucky and have both … but don't count on it.

If you are really stuck the final roll of the dice (pun intended) is to have a flutter. Every 'high rolling' $15 buy-in poker game around town is almost guaranteed to have at least two or three local agents involved trying to bolster their meagre returns. Of course, they will tell you it is just a pastime, like stamp collecting you understand. They obviously don't *need* to be there, thinking that somehow their real estate poker face and natural ability to bluff will automatically give them a shot at the big pot each week. Or every evening if you are spreading it around a bit at different venues—but again, just for the social and a bit of fun, of course.

Another bonus is some dubious quality networking as, in between hands, you can let casually drop in idle conversation to your fellow players that you are in real estate. You might get lucky with someone coincidently looking to sell. I don't know any statistics for whether that ever works, as the normal routine is many people love to talk real estate with you informally, pumping you for free advice and information, but still go with whoever else they already had in mind when it comes to the crunch.

Expand your horizons further and have a go at the casino or take a regular punt on the horses, all easy enough to do these days in between any real work. After all, the day job is a bit of a gamble at the best of times!

26 | ACCIDENTAL MILLIONAIRES

Most of my experience, and indeed subject matter of this book, relates to residential sales. Commercial real estate is a separate beast altogether with its own specialists, dedicated offices, and methods of operation. As the saying goes, *business is business,* and this tends to be a more—if that's possible!—cutthroat world of wheeling and dealing, often with very big numbers involved. All well and good for the most part, with both residential and commercial activities (and agents) co-existing within the same geographical areas without too much need to interact. The intricacies of selling/leasing commercial sites and/or ongoing business concerns presents a degree of complexity that most residential agents are happy to steer clear of and leave to the experts in their field. What happens, however, when some self-appointed 'experts', aren't and their 'field', is just that—a field (of grass)!

Confused? Well, the relentless expansion of the urban sprawl has created a certain set of properties that can cross the divide, being still residential in nature, but having interest and potential value to the commercial sector. These are typically within newly identified development areas, where current rural style residences are reclassified as potential future subdivisions, or even high density living/retail sites. Aside from the obvious environmental issues and deliberations over the need or merit for some of these proposed developments, there are other more pressing problems for most agents (who aren't too fussed about the forementioned issues of conscience, just whether the property is now more sellable).

You see what we have when this happens is typically existing 'mum and dad' owners who, more by luck than judgement, are now suddenly sitting on a potential goldmine—or so they very quickly think. Good luck to them, I hear you say. Of course, but with very good fortune comes the loss of rational thought, it appears. These people are no longer *just* owners, they are instantaneously business-savvy entrepreneurs at the cutting edge, who *always knew* this was going to happen (sure, even when you inherited the house 30 years ago from Auntie Dot). If you have only driven a modest SUV all your life and are suddenly dropped into the cockpit of a finely honed Formula 1 car, unfortunately, you *are not* automatically Lewis Hamilton. *Stalled without moving* or *fiery wreck* are the only likely outcomes, and it's often much the same in this instance!

Despite their recently acquired status, should these new land barons want to cash out and sell they will, most likely, still utilise the services of an Average Joe residential agent in the first instance. This is because they are cheaper, and easier to understand ... plus they don't know any commercial agents or, in truth, appreciate the difference. Your typical agent isn't going to turn down any opportunity, in particular one where a relatively routine property might sell for considerably more money, and so the scene is set once again.

So, now we have a residential operator delving into areas where some understanding of zoning implications, future commercial potential, etc., will be needed, whilst trying to deal with an empowered owner who is now apparently on a par with the likes of Gates, Musk and Bezos in terms of business acumen and economic foresight. What could go wrong? Well, enough that I felt it warranted a whole chapter by itself, having been involved with a number of these type of properties over time. Protracted and messy listings, arguments over who pays commission—and how much—endless buyer 'due diligence' and aborted option contracts are all common place, but the elusive pot of gold at the end of the rainbow always draws you back in.

There are a few fundamentals to grasp here before we go further. Owners, unlike individual residential buyers, automatically assume that developers and/or companies that are potentially investing in the land for future use somehow have almost unlimited funds. Therefore, they can—and should—'pay anything' to get what they want. Of course, for any well-run business, that is the last thing they will do if they want to stay solvent! This aligns closely with the notion they now own something magical and rare, which represents an honour for anyone else to be bestowed the privilege to be involved with, be it agent or buyer. Many owners also think that once their overgrown, unused paddock is rezoned, the job is already done, and it should be worth the collective resale value of whatever smaller blocks can be subdivided out of it.

Before rushing to the calculator, the slight problem with that perception is that by the time you factor in physical site works to prepare the land (including access roads, drainage and utility provision) plus hefty council head end fees for legal subdivision and registration, the net value of each finished lot is many, many tens of thousands less than the final individual resale price. Another common problem exists where there are a number of properties in a potential development area, and an unofficial sellers co-operative is formed. Each owner thinks if they band together and produce a united front—typically of initial defiance and suspicion—they will push the eventual prices up. This is all well and good, but different properties command different money for any number of reasons (some not so obvious, like planning overlays) and knowing each other's business inevitably leads to problems later, as we shall see

On the flip side, most developers' default position is to think these owners are just money hungry, selfish, and ignorant. Wanting all the big end dollars, but not wishing to understand, or undertake, any of the associated risks and hard work themselves that is required to get there. They see a block of dirt as just that, with limited additional value until they have a Development Approval (DA) in place which, in itself, costs not inconsiderable time and money. It is the work of the developer in designing, securing authorisation, and producing the end product which essentially creates the extra wealth.

Whilst some smaller developers will approach owners directly in these circumstances, many larger established players are happy to go through agents as they simply do not have the time or patience to deal with much of the endless pettiness and humouring that has to be undertaken with a group of individual owners. Better to get some other mug to do that instead! Key also is that developers/investors typically utilise a 'due diligence' period as part of any approach. This allows them to secure a property in principle, so they can then undertake whatever investigations they need to over an agreed period of time. As even initial analysis and council interaction costs money, it is unlikely most companies will do this work first, without at least a basic commitment from the current owner. A sensible and typical vehicle of acquisition across many areas of business, but it's also open to manipulation.

With respect to the properties themselves they are essentially characterised as being one of two major types. Those which exist within *existing developed areas*, with associated density zoning and infrastructure services already in place, but for whatever reason, have yet to be exploited. They offer a quicker return as they can be developed almost immediately, subject to the application, and granting, of a suitable DA. To this end they will command more money and a wider interest, but the big dollars will still be linked to the granting of a DA, to begin with. The DA ultimately confirms what the final footprint of any development can be and, thus, the bottom-line expected return.

The second type are those properties in *areas identified for future development,* but where all the surrounding properties are of a rural or low-density nature, typically with limited infrastructure, such as water and sewerage, which hinder any immediate development. By setting 'future zoning', councils can 'ring fence' an area to stop piecemeal development in the short term, whilst identifying it as a longer-term area of expansion. This type of property is the more intriguing with the owners typically focused only on the end game, failing to appreciate the limitations for would-be purchasers in the short-term (unable to obtain finalised DAs and needing to 'land bank').

Okay, enough of the scene setting, as we don't want this to drag on like an actual real estate training session, perish the thought! Whilst I have experienced both sales of currently developable land and negotiations on future zoned development sites, it is the latter I have had, by far, the most exposure to (and has created the most 'fun'). The first thing you notice early on is the widespread and instantaneous paralysis in spending *any* further money on their humble dwellings once these properties have been rezoned and a future of glittery gold has been set in (slow) motion. The owners realise that it is now their land that has the future dollars, not the dated old house upon it (which will most likely be flattened the moment a developer buys it). Why pay out money in terms of any significant ongoing maintenance or renovations, if this will not be returned as an increase in sale price, that is, an improved house will not add anything to the underlying subdivision value.

Why indeed? Well, perhaps so the house doesn't fall down around you while you are 10 years plus in the waiting! Slight exaggeration? Well, no, as it turns out. We had a large company with holdings already in the area looking to acquire more adjacent land for consolidation and future development. We identified a number of target properties and attempted to contact the relevant owners. One older couple seemed quite keen to discuss selling, but were equally hesitant about onsite visits. I explained that I needed to take a quick look at the property so I could assess it and report back to the buyer for any final determination from there.

Reluctantly they agreed and so one afternoon there I was walking up their driveway. One of the owners came out of the house and approached me. He was okay for me to look through the house if I wasn't going to "report anything back to council". Somewhat strange comment I thought, but I assured him I was only there to appraise the property and to provide general overview/feedback to the buyer. Once I ventured into the house (I use the term loosely) his request made a lot more sense! The first indication of their somewhat unusual situation was a spare bed set up in the small living area at the front of the home. He advised that was where is wife slept as their main bedroom was currently unusable. On opening the adjacent door to the offending room, I could see why! All over the floor (and the bed that was still in there) were the remains of the ceiling that had collapsed some time previously. Looking up, I was greeted with the sight of the exposed beams and the roof void, punctured with odd pin-sized rays of sunlight coming through (watertight still, then!).

Oh dear me, and the show went on; as we walked into the main lounge area I had to dodge two large step ladders in the middle of the room. Good, at least some remedial work under way here then? No! The ladders were in fact acting as 'temporary' supports for the failing ceiling in this room, with various wooden blocks wedged between the top steps and sagging plasterboard above. The somewhat coy owner explained they hadn't done any maintenance over the last few years thinking they were imminently selling, and it was a waste of money. But things had by now got a little "on top of them" (yep, like most of the ceiling, for starters!).

There were a multitude of other horrors including widespread mould, leaking pipes, and termite damage. They were an older couple and in many respects I did feel quite sorry for them and the way they were living. But equally they were not destitute and were perfectly capable of improving their lot, they just chose not to. Caught in limbo, waiting for—and trying to maximise—the big payment, whilst their home disintegrated around them.

Eventually our purchaser did indeed buy this property—and demolish the house—and the owners got close to a $1,000,000 payout for a property that was worth maybe $500,000 (at best) as a rural block in very poor condition. It can be argued their approach was justified given the outcome, but I am not sure whether the years of self-inflicted discomfort prior were really beneficial to their long-term physical or mental health.

This is, perhaps, the most extreme example but, as already touched on, they were in good company. Whether living at the property themselves or renting it out, many of these owners try to avoid spending anything unless they really have to.

Around the same time as the previous example, I had another property in the same future development area come up for auction. It had been purchased sometime prior from the original owners as a general investment, and had been subsequently rented out for many years (most recently through our real estate office). With recent re-zoning the current owners were excited about the extra potential, but simultaneously had limited any expenditure to a bare minimum. The house was square in the middle of one hectare of land and clearly would be removed eventually.

The constraints of property management and rental obligations, however, forced them to begrudgingly cover just the necessary maintenance, but nothing more (just enough so they were not sued). Furthermore, they adopted a 'no questions asked' policy of their tenant's activities in return for a relatively quiet life of minimal requests. Example? Well, the final tenants there managed to set fire to the four-bay shed on site (don't ask) and this was simply put out and left as was (nicely charred, blackened and twisted metal in one section). There were roof leaks in a separate utility building, which took on the appearance of an indoor swimming pool after heavy rain, and large tree roots dislodging most of the paving around the house, causing potential trip hazards and undermining of foundations.

Unfortunately, while waiting for their pot of gold these particular owners ran out of money elsewhere and the property was repossessed (hence the auction). The tenants were evicted but left with rubbish and discarded items all over the property. This added to the general look of a very tired and run-down property. The trustees responsible for the property liquidation allowed for a small budget to clear most of the rubbish, cut the grass and clean the house to an acceptable level. But beyond that, any further work was deemed too cost-prohibitive given the likely buyer profile (yes, even *they* wanted to spend as little money as possible!).

For the more attentive amongst you, this was the property referenced in Chapter Eight (Boom Or Bust!) as my finest hour for an auction outcome. Yes indeed, as covered, we had two future developers fight it out tooth and nail with a result substantially higher than anyone expected, some $400,000 above reserve. As you may recall, the auctioneer had remarked about 'drugs in the walls' at that price. Well, given the evidence of some of the discarded items we had needed to clear away, he may not have been too far wrong! He couldn't quite comprehend this ramshackle property, some distance away from the swanky inner city, and with no discernible attributes had just smashed it's reserve price in a frenzied bidding war (in truth, neither could I). Again, you could argue the previous owners got it right as good money was there without ongoing investment in the house, but it is a calculated risk.

These two stories represent the financial successes (albeit one repossessed) but there are plenty more examples of failures and properties still languishing after many years through:

i.   excessive greed of the owners, and
ii.   poor quality of their would-be suitors

These two fundamentals, by their very nature, conspire together with depressingly predicable results. As already mentioned, many owners become fixated with this *blank cheque* of a property they now own. It is their ticket to early retirement and a life of leisure, but you only get one shot at the title, so when do you stick and when do you twist? You see, FOMO doesn't just exist for buyers. For these sellers it is not a physical property they stress about missing out on, but that endless extra $500,000 (if they just hold out a bit longer).

We have already established that these owners are overnight business entrepreneurs, so, clearly they can determine the wood from the trees and skilfully negotiate the highest workable price from a qualified buyer with suitable credentials and runs on the board. Surprisingly no, on all counts. Their initially desired figures are nearly always far too high, with no relationship to practical matters. Yes, a developer may hopefully pay more than a residential buyer, but the genuine ones—that is, those who actually complete these type of acquisitions, run projects and (crucially) stay in business whilst doing so—will have clear limits on their expenditure. These limits will be dictated by the costs and work required versus the projected resale returns on completion.

Where land is to be held first, again sensible valuations will be determined based on the interim cost of carry versus the long-term outcome/profit. As a seller, however, you do not need to worry yourself with all that dreary nonsense. These companies have unlimited money and should pay whatever you ask for, as you have what they need. Easy? If only! The irony is, even if you get someone who will finally agree to your inflated figure (which in itself should start some alarm bells ringing), then decision paralysis sets in. Hang on, they are *actually* paying what we want? Something must have changed, perhaps there will now be others following in the next few months, prepared to pay even more. It has only been 12 years so far, let's not be *too hasty* (step ladder can support the ceiling for another year)! As much as you want to sell, you simultaneously don't because tomorrow could be even better.

Into this arena of greed then come the chancers and disruptors, who dangle higher figures in front of the owners (in comparison to serious developers or investors) in the hope of snagging the property on some long, option-based contract with built-in 'get out' clauses liberally embedded and cast in stone. Typically with very little up-front commitment to the owner financially, either. Many of these buyers simply don't understand the zoning properly, but want to lock the property out before bothering to speak with council about what is possible. Only to find out it is nothing in the short-term, and not as profitable as hoped in the long term. After which they simply drop the property cold via 'due diligence', or similar clause and the owner is back to square one.

Others who are more calculating may have an inkling, but still won't make any serious investigation until they have a property already secured. So, they make a higher-than-market approach which they can potentially try and reduce at a later date once the 'results' of detailed council discussions are known. That is, "We can go ahead still, but only at *$X*, because of our investigations and the subsequent planning issues that have come to light". In some respects this is no different to a residential buyer trying it on after agreeing a higher-than-wanted contract price (perhaps under competition) then claiming issues with the building and pest inspection to try and reduce the figure after the fact.

The problem is, once these fictional figures are thrown out there—however dodgy the buyer subsequently turns out to be— even after abject failure, the number remains ingrained in the seller's head. You then appear with your more qualified buyer only to be told they have already had a 'contract' for much more. Really, how did that go for you? Any 'purchase' figure only becomes real at settlement, let me tell you. I could put a contract on a development block for $5,000,000 if I wanted to for giggles. As long as a due diligence clause is there, it will never get to the point of needing the funds.

In the areas I was most involved with some of the 'contracts' agreed by owners directly with random buyers in the early days just after rezoning, were amazing. Huge figures on paper, but equally matched by huge (long) due diligence periods of up to 24 months, with little or no non-refundable deposit. Two years locked up in limbo and all were then dropped like a stone. Being burnt over time, some of these owners became a little more wary of the fine print in subsequent offers that were too-good-to-be-true.

Decision times have since been reigned in somewhat, combined with better commitments in terms of up-front non-refundable deposits (effectively paying for their time whilst checks are completed). Nonetheless, big-ticket numbers still dazzle and, even recently, I was involved with some sales in this area with good quality buyers and well-structured contracts. Most developers requested—quite reasonably—that any price negotiations remained confidential. Each owner would agree, but where two or three were selling at the same time, predictable 'over the fence' conversations would still *miraculously* take place resulting in the inevitable, "I want what they are now getting!" demands to this—by now—somewhat beleaguered agent (regardless of those *subtle* differences in land size or overlays between properties!). Hence, it was nothing for the owner to want another $100,000 at the very last minute, or try to introduce some other *random*—as 'competition'—who had just called them the day before offering the world (again). The world is not enough, as 007 may tell you.

Ironically the massive price increases in the Queensland market during the 2020/2021 COVID-19 period created quite a few more unexpected millionaires—before their time was due—across a whole range of properties. It was also a massive get-out-of-jail card for a lot of investors with previously (consistently) underperforming properties. Many, particularly interstate, who had paid overinflated prices for newbuild house & land packages or units through a combination of poor research or bad advice had been struggling. Suddenly, with an extra $150,000 in less than 18 months added to their bottom line, most albatrosses turned into soaring eagles! Shackles finally removed, and in the black.

After the event, all would probably claim this was calculated all along and they were, indeed, the savvy entrepreneur they always said they were. To a point yes, if you remain disciplined and retain something over the long term it should see eventual returns. Nonetheless, many others had already blinked prior to 2020, unable to keep investment repayments going and—with little immediate improvement then in sight—had sold at a loss. Hindsight, as they say, is a wonderful thing.

It is worth noting here that us real estate agents might pretend to know what is going on, but if we really did—and had foreseen 2020/21—we would have all retired from the industry by now, having mortgaged to the hilt and purchased every possible property we could for ourselves in early 2020 as investments! Oh well, back to the Uber driving and book writing.

27 | THIS IS THE END?

Well, there we have it. I could go on (and have often been known to) but essentially, I think we have covered all the key areas and relevant experiences in a delightful crash course of information overload. Given there is probably more guidance contained in these few rambling pages than many a hapless new agent will ever receive—plus some helpful, but uncomfortable, home truths—then, perhaps, dear reader you are now sufficiently qualified should you ever get the urge!

What have we learnt? Questionable. Hopefully a few common themes have at least come through. Most importantly I repeat, as with life, agents vary a great deal so don't judge all by one bad experience or clichéd industry stereotype. There are many good people out there doing very good work if you just look carefully enough. I came into this industry in the belief a different path could be made through professional behaviour and reliable service first and foremost, as opposed to aggressive hard-selling techniques with high-turnover listing volumes and low care-factor. At times this belief has been severely tested but, nonetheless, here I am with a reasonable career spanning more than 16 years sustained by plenty of return and referral clients, demonstrating they, at least, do value such qualities. I even have some ex-clients I would genuinely class as friends.

This can be a brutal and cutthroat job at times, always under scrutiny, aways in competition, but not always with a paycheque. So, before you judge the character of an agent too harshly, understand they must be up to the job, in the first place, with its sacrifices of time, family, and *consistent* cashflow to deliver the personalised 24/7 service the public wants. Ask yourself truthfully whether you would be prepared to do the same before being too critical.

What else? There is the theory that goes, *we only get the government we deserve,* and frankly it pains me to say it but, by and large, the public only get the agents they deserve. You cannot complain about agents overpricing homes just to get listings when they have to *overprice* homes just to get listings! If 90% of our potential target market is going to be oh-so-predictably swayed by the lure of the highest suggested dollar, then apologies to the other independently thinking 10%, but we can't pin all our hopes on you alone. Well, we can, for the three months we will last doing so. How about if you want agents to be better communicators, then be better communicators yourselves ... as in not just when it suits, but all the time. If you have lost interest in a property you were previously all over 10 minutes prior, just return the agent's call and tell them! Not hard, honest.

Trust is a two-way street; treat the industry with general disdain and any agent with contempt from the outset, then don't expect too much love in return. Set the bar low and you will not be disappointed, as we can all gravitate to the lowest common dominator easily enough. Ultimately, we are shaped totally by what we need to do to survive. If everyone appreciated thoughtful, honest and non-pushy agents then, over time, that's what you would get because that approach would be exclusively needed to achieve any success. Put simply, natural selection exists here and the 'species' adapts based on the demands of its environment. Fail to do so, and you will become extinct! I would like to be optimistic and think that things could improve; perhaps the mass populous will suddenly become more insightful in this digital age with greater access to independent research and verification but, alas, I fear not.

As again with the political arena, we are less about substance these days and more about the show and abstract soundbites, with little relation to fact. 'Flashy' agents, up themselves, with big egos? Yes, because this attracts people, even though some might not like to admit it! As the cost of living rises and financial constraints increase, the notion of loyalty and character drop down the list of requirements quite quickly, sacrificed in the pursuit of the (perceived) absolute best dollar outcome. The ultimate desire is simply lowest dollars spent for the highest possible return. We all have a better vision of ourselves, but in truth, saving (literally!) a dollar has become a significant factor in any decision making over the last few years. The 'promise' of a higher sale price compared to others, undeniable 'success', and suitably vague—but seemingly cheap—marketing costs will often win the day, regardless of the detail to back this up. Nothing wrong in wanting to get the best outcome, but questioning things first should be a prerequisite.

Ultimately, as in life, we probably still need a broad range of personalities and approaches. Experience has taught me one single style of operation will never capture all possibilities. The aggressive, in-your-face agents will inevitably win business that the more passive agent will not (as many principals love to bang on about endlessly). This will be through a mixture of bulldozing some people and genuinely appealing to other like-minded individuals who may view them as hard, no-nonsense characters who will take no prisoners and, therefore, get them the best money (perhaps). Other, more reserved, potential clients will never warm to, or want to work with, such personalities and will gravitate towards those with a far less abrasive manner and the time to understand their situation and point of view. Different techniques yield different outcomes and, you know what, that's okay in my book. There should be enough listings out there to go around, and to believe you can single-handedly capture everyone who might cross your path is a little naïve or somewhat of an ego trip. Yes, you have to adjust your dialogue and presentation in parts to match your client, but my advice to anyone coming into the industry is, *simply be yourself*, whatever those traits may be. Trying to create a false persona is difficult to maintain and most people will see through it for exactly what it is.

What can we expect in the future then? Are agents a dying breed, as we have already touched on and some would suggest and dearly hope? Personally, I think not, we will just continue to evolve. Looking back 30 years or so, before the internet, the agent's activities have already changed. Back then the office was central, people coming in and setting out their requirements, being given a set of corresponding brochures to look through. And then arranging inspections of selected properties, based on relatively limited visual information, and a greater degree of verbal description from the agent. The agent may then even have utilised their own vehicle to drive their potential customers around to various locations on a personalised stock run. These days, in many cases, the office is more of an administration hub and access point for rental related activities.

Much of the initial activity undertaken by buyers is now done in cyberspace. This is partly for convenience and also because of the comparatively large amount of information available to digest prior to any physical inspection (videos, aerial shots, virtual tours, etc.,). The agent's time has transferred from these face-to-face meetings to simply providing the same information online for primary determinations to be made. These days the first contact we have with most buyers is when they have already researched and pre-selected properties for viewing, and they are simply wishing to arrange an inspection, or attend an open home.

By and large the process from here on is currently much the same as it has always been. Again, it is suggested automated buying applications/services will replace the human element in offers and contract negotiations, and this will move fully online, thereby removing the annoying agent from the process. Indeed, there are services that already offer automated online auctions for some properties. After all, we have advanced to the point where we can already buy virtually any consumer product and just about anything to eat, drink and be merry with from the comfort of our sofa and onesie (couldn't be bothered to dress today). So, why not buy a house?

Perhaps all physical transactions can be automated, but I genuinely struggle to see a point when the need for an agent, in some capacity, is not required. There is a view the role may evolve more into a property broker situation, advising from the sidelines on properties and being able to assist with questions through the process. Perhaps we will just all be influencers, divulging our pearls of wisdom online instead, in 90-second sound bites. Removing the agent completely from all potential sales, based on my experience of buyers and sellers, just does not seem realistic. This is not a cheap pair of shoes on eBay; it is usually the biggest financial commitment of your life and has many complexities, emotions, and stresses involved before reaching successful completion.

I refer to our purple-coloured friends again who tried (and failed) to offer a dirt cheap capped-price sales product with minimum service and intervention. It ultimately failed because most people still needed more support and assistance through the process. Limited and soulless online support from a website isn't going to resolve many of the situations I have recounted in this book. Buyers and sellers directly interacting without any wriggle room will result in some interesting outcomes! We all want someone to blame when things don't go as planned—certainly not ourselves—so without the patsy in the middle who can probably resolve said issue, you will have direct conflict. If neither party can stand down or agree, I think many people's dream 'auto' purchases will be going up in smoke. Perhaps I am a dinosaur, but then so are many of our clients still, and until we are all extinct, I would be surprised if a whole lot changes.

Ever more sophisticated websites fight to offer easier ways to do just about everything online, and it seems as if everyone is transitioning towards a world of minimal direct contact. Many buyers already prefer negligible interaction wherever possible. As mentioned previously, perhaps sending an 'enquiry' online which just ticks, 'Would like to inspect', with no comments and often no contact number given, is enough for some. You respond with a terrifying *written sentence,* and all goes silent—too hard! A quick, blunt text message with no preamble is now as likely as anything else. "Available?", might be the extent of the narrative engagement with a link pasted to the property they mean.

Ultimately we adapt, and if short, sharp, direct messaging is the new standard, then so be it. The way we communicate information to customers has already changed over the years and will continue to do so. Perhaps this is the ultimate future with desensitised, faceless transactions the preferred option as the generations age. Conceivably, but even the minimal conversationalists will still feel the need to 'fire up' when there is a problem incurred or a perceived injustice, whether it be directly or via their socials to vent and name/shame. So there is still an argument to have some form of third party outlet in the thick of battle.

Ironically, the lack of time or desire to deal directly with agents has led to a relatively new phenomenon which, if anything, doubles up the involvement. Buyer's agents have existed for some time already. Typically employed by investors, for a fee, to do the hard yards for them. Research the best target areas, search homes for sale, deal with all those annoying selling agents on their behalf. Just present the purchaser with the result in terms of a short list, already vetted, with some form of price pre-negotiation potentially done.

This concept now seems to have spread to employing a seller's agent. They offer the busy property owner a managed service, by which they go out and research the local agents/agencies and decide on behalf of the owners as to who to select and use to actually sell the home. They then deal with them directly on all the mundane issues until such times as there is a contract to sign, of course, while ensuring the best interests of their client. The seller effectively disengages from the process. The *seller's* agent takes a fee or commission split from the *selling* agent. Therefore, you employ a service company as broker/arranger, so you don't have to deal directly with an individual selling agent. Wow, an agent to deal with an agent, two layers of middlemen! Perhaps we're not dead just yet. I suppose it is no different to getting the Uber Eats guy to do the leg work and interact with the restaurant directly on your behalf for your takeaway order. I mean you could do it, but hey?

One other evolving paradox seems to be that the more information we have available to research and make educated decisions, the less this seems to be happening. Yes, I am an old git, but in this new world of influencers, Tik Tok, and limited attention spans, it seems many do not worry about the devil in the detail. During the unstoppable surge of buying and outrageous price escalation that was the pandemic, at times it felt like some people were just buying out of blind panic because they felt they had to. There appeared to be little groundwork or plan to this desire, but 'that's what *everyone* was telling them to do' before the price increased even further. Ironically, by then proceeding to pay another $50,000 extra in a bidding frenzy, they self-fulfilled the prophecy anyway!

It was very apparent, to anyone with even a basic following of the economic cycle, that rates were going to rise imminently with an inevitable impact on demand and prices. But still people jumped in, *all guns blazing,* because certain television news broadcasts were running their generic 'market is hot' and 'best suburbs to buy' soundbites every other night. Naturally, this was in between giving out codewords for whatever ratings-boosting competition they were running that week. Got to love some hard journalism. Gung-ho right up to ... oh yes, the first rate-hike! Then, shock, horror, who saw this coming?! Well, any informed people, actually.

Our media friends instantaneously switch to their pre-determined 'rates to sky rocket' and 'markets cooling and prices to drop' drama pieces instead. Only black or white remember, never grey. Give the punters excitement and, hey presto, everything has changed! Oh no, if only we had a crystal ball ... or perhaps five minutes to research some basics. By and large, we are becoming *reactive*, as opposed to *proactive*, I suppose.

In concluding, this might all sound like the slightly embittered ramblings of a cynical, ageing exponent of the industry who never quite made it to highest grades (damn, that was a bit *too* incisive!). Well perhaps, but in truth bemused, rather than embittered, and entertained through observation, rather than cynical. I have absolutely no regrets on choosing to take this path so many years back. Overall, it has given me more flexibility for valued time with family, a wonderful window on the culture, colour, and diversity of Australia, good friends, and a host of interesting—and often humorous—memories to cherish, as shared in this book.

Whether it was standing back to admire a newly installed corflute sign—forgetting I was on a retaining wall—and falling backwards headfirst (and disappearing) into the owner's hedge below, or desperately trying to open a property for inspection on a stock run with the key to the office toilet, there was always a story to be had. As a contrast and tonic to many years previously spent on a long daily commute to city-based desk jobs, it has been invigorating and has opened up a whole world of new experiences. Is it for everyone? Probably not, but equally as they say, don't knock it until you've tried it!

About The Author
Michael Blackmoor

London 1991. Another day in the office.

Life's indeed a journey and we never quite know where it will lead. 30-plus years ago, slowly working my way up the corporate ladder in international banking, I could never have imagined the alternative path that lay ahead, culminating in a dynamic new country, culture, and occupation.

Real estate has also been a journey, of sorts, and hopefully these writings have given some sense of its colourful & cosmopolitan inner soul.

Australia has proved to be a wonderful environment for my family, and offered opportunities I could never have envisaged. Be it running marathons for the first time in my 40s, or becoming an author in my 50s!

There are compromises, of course, and I still visit the UK regularly to catch up with other family members and have the occasional 'warm beer' at a 'proper' pub! Nonetheless, I feel privileged to have experienced living and working at opposite ends of the world, and I suppose with Queensland home for the last few years, I am now *SOLD on the Sun* ... hmm, that gives me an idea!

More From Michael Blackmoor

Podcast series

Intrigued? Well, if you'd like to hear from the horse's mouth, so to speak, catch *SOLD On The Dream*—the accompanying podcast series—from Michael Blackmoor.

Contact me

Website: michaelblackmoor.com

Email: michael@michaelblackmoor.com

ACKNOWLEDGEMENTS

This book would not have come to fruition without the support and expertise of several people.

Firstly, I would like to thank Deborah Fay at Disruptive Publishing for her time, valued guidance and diligent execution of the myriad of practical matters required on my behalf to get this publication over the line. To utilise her as my publisher was both a highly enjoyable and rewarding experience.

Likewise, my editor, Jo Scott, provided a comprehensive service of such excellence and easy-going communication that creating the final polished product from my original rough-cut manuscript was a breeze. Furthermore, her generous encouragement coupled to likeminded humour and outlook was a major inspiration to push forward with this project from the outset.

To my current Principal, who freely endorsed my creative side be set free without restriction or prejudice, having been in the game long enough (and of such genuine character) to see the funny side and not take everything in life quite so seriously.

To a couple of specific agents who have become good friends over the years, both of whom approach this business in the right way, with honestly, integrity, and a genuine ambition to provide the best service, without any ego trip. Their own wry wit and observations have inadvertently help shape this book. Yes, Carlton, that's you and 'our man in Hobart'!

Finally, to my dear wife and family who have always remained fully supportive of me during the many twists and turns of my chosen profession, and who have been equally positive about my foray into the word of writing. Without them, there would be no book and I thank them always.

www.ingramcontent.com/pod-product-compliance
Lightning Source LLC
Chambersburg PA
CBHW060322200326
41519CB00011BA/1803